BUDDHISM IN MODERN INDIA

Bibliotheca Indo—Buddhica No. 82

BUDDHISM IN MODERN INDIA

D.C. AHIR

SRI SATGURU PUBLICATIONS
A Division of
INDIAN BOOKS CENTRE
DELHI—INDIA

Published by :
SRI SATGURU PUBLICATIONS
a Division of
INDIAN BOOKS CENTRE,
Indological and Oriental Publishers
40/5, Shakti Nagar,
Delhi—110007
INDIA

ISBN—81-7030-254-4

Printed in India at :
Kiran Mudran Kendra,
A-38/2, Maya Puri, Phase-I,
New Delhi-110064

DEDICATED

to

the sacred memory of

DR. B.R. AMBEDKAR,

the modern Bodhisattva,

on

the occasion of

his

Birth Centenary Celebrations

Contents

Preface

AFTER a long spell of darkness, light dawned on Buddhism in India in the early years of the nineteenth century when the archaeologists and scholars started digging its hidden treasures. A systematic campaign to revive Buddhism in India was launched by Anagarika Dharmapala, a missionary from Sri Lanka, in 1891. For the next 65 years, the revival movement made slow but steady progress. Then it took a great leap forward. This happened on 14 October 1956 when the great Dr. Ambedkar gave a clarion call to millions of his followers to seek refuge in the Buddha—Dhamma.

With a population of over 4.7 millions, the Buddhists are now 0.71% of the total population of India as against 0.05% in 1951, and now rank as the fourth religious Minority; the first three being the Muslims, Christians and Sikhs. Inspite of this unprecedented increase in their population in recent years, an impression still persists in certain quarters that Buddhism is not a living religion in this country. Not only that, even the Buddhists themselves seem to be ignorant about their co-religionists in other parts of this ancient land of the Buddha. Therefore, the object of writing this largely factual History of Modern Buddhism is two-fold. Firstly, it is to expose the myth that Buddhism in India is still a religion of Museums only. Secondly, it is to provide the Buddhists a deep insight into the living cells of their religion. The enormous material presented here will, it is hoped, serve both the purposes in view.

Besides the chapters on modern Buddhism: its history, monasteries, societies, institutions and literature which have been treated extensively, two chapters—one on the history of the Himalayan Buddhists, and the other on Buddhist Customs and Manners have also been added. With this additional information, the utility of this comprehensive work on Buddhism in modern India has been further enhanced.

D.C. Ahir

Buddha Purnima
May 9, 1990

Acknowledgements

I record my grateful thanks to Ven. Bhadant Anand Kausalyayan (1905-1988), the founder of the Bhikkhu Niwas, Deeksha Bhoomi, Nagpur, Maharashtra, who had inspired me to undertake this study about the living Buddhism in India, and also published the same in 1972.

I am also indebted to the following Societies which had furnished the requisite information in response to my request at the time of preparation of the first edition of this work :

All Assam Buddhist Association, Desangpani;
Ancient Buddhist Society, Kanpur;
Andaman Buddhist Mission, Port Blair;
Asoka Mission, New Delhi;
Baudh Dharma Sangh, Vanasthali, Nilgaon, Sitapur;
Bhartiya Baudh Maha Sabha, Meerut;
Buddha Bharati, Siliguri;
Buddhist Centre, Aurangabad;
Burmese Buddhist Society, Rajgir;
Council of Religious Affairs of His Holiness the Dalai Lama, Dharmsala;
Himalayan Buddhist Society, Kulu;
Japan Buddha Sangh, Bombay;
Ladakh Buddhist Association, Leh;
Maha Bodhi Society of India, Calcutta, Sarnath, Bombay, Lucknow, and New Delhi;
Maha Bodhi Society of Ceylon, Madras;
Maha Bodhi Ashoka Mission, Ajmer;
People's Education Society, Bombay;
South India Buddhist Association, Madras;
Tripura Rajya Buddhist Association, Agartala.

I am also indebted to the authors of the following works : The Himalayan Borderland by Ram Rahul, Vikas Publications, Delhi, 1970; and Ladakh-Crossroads of High Asia by Janet Rizvi,

Oxford University Press, Delhi, 1983.

Lastly, I would like to record my thanks to Ven. L. Ariyawansa Nayaka Maha Thera, New Delhi for helping me in various ways.

D.C. Ahir

A Vow

There are beings without limit,
Let us take the vow to convey them all across.
There are depravities in us without number,
Let us take the vow to comprehend them all.
There are truths without end,
Let us take the vow to comprehend them all.
There is the Way of Buddha without comparison,
Let us take the vow to accomplish it perfectly.

Dr. B.R. Ambedkar
in
The Buddha and His Dhamma

Prologue

ONE of the greatest epoch-making events in the history of India took place in the sixth century B. C. when Gautama the Buddha delivered the First Sermon at Isipatana (Sarnath), and exhorted His disciples to "Go and wander forth for the gain of the many, for the welfare of the many, in compassion for the world, for the good, for the gain, for the welfare of gods and men, and to preach a life of holiness, perfect and pure." Soon His message of equality; of hope and peace; of kindness and compassion became the talk of the day; and the name and fame of the Buddha spread far and wide. As small rivulets flow towards the ocean, so rushed people from all walks of life; rich and poor, high and holy, low and lowly; and the Way of the Buddha became a highway to salvation for all—the recluses, scholars, philosophers, kings, queens and lay men and women.

That the popularity of the Buddha reached its zenith during the life time of the Master is more than evident from the incident which took place at Kushinara, immediately after His Mahaparinirvana. There, a dispute arose about the division of the body-relics of the Buddha. Besides the Mallas, a number of neighbouring rulers demanded a share of the ashes of the Blessed One. The Mallas were at first reluctant and the dispute threatened to end in a war. But later the wise counsels prevailed and the relics were shared equally by the Mallas of Kushinara; Ajatasatru, the king of Magadha ; Licchavis of Vaisali ; Sakyas of Kapilavastu ; Bulis of Allakappa; Koliyas of Ramagrama; the Mallas of Pava and a resident of Vethadipa. The urn was taken by Drona who was instrumental in dividing the relics to the satisfaction of all.

After the Mahaparinirvana of the Buddha in 483 B.C., the rise and fall of Buddhism in India can be said to have passed through the following phases :

1. Consolidation (483 B.C.—275 B.C.)
2. Systematic Propagation (275 B.C.—200 B.C.)
3. Popular Religion (200 B.C.—500 A.C.)

4. Struggle for Survival (c. 500 A.C.—700 A.C.)
5. Decline (c. 700 A.C.—1150 A.C.)
6. The Dark Age (c. 1150 A.C.—1800 A.C.)

1. When the Master had gone, His disciples thought of codifying His Teachings with a view to preserving their pristine purity. So they convened at Rajgir (Rajagaha) a Sangiti or Council under the Presidentship of Ven. Maha Kassapa. After a great deal of scrutiny, this Council settled the full text of the Scriptures. Another effort to codify the Buddha—Word, and dispel doubts about it were made at the Second Council held at Vaisali after a hundred years of the passing away of the Buddha. The occasion for this Council was provided by the difference of opinion between the Vajji monks, and others led by Yasa. This Council was held under the Chairmanship of Ven. Sabbakami, and it gave verdict against the Vajji monks.

2 The emergence of Asoka the Great (273 B.C.—232 B.C.) was an important turning point in the history of Buddhism. Soon after ascending the throne of the Maurya Empire, which covered almost the whole of India, and even more, Asoka embraced Buddhism, and declared that hence-forth he would make the Buddha-Dhamma the basis of all his actions in the spiritual as well as temporal fields. To devise ways and means to accelerate the propagation of Buddhism, therefore, he convened the Third Buddhist Council. After the Council, which was held at Pataliputra (modern Patna) under the Presidentship of Ven. Moggaliputta Tissa, Asoka launched a vigorous campaign to preach and propagate the message of the Buddha, and sent missionaries to various parts of India and the neighbouring countries. In order to supplement the efforts of the missionaries he also issued a number of Rock and Pillar Edicts which stand even to-day to prove his qualities of head and heart. With his systematic and energetic efforts, therefore, Asoka took out the gospel of the Buddha from the caves and monasteries, and made it a national religion.

Asoka passed away in 232 B.C. leaving behind a vast empire devoted to the cause of Buddhism. After about 45 years of his death, however, the Maurya Empire crumbled when Pushyamitra, Brahmin commander-in-chief of Brihardartha, the last Mauryan King, treacherously assassinated the king and usurped the throne.

3. The systematic efforts of Asoka the Great to popularise the gospel of the Buddha created a stir amongst the Buddhist masses. They became conscious of their duty towards their sacred religion, and despite persecution by Pushyamitra they stuck to their faith, and gave unreserved support to the Sangha after the decline of the Mauryan rule. No wonder, most of the stupas and railings which we see today at Sanchi and Bharhut are the creation of the pious lay devotees of the Buddha who came about 50-100 years after Asoka. It is said that the village committees were formed to help building the railings at these places. The religion of the Buddha had, thus, by the second century B.C. become a force to reckon with. Its popularity further increased when the Greeks and the Kushanas, who established their hold over North—West India in the second century B.C. and first century A.C. respectively, embraced Buddhism and did their utmost to further popularise it. Of them, the names of the Greek King Menander or Milinda, who embraced Buddhism at the hands of Ven. Nagasena around 160 B.C., and the Kushana ruler, Kanishka, who ruled from 78 A.C.—101 A.C., shine above all.

This period (200 B.C.—500 A.C.) saw the emergence of a number of illustrious saint-scholars who made an immense contribution to the Buddhist philosophy and religion. Here, mention may be made of 1. Ashvaghosha, who was contemporary of Kanishka. gifted as he was, a poet, dramatist, musician, scholar and debator, he went on foot from village to village, town to town and city to city playing on his instruments and singing songs in praise of the Buddha. Thus he took Buddhism to every hearth and home. 2. Nagarjuna who was a friend and contemporary of the Satavahana King, Yajnasri Gautami-putra (166-196 A.D.) of Andhra. He propounded the Madhyamika school of Buddhist philosophy, popularly known as Sunyavada. He thus gave a new and definite turn to the Buddhist philosophy. 3-4. Asanga and Vasubandhu, who were brothers, flourished in Punjab in the fourth century A.C. Asanga was the most important teacher of the Yogacara or Vijnanavada school founded by his guru, Maitreyanatha. Vasubandhu's greatest work, the Abhidharmakosa is still considered an important encyclopedia of Buddhism. 5. Buddhaghosha, who lived in the fifth century A.C., was a great Pali scholar. The commentaries and the Visuddhimagga written by him are not only a great achievement in the post-Tripitaka literature but are also a key to the Tripitaka. 6-7. Buddhapalita and Bhavaviveka were important exponents in the fifth century, of the Sunyavada doctrine propounded by Nagarjuna. 8. Dinnaga, the last mighty intellectual of the fifth century,, is well-known as the founder of the Buddhist logic. He wrote about 100 treatises on logic and is often referred to as the father of the Medieval Nyaya as a whole.

To what extent Buddhism was popular during this period can be well-judged from what says Sir R. G. Bhandarkar. According to him, "The period that we have been speaking of (that is from the beginning of second century B.C. to the fifth century A.C.) has left no trace of a building or sculpture devoted to the use of the Brahmin religion. Of course, Brahminism existed and it was probably, during this period, being developed into the form which it assumed in later times. But the religion certainly does not occupy the prominent position, and Buddhism was followed by the large mass of the people from princes down to the humble workman." In other words, during this period the religion of the Buddha was always the first choice of the thinkers and philosophers. And the princes, nobles and the masses always considered it honour to associate themselves one way or the other with the great name of the Buddha.

4. The successive invasions of the savage Hunas in the fifth century desecrated and destroyed almost all the Buddhist places of worship in the North-West India, In Kashmir, the Buddhists were mercilessly persecuted by Mihirkula, a Huna Chief, who came to power in 515 A.D. Not only that, the Huna invasions also weakened the Gupta Hindu Empire founded by Samudragupta in 330 A.D. and hastened its disintegration. Taking advantage of the slackening grip of the latter Gupta Kings, some of the local chieftains carved out Independent States. A few of them were Buddhists, and they endeavoured to rehabilitate their sacred religion. Three of such powers were: the Samanta rulers of Valabhi (Gujarat), the Maukharis of Kanauj (U.P.) and the Vardhana dynasty of Thanesar (Punjab). On Mihirkula's death, Kashmir also came under the Buddhists as Meghavahana, the first ruler after the Hunas, was a staunch Buddhist, and undertook the propagation and preservation of Buddhism with great zeal.

Harsha (606-647 A.D.) was the most illustrious King of all the Buddhist rulers of this period (500-700 A.D.). He was barely 16 when he had to assume power of the Thanesar and the Kanauj dynasties under dramatic circumstances. This happened after the assassination of his elder brother, Rajyavardhana, at the hands of the king of Malva who had earlier assassinated his brother-in-law, Grahvarman and imprisoned his sister Rajyashri. Later on, Harsha extended his sway over other areas and in due course his kingdom included present day Punjab, Haryana, part of Rajasthan, U.P., Bihar, Bengal and Orissa, with Kanauj as capital.

The second Chinese pilgrim, Bhikshu Yuan Chwang (Hiuen Tsang), who was in India from 629-644 A.D., was treated with utmost reverence and hospitality by Harsha. To honour the distinguished guest, he convoked a grand assembly at Kanauj which was attended by thousands of Bhikkhus from all over India. It seems the Brahmins were not happy about the way Harsha honoured Hiuen-Tsang, and showed his respect and reverence to the Buddha. So they conspired and tried their utmost to make the celebrations a failure. Firstly, they put on fire the tower and the pavilion over the gate of the hall erected at an immense cost. There was some damage but the fire was immediately extinguished. Later, the opponents of Buddhism thought of another conspiracy and hired a lunatic heretic to kill Harsha. So when after inspecting the damaged tower Harsha was coming down the steps the hireling tried to stab the King with a knife. The attempt was, however, foiled by the alertness of Harsha who promptly seized the knife from the hired culprit.

According to Hiuen Tsang, there were about 1000 monasteries and about 50,000 monks in India during the reign of Harsha. Thus till then the whole of India was studded with Viharas, and there were a number of eminent Buddhist scholars and teachers. Inspite of all that, however, Buddhism was showing signs of decline. And after the death of Harsha in 647 A.D. it began declining rapidly.

5. The history of Buddhism in India from the eighth century onward is a sad story of degeneration, decline and ultimate disappearance. In fact, the decline trend had commenced as early as the fifth century A.D. The rise of Harsha and his efforts to rehabilitate Buddhism in North India were like a last flicker, a powerful flicker no doubt, as is evident from the testimony of Hiuen Tsang. But once the protection and patronage of Harsha was gone, Buddhism crumbled. Thereafter, the decline was so rapid that I-Tsing, the last Chinese traveller, who came just after 30 years of the departure of Hiuen Tsing in 644 bemoans the dying religion which he loved. (I-Tsing was in India from 673 to 685 A.D. and stayed at Nalanda for 10 years). Thus, during the period from

700 to 1150 A.D., we hear very little of Buddhism outside Kashmir, Bengal and Bihar where the religion of the Buddha was still flourishing. The Khadgas was the first Buddhist dynasty to rule Bengal from 625 to 725 A.D. After 25 years gap, another Buddhist family came to power. We refer to the Pala rulers who ruled from 750 to 1162 A.D. During the long reign of the Pala Kings, who had sway over Magadha also, Buddhism in this region was bound to flourish, and it did. These pious and virtuous kings not only patronised the Nalanda Maha Vihara but also established the famous monasteries of Vikramasila, Odantapuri and Somapuri.

After the downfall of the Palas, Buddhism passed into oblivion, as everywhere else, in the North-Eastern region also. And soon it was a forgotten creed in the whole of India.

6. As stated above, by the twelfth century A.D. Buddhism in India was only confined to a small pocket in North-East India. Even there it was almost closetted within the monasteries. So when the Muslim army advanced towards Bihar; sacked the Buddhist establishments at Nalanda, Vikramasila and Odantapuri; massacred most of the monks residing in them, the rout of Buddhism was complete. The Bhikkhu-Sangha having been wiped out and the Buddhist shrines having been destroyed, the Buddhist laity were left without any guide; and in due course they went back to the fold of Hinduism.

The Dark Age was in fact the darkest. During this period (1150-1800 A.D.), thousands of Buddhist Viharas, Stupas and Monasteries were destroyed and plundered by the opponents of Buddhism on the one hand and completely ignored and allowed to decay by the masses on the other hand. To what extent the Buddhist sacred shrines were neglected and even desecrated by the people of Varanasi, the Hindu holy-city, can be judged from the fact that the Asokan Stupa at Sarnath was dismantled in 1794 by Jagat Singh, the Diwan of Raja Chait Singh of Banaras, merely for the sake of bricks required for the construction of a market in Varanasi. This market is now known as Jagat Ganj. A good number of the Buddhist temples were also converted into Hindu or Muslim places of worship. These included the Mahabodhi Temple at Bodh Gaya as well which was occupied by a Hindu Mahant some time in the 16th century. Thus, by and by every trace of Buddhism was effaced from the land of its birth.

Leaving behind such a dark age, we proceed further to unfold the romantic story of the revival of Buddhism in modern India.

CHAPTER I

History of Revival Movement

THE history of the revival movement can be conveniently divided into three distinct phases, namely :

(a) Renaissance (1750-1890) ;

(b) Systematic Revival (1891-1947); and

(c) Mass Movement (1947-1990).

(a) Renaissance

The renaissance of Buddhism can be said to have commenced in India towards the middle of the 18th century when the British Civil Servants started bringing to light its treasures hidden under dust and debris. The romantic story of the archaeological discoveries goes back to 1750 when Padre Tieffenthaler discovered fragments of an Asokan inscription on the Delhi-Meerut Pillar which now stands on the Ridge, Delhi. In the same year, the Allahabad—Kosam (Kausambi) Pillar at Allahabad was discovered. This was followed by the discovery of the Lauriya—Araraj (Radhia) Pillar in 1784 and the Barabar Hill Cave inscriptions in 1785. In 1785 again, the Delhi-Topra Pillar at Ferozshah Kotla, Delhi was discovered by Captain Polier. He presented some drawings of its inscription to Sir William Jones who had founded in Calcutta in 1784 the Asiatic Society of Bengal to collect, decipher and interpret the archaeological, ethnological, geological and zoological specimens discovered by its members.

In 1801, Captain James Hoare published for the first time in the Asiatic Researches, Journal of the Asiatic Society of Bengal, fascimiles of the Delhi—Topra inscriptions. This attracted the attention of the scholars, and attempts to decipher the Asokan lipi began in right earnest.

In the year 1819, a discovery of highest importance was made accidently by a pair of British soldiers who were on patrol duty. They stumbled on the caves at Ajanta which had fallen into disuse and lost sight of more than 1000 years earlier. The Ajanta Caves are now well-known throught the world. They are unique as they combine three forms of art: architecture, sculpture and painting. Following the discovery of the Ajanta Caves, a number of caves carved out of natural rock formations in several distinctive styles were discovered at Ellora, Nasik, Karle, Bhaja and Junnar etc.—all in Western India.

In 1822, Major James Todd discovered the first Rock Edict at Girnar, sacred mountain near Junagadh in Gujarat. In 1834, a copy of the Allahabad Pillar inscription made by Lt. T.S. Burt was published by the Bengal Asiatic Society's Journal. Two years later, the Shahbazgarhi Rock Edict (in Peshawar District, Pakistan) was discovered by M.A. Court, a French Officer in the service of Maharaja Ranjit Singh.

By 1836, a number of Rock and Pillar inscriptions had been discovered in various parts of India. But no body knew either their contents or the name of their creator. No Indian scholar was competent enough to decipher the most ancient inscriptions of India which were found not only on the rocks and pillars but on the coins as well. In 1837, a high official of the Indian Mint and Secretary of the Asiatic Society of Bengal, succeeded, after several years of assiduous study and hard work, in deciphering the inscriptions which were written in Prakrit. As Prakrit stood between Pali and Sanskrit, Prinsep consulted the Pali and Sanskrit scholars. With their help he was able to evolve the deciphering method. In July 1837, Prinsep published fascimiles, phonetic transcriptions and English translation of the seven Pillar Edicts, the opening words of which were: 'Thus spake the beloved of gods, King Piyadasi!' Who was King Piyadasi still remained a mystery. Luckily, in the same year, George Turnour translated and published in English the Mahavamsa, a Pali chronicle of Sri Lanka. The occurrence of the word Piyadasi in the Mahavamsa helped James Prinsep in identifying King Piyadasi as the great Buddhist Emperor Asoka. The deciphering of the Asokan lipi and the identification of Asoka was an epoch-making event. It enriched the history of India and of Buddhism to such an extent that all history books had to be re-written.

In 1838, James Prinsep deciphered and published the Rock inscriptions discovered at Girnar, and Dhauli in Puri Distt., Orissa (discovered by Lieutenant Kittoe in 1837). Thus, James Prinsep, working almost single-handed, made available just within a period of ten months the major portion of the Asokan inscriptions This was truly a herculean task, and over-work affected Prinsep's health. He fell ill, left India for his home in England in 1840, and died soon thereafter.

In 1840, the Bhabru Edict on the rock at Bairat near Jaipur was discovered by Captain Burt. This was transcribed and translated by Captain Kittoe. Ten years later, in 1850, the Jaugada Rock inscription (in Ganjam Distt., Orissa) was discovered and copied by Sir Walter Elliot who recognised it as another version of the Asokan Edicts discovered at Dhauli, Girnar and Shahbazgarhi. In 1860, yet another Asokan Rock inscription was discovered at Kalsi near Dehra Dun by Forrest,

In 1851, an important discovery was made at Sanchi, near Bhopal. Though the monuments at Sanchi were discovered and rescued from oblivion as early as 1818 but it was in 1851 that the Stupas were opened by Cunningham. From inside the Stupa 3 he discovered the sacred relics of the two chief disciples of the Buddha, namely, Sariputta and Mahamoggallana. These sacred relics were taken to London and kept there in safe custody till their return to India a century later, i.e. in 1949.

The advent of Sir Alexandar Cunningham accelerated the discovery and restoration of the archaeological sites in India. He was undoubtedly the greatest archaeologist and hero of the renaissance period. In 1861, the Government of India appointed him as the first Director General of the Archaeological Survey. Cunningham's zeal and interest in the archaeological material opened a new vista in the study of Indian Archaeology. He himself went round; visited all the ancient sites; and prepared a systematic geographical map of ancient India. In his monumental work 'Ancient Geography of India, Part I, the Buddhist Period,' Cunningham recapitulated the glorious history of the Buddhist remains and monuments scattered all over the country. In 1870, he excavated the vicinity of the Maha Bodhi Temple, and published his conclusions under the title 'Maha Bodhi or the Great Buddhist Temple at Buddha Gaya." In 1873-74, Cunningham excavated the Mahastupa of Bharhut and rescued the finest Buddhist art from further oblivion. His publication 'Stupa of Bharhut' throws a flood of light on this most ancient Buddhist shrine in Central India. Cunningham's another important publication based on his researches was on the Bhilsa Stupa. The Asokan inscriptions also received Cunningham's proper attention as it was he who in 1877 published all the then known inscriptions in one volume titled 'Corpus Inscriptionam Indicarum.' In this volume all the inscriptions were presented in fascimile, phonetic transliteration and English translation. By this time, the Bairat Minor Rock Edict, the Rupnath Minor Rock Edict and the Rampurva Pillar Edict had also been discovered.

In 1882, a fragment of an Asokan Rock Edict was discovered at Sopara in Thana Distt., Maharashtra by Dr. Bhagwan Lal Indraji. The Mansehra Rock Edict (in Hazara District, Pakistan) was discovered by Captain Leigh in 1889. In 1890, the three Mysore Minor Rock Edicts were discovered by Lewis Rice.

So much about the archaeological discoveries. A further fillip to the renaissance movement was given by the literary activities of the Western scholars who were responsible for creating a congenial atmosphere for the study of Buddhism in India and abroad.

The pioneers of the literary movement were M. Winternitz, E. Burnouf, V. Fausboll, Prinsep, Kern, Cosma de Kores, Oldenburg, Poussin, Levi, Stcherbatsky and Mr. and Mrs. Rhys Davids. The discovery of Buddhist literature commenced with Winternitz who attempted a history of Buddhist literature in French as Volume II of 'History of Indian literature'. In 1844, Burnouf published the first history of Buddhism. His second book was a French translation of the Saddharma-pundarika which appeared in 1852 Burnouf concentrated on Sanskrit Buddhism. The study of Pali texts was undertaken by Fausboll who published a Latin translation of the Dhammapada. His English translation of the Sutta-Nipata was published in 1881. Fausboll's monumental work was the translation of the Jatakas (Birth stories of the Buddha) which were published in six Volumes between 1877 and 1897. Hermann Oldenberg was another giant Indologist. He translated into English the Vinaya-

Pitaka-Discipline of the Buddhist Order from 1879 to 1883. His English translation of the Patimokkha, the Mahavagga and the Cullavagga, in collaboration with Rhys Davids, appeared in Volumes XIII, XVII and XX of the Sacred Books of the East (1881-85). Rhys Davids was a renowned scholar of Pali He had learnt Pali in Ceylon where he was a civil servant. In 1879, he published a translation in English of the Nidanakatha (Buddhist Birth Stories). In 1881 he founded the Pali Text Society in London. Under the auspices of this Society Mr. and Mrs. Rhys Davids did a yeoman's service to the study of Pali and Buddhism. Rhys Davids himself edited a number of texts like the Digha Nikaya (1889) the Abhidhammattha-Sangaha (1884), the Dathavamsa (1884) and a Manual of Yogavacara (1896). He translated Milinda-panho and Digha-Nikaya also.

The researches of all these explorers, archaeologists and scholars were helpful in creating a new awakening amongst the people but no body had as yet thought seriously of the Buddhist revival in India. In 1885, Sir Edwin Arnold. the world famous author of the Light of Asia visited Bodh Gaya and was shocked to see the deplorable condition of the most sacred shrine of the Buddhists. He, therefore, wrote a number of articles in the Telegraph, of which he was the editor, and drew attention of the Buddhists to the pitiable condition of the Maha Bodhi Temple, and urged them to save it from further desecration.

(b) Systematic Revival

The systematic revival of Buddhism in India began in 1891 with the arrival of Anagarika Dharmapala, a young Sinhala Buddhist, who turned out to be the first great missionary of modern times. Inspired by Sir Edwin Arnold's articles on Bodh Gaya, Dharmapala visited Sarnath and Bodh Gaya in January 1891 to see for himself the condition of the Buddhist shrines. He was shocked to see the horrible condition of the most sacred shrines. At Bodh Gaya he was visibly moved as under the Mahant's charge the Maha Bodhi Temple was being shamefully negelected and desecrated. He, therefore, resolved to restore the sacred shrines to their former glory, and to make them living centres of Buddhist culture. He also resolved to regain the control of the Maha Bodhi Temple from the Saivite Mahant, whose ancestors had converted it into a Shiva temple around the close of the 16th century. With this object in view, he established the Maha Bodhi Society of India on the 31

May 1891. After a brief visit to Ceylon (Sri Lanka), he returned to India and installed four monks from Ceylon in the Burmese Rest House constructed by King Mindon in 1875 to look after the Maha Bodhi Temple. He also decided to organise an International Buddhist Conference. This Conference was held at Bodh Gaya on the 31 October 1891. The representatives from Ceylon, China, Japan and Chittagong (Bangla Desh) attended this Conference and pondered over the ways and means to save the Seat of Buddha's Englightenment from further desecration.

The year 1891 is most memorable in the history of Indian Buddhism. Same year, Ven, Kripasaran Mahasthavir, a Bengali Buddhist monk, founded the Bengal Buddhist Association (Dharmankur Sabha). It was again in 1891 that a casket containing the bones of the Buddha was discovered by Mr. Rea at Bhattiprolu in Andhra Pradesh. Another important event of the year 1891 was the birth of Bhim Rao Ambedkar (on 14 April), a great man who was to change the course of the history of Buddhism after about 65 years. Further, about the same time Ven. Mahavira, the first Indian to become a Bhikkhu, took up his residence at Kushinagar, the site of the Mahaparinirvana of the Buddha. At that time Kushinagar was completely in ruins. In fact, it was a haunted place and the people were afraid of going there. Mahavir Swami's arrival, therefore, made Kushinagar an accessible shrine.

At the beginning of 1892, the office of the Maha Bodhi Society was shifted to Calcutta, and from May 1892, Anagarika Dharmapala started the Maha Bodhi Journal; a journal which is still preaching the Dhamma in various parts of the world. In the same year, the scholars of India, who were awakened by the labours of the Western scholars, founded in Calcutta the Buddhist Text Society. The Buddhist Text Society published many Buddhist texts in Indian languages based on the laborious researches of Rajendra Lal Mitra, Hara Prasad Shastri, Sarat Chandra Das, and Satish Chandra Vidyabhusan. The year 1892 also recorded the discovery of three Asokan Rock Edicts at Brahmagiri, Jaitinga – Ramesvara and Siddapura in the Chitradurga Distt., Karnataka.

In September 1893, Dharmapala attended the Parliament of Religions in Chicago, U.S.A. On his way back he visited Hawaii, Japan, China, Thailand and Malaya. At Honolulu, he met by chance a lady, Mrs. Mary E. Foster, who became in later years the most active supporter of Dharmapala and donated more than Rs. Ten Lakhs to the Society.

The year 1896 witnessed the discovery of the Asokan Pillar at Rummindei (Lumbini) by Fuhrer. This Pillar added further historicity to the Buddha as the inscription on it says, "The Buddha Sakyamuni was born here." Two years later (in 1898), a relic casket was discovered in the Lumbini garden by the owner of the estate. The words inscribed on the casket are, "This relic casket of the Divine Buddha is that of the Sakyas."

The year 1900 was also an eventful year for the revival movement. In that year, two branches of the Maha Bodhi Society were opened at Madras and Kushinagar. The same year Pandit Ayodhya Dasa founded the South India Buddhist Association with headquaters at Madras. This Association, of which second President, after Pandit Ayodhya Dasa, was Professor P. Lakshmi Narasu, has been propagating the Dhamma in the South ever since. It has six branches in the Karnataka and Tamil Nadu States.

In 1902, the first Buddhist Vihara of modern India was constructed at Kushinagar by Mahavir Swami. He also did much to repair, restore and rehabilitate Kushinagar. Same year, the Asokan Pillar at Rampurva in Bihar was discovered. In 1903, Kripasaran Mahasthavir founded the Dharmankur Vihara at Calcutta. Since then this Vihara has served as the headquarters of the Bengal Buddhist Association, an Association which has done much to awaken the Barua Buddhists of Bengal who, though Buddhists by birth, had forgotten the essence of the Buddha-Dhamma. In 1904, the famous Asokan Pillar, the Lion Capital of which has been adopted as National Emblem, was discovered at Sarnath.

In 1909, Dr. D.B. Spooner of the Archaeological Survey of India, after tremendous labour, discovered at Shahji-ki-dheri (Kanishka Stupa) at Peshawar, an ornamental metal casket on the top of which was a small image of a seated Buddha. Inside it was a small barrel shaped vessel of polish crystal, the mouth of which was closed with a clay seal bearing the figure of an elephant. The bottom of the vessel contained an image of Kanishka himself. This vessel contained relics (small pieces of burned bones) of the Buddha which, according to the inscription on it, were enshrined by Kanishka. The discovery of these relics created a sensation in the Buddhist world on the one hand and added a new chapter to the Indian Buddhism on the other hand. These relics were eventually replaced in a beautiful gold casket and presented by the Government of India to the Buddhists of Burma. In 1914, Sir John Marshal discovered the relics of the Buddha while excavating the Dharmarajika Vihara at Taxila. According to the inscription on the golden reliquary, these 'relics of the Holy One (Buddha) were enshrined by Urasaka, Scion of Imtavhria, a Bactrian, resident of the town of Noacha, in the year 136 of Azes, on the 15th day of the month of Asadha.' Two more caskets of the relics of the Buddha were discovered from two minor Viharas near Dharmarajika Stupa. These relics were presented by the Government of India in 1917 to the Buddhists of Ceylon and were enshrined in the Temple of the Tooth (Dalada Maligawa) at Kandy. Yet another relic casket was discovered about the same time from the only brick stupa of probable pre-Asokan date at Piprahwa in Basti District of Uttar Pradesh. According to the inscription in pre-Asokan characters on this relic casket the relics found in the stupa pertain to the Buddha. With the discovery of so many relics from different parts of India, the Buddhist heritage and culture were fully brought to light.

The first Vihara to be built by the Maha Bodhi Society of India was the magnificent Sri Dharmarajika Chaitya Vihara in Calcutta which was opened in November 1920. In this Vihara the sacred Relics of Lord Buddha, discovered in a rock crystal casket during the excavations at Bhattiprolu in Andhra Pradesh, were enshrined. The consecration ceremony of the Vihara was presided over by Lord Ronaldshay (Marquis of Zetland). The Dharmarajika Vihara, being the headquarters of the Maha Bodhi Society, has over a number of years become a symbol of the Buddhist revival movement in India.

We have already highlighted the contribution of Ven. Mahavir Swami and Ven. Kripasaran Mahasthavir in the revival movement. Another Bhikkhu, who was equally illustrious, was Ven. Bodhanand Mahasthavir. Ven. Bodhananda was first attracted towards Buddhism in 1896 when he met some Buddhist monks in Varanasi (Banaras). He became a Bhikkhu in 1914 at the hands of Ven. Kripasaran Mahasthavir. Since at that time there was no consecrated Sima in India for this purpose, the Upasampada ceremony of Ven. Bodhananda was performed in a boat on the Ganges near Calcutta by the Bhikkhus of Burma, Ceylon and Chittagong. Anagarika Dharmapala was also present on the occasion of this historic ceremony. On becoming a Bhikkhu, Ven. Bodhananda returned to Lucknow and made it the centre of his activities thereafter. In 1916, he established the Indian Buddhist Association (Bhartiya Baudh Samiti), In 1925, he erected a beautiful Vihara in Risaldar Park, Lucknow. As a result of the preachings of Ven. Bodhananda Mahasthavir, a congenial atmosphere was created for the revival of Buddhism in North India which gave inspiration to many to adopt the Buddhist way of life.

In Western India, the revival movement was pioneered by the two grand personalities, namely Dr. Anandrao L. Nair and Dharmananda Kosambi. Dr. Anandrao L. Nair founded the Buddha Society, Bombay in 1922. He also built the first Vihara (Ananda Vihara) in Bombay in 1931. The Buddha Society popularised Buddhism in Western India through its spokesmen in print, first 'Buddha Purnima' and then "Dharma-Chakra : the Wheel of Moral Law". Dharmananda Kosambi was the first Indian scholar of Pali. He wrote several books on Buddhism in Marathi and Gujarati. All his works reflected his zeal to popularise Pali literature and the Buddha-Dhamma. In 1937, he built a small Vihara at Parel, Bombay and called it 'Bahujana Vihara' as it was intended to satisfy the spiritual needs of the workers and labourers living in the area. Another pioneer Buddhist in Western India was Professor N.K. Bhagwat, a disciple of Dharmananda Kosambi.

The religion of the Buddha made significant progress in Kerala with the conversion of C. Krishnan, Editor of the Mitavadi, who was elected President of the Kerala Buddhist Association established in 1925 with headquarters at Calicut. Bhikshu Dharmakkhanda, a Malyali monk trained in Ceylon helped Krishnan and his colleagues in taking Dhamma to the masses in that State.

In December 1928, an All India Buddhist Conference was held in the Maha Bodhi Society Hall at Calcutta under the Presidentship of Shiv Charan Lal of Lucknow. Nearly 300 delegates attended the first National Conference of the Buddhists. Prof. B.M. Barua was the Chairman of the Reception Committee.

One of the resolutions passed by the Conference related to the return of the relics of Sariputta and Moggallana which had been taken to London and were lying in the Victoria and Albert Museum.

In the year 1928, the Great Stupa at Nagarjunakonda was excavated, and from it some interesting antiquities were discovered. These included a broken earthenware pot (relic-casket) which contained a fragment of a bone of the Buddha himself. The excavation revealed that the Stupa, which was probably built in the third century A.D., was in the form of a wheel, Dharma—Chakra, the well-known symbol of the Buddhists.

In 1929, two Asokan Rock Edicts were discovered at Yerragudi in the Kurnool District of Andhra Pradesh. Two years later, in 1931, the Rock-Edicts of Asoka were discovered at Gavimath and Palkigundu in the Raichur District of the same State.

In 1931, the beautiful Mulagandhakuti Vihara built at Sarnath at a huge cost by the Maha Bodhi Society of India was opened. The sanctity of this Vihara was enhanced as the sacred bone-relics of Lord Buddha discovered from the Dharmarajika Vihara at Taxila and presented to the Maha Bodhi Society were enshrined in it. The completion of the Mulagandhakuti Vihara was the crowning and most glorious achievement of Anagarika Dharmapala. He decided to make Sarnath a living centre of Buddhist learning and culture. For this purpose, he established a library also to which Pandit Sheo Narain, a pioneer Buddhist of Punjab, transferred all books in his personal library.

Anagarika Dharmapala, who had assumed the name of Sri Devamitta Dhammapala on entering the Sangha in 1931, passed away in 1933. His unfinished mission of the revival of Buddhism in India was continued uninterrupted by his colleagues and followers, notable amongst them being: Devapriya Valisinha, Ven. Sangharatana and Ven. Jinaratana From the year 1931 onward, Sarnath also became an important centre for propagating the Dhamma, especially amongst the masses. The Hindi Journal 'DHARMADUTA' which first appeared in 1935 proved to be of immense help in spreading the message of the Buddha amongst the Hindi speaking masses in North India.

In 1939, the Maha Bodhi Society opened a centre at New Delhi in the first Vihara constructed in the Capital of India. The other notable Viharas constructed in the pre-Independence era were Desangpani Temple, Assam (1939); Buddha Vihara, Bangalore (1940); Venuvan Vihara, Agartala (1946); and Madras (Kennet Lane) Vihara (1947).

Among the writers who played a prominent role in the revival movement, the names of Mahapandit Rahul Sankrityayan, Ven. Anand Kausalyayan and Ven. Jagdish Kashyap are most important. Rahulji was a prolific writer in Hindi and he wrote novels, histories, scientific and philosophical books, travel records, biographies etc. He was a great explorer also. Thrice he undertook the hazardous journey to Tibet and brought back valuable old manuscripts. Some of which he himself edited and published. Rahulji's efforts to fill the long felt need of Buddhist literature in Hindi, the National Language of India, were supplemented by his worthy colleagues, namely, Ven. Bhadant Anand Kausalyayan and Ven. Jagdish Kashyap.

Inspired by the activities of the Maha Bodhi Society of India, the Buddhists of the hilly tracts, who have all along been professing the Buddha-Dhamma, also became conscious of their duty towards the preservation of the Buddhist way of life, and thought of organising their religious affairs on proper lines. Accordingly, they established their own societies to preach and propagate the Dhamma. Of these societies, mention may be made of the Ladakh Buddhist Association established in 1937 by Kalon Tsewang Rigzin and Munshi Sonam Tsewang; All Assam Buddhist Association established in 1939 by Rev. Nandabansha Mahasthavir and Rev. Jinaratana Mahasthavir; and Himalayan Buddhist Society, Kulu/Manali which was established in 1942 with Rev. Kushak Bakula as President.

By 1947, the revival movement, which began on modest lines in 1891, had come a long way and was well-trenched. But the Buddhists were still a small fry in a big ocean as till then the revival movement had not become a mass movement.

(c) Mass Movement

After Independence, the revival movement took a new turn as Buddhism came to be associated with nationalism and ancient Indian culture. When the Constituent Assembly was busy in drafting a Constitution for free India, the question of the National Flag and the National Emblem baffled the Constitution makers. Their eyes ultimately turned towards the Buddhist heritage which represented the glorious days of India under the aegis of the Buddhist kings. Thanks to the wisdom of the Constituent Assembly, of which President was Dr. Rajendra Prasad, the Buddhist Wheel of Law and the Lion—Capital of Asoka were adopted as National symbols of free India. The inspiring personality behind the adpotion of these symbols of Buddhist culture as 'National symbols' was none else but Dr. B.R. Ambedkar, who was Chairman of the Committee which [drafted the Constitution. The Constitution of free India was finally adopted by the Constituent Assembly on 26 November 1949. Another event of importance in 1949 was the return of the sacred relics of Sariputta and Mahamoggallana from London where they were taken in 1851. Again it was in 1949 that the Government of Bihar enacted the Buddha Gaya Temple Management Act. Under this Act, a Committee called the Buddha Gaya Temple Management Committee, consisting of four Buddhists and four Hindus was constituted. Though not a very happy and satisfactory solution : by it, however, the Buddhists succeeded to some extent in gaining the control of the management of the Maha Bodhi Temple which was hitherto completely under the control of the Mahant.

In 1950, the revival movement took another favourable turn. Hitherto. Babasaheb Dr. B.R. Ambedkar was only known as an acknowledged Leader of the Scheduled Castes, the down-trodden masses. as he had confined his attention to their economic, social and political problems only. But in 1950 he made known publicly his determination to revive Buddhism in India. In that year, he asked his followers to celebrate the Buddha Jayanti in future every year. Same year, he contributed an article to the Vaisakha Number of the Mahabodhi Journal under the title 'The Buddha and the Future off His Religion' concluding which he said that Buddhism was the only religion which the world could have because of its emphasis on reason, morality, liberty, equality and fraternity.

An important event in the post-Independence era which focussed the attention of the Indian masses on the virtues of the Buddha-Dhamma was the restoration of the sacred relics of the two chief disciples of the Buddha, namely, Sariputta and Mahamoggallana at their original resting place. These relics were returned to India by the British Government in January 1949 at the request of the Maha Bodhi Society. Prior to their enshrinement at Sanchi the relics were taken round to various parts of India as well as to various Buddhist countries with a view to enabling the Buddhists of various lands to pay their homage to the two chief disciples of the Blessed One. In India, the most spectacular welcome given to these relics was by the people of Bihar, the birth place of both the saints. On March 26, 1949 the sacred relics of Sariputta and Moggallana reached Patna and were welcomed by more than 50,000 people with great joy and enthusiasm. Speaking on the occasion, Dr. Sri Krishna Sinha, the Chief Minister of Bihar said with genuine pride and feelings of thankfulness, 'the history of Bihar was the epitome of the history of India and nay, in a way, the history of the world itself. India has been the leader of the world through the ages and the credit for this leadership goes to Lord Buddha and His band of selfless disciples'.

The celebrations of the home-coming of the relics of Sariputta and Moggallana were concluded with a grand function at Sanchi, near Bhopal, in November 1952 which was attended by the Prime Ministers of India and Burma, World Buddhist leaders and Venerable Bhikkhus Speaking on this occasion, the Prime Minister of India, Jawahar Lal Nehru said that he saw in the teachings of the Buddha a path leading to progress and prosperity and that he had made it his life mission to make others conscious of this revelation to him. He further said that the incident of the home-coming of the relics had a deeper significance to his mind and that the significance would be realised when all of them had made a living temple in their hearts enshrining ancient memories for guidance in this confused world. Concluding, Nehru said : "Out of this Conference a seed will bloom and spread happiness." Thus the Sanchi celebrations opened a new vista for the revival of Buddhism in India.

The year 1956 marked a milestone in the chequered history of Buddhism. In that year, the Buddhist Era, which commenced on the day of the Mahaparinirvana of the Buddha, completed 2500 years. This historic event was celebrated with great enthusiasm throughout the Buddhist World. The Buddha Jayanti Celebrations of 1956 undoubtedly marked the beginning of a New Era, an era of hope, peace and prosperity for Buddhism. This is particularly true about India. To celebrate the historic Buddha Purnima in a befitting manner, the Government of India appointed the Buddha Jayanti Celebration Committee headed by Dr. S. Radhakrishnan, Vice-President of India. Other members of this Committee were : Dr. Sampurnanand, Chief Minister of U.P. ; Dr. Sri Krishna Sinha, Chief Minister of Bihar; S.D. Sharma, Chief Minister of Assam, Ven.

Kushak Bakula, Head Lama of Ladakh; and the Maharaj Kumar of Sikkim. Shri Nehru, Prime Minister, was an associate Member. Under the auspices of the Celebration Committee, the Government of India and various State Governments drew up ambitious programmes. The Buddha Jayanti Celebrations lasted for full one year i.e. upto May 1957. The programme of the Government of India, inter-alia, included the following :—

(*i*) *23rd May 1956* : Laying the foundation stone of the Memorial Monument in New Delhi by Jawaharlal Nehru, Prime Minister of India. (The monument which is still to be constructed in the Buddha Jayanti Park will be an abstract form of a lotus flower in reinforced concrete).

(*ii*) *24th May* : Mass public meeting under the Chairmanship of Dr. Rajendra Prasad, President of India.

(*iii*) *3rd November* : Opening of the Buddhist Art Exhibition at New Delhi. The exhibition was later on taken to other important cities and towns.

(*iv*) *17 & 18th November* : (*v*) Buddhist Symposium.

(*v*) *Publications* :

(1) 2500 years of Buddhism.

(2) Album containing illustrations of important Buddhist monuments etc.

(3) Edicts of Emperor Asoka, and

(4) Tripitaka in Devnagari Script.

(*vi*) Documentary film showing the life of Lord Buddha in Indian sculpture and paintings.

(*vii*) Issue of commemorative stamps.

The Maha Buddha Jayanti Celebrations commenced with a message from the President of India. In his message Dr. Rajendra Prasad said, "On this auspicious occasion of the 2500th anniversary of Lord Buddha, I send greetings to my countrymen and indeed to every citizen of the world. It is a solemn day for all those who believe in the supermacy of virtue and the superiority of human spirit over things mundane and ephemeral. People of the land, where he underwent a process of rigorous penance in search of truth and where he preached the gospel of absolute tolerance and universal peace, are bound to experience a special joy on this occasion".

During the course of the year-long celebrations, thousands of religious and cultural functions were held and millions of pages were written in praise of the Buddha as almost all the Daily Newspapers and Periodical Journals in the country brought out special supplements devoted to the Buddha and Buddhism. In addition, hundreds of books and pamphlets were published in various languages of India. The All India Radio throughout the year broadcasted a number of features, talks and dramas on Buddhism. Two Hindi feature films i.e. Anjali and Angulimala, based on the Buddhist history, were also produced in connection with the 2500th anniversary of Buddhism. Dr. B.R. Ambedkar arranged the production of two Gramophone records, through the H.M.V. Company in Pali relating to Trisarana, Panchsheel etc. The celebrations at the Buddhist shrines, which were generally organisad by the Maha Bodhi Society, were more solemn and religious in character. As was natural, on the occasion of the 2500th Celebrations the Buddhist shrines in India got a face-lift. They were restored, repaired and renovated by the Government with a view to making the visit of the large number of Buddhist pilgrims from India and abroad more comfortable. Approach roads to these centres were repaired; rest houses and canteens were constructed ; and gardens were laid out. Thus the entire country during the Maha-Jayanti year was swept by the Buddha-spirit.

Another important event of the year 1956 was the homecoming of the Sacred Relics of Arahat Moggaliputta Tissa and others which were in the possession of the British Museum, London. These relics were of the Arhans (Arahats) who lived at the time of Asoka and were placed in three replicas of the original caskets in which they were discovered. The first casket contained the relics of (1) Moggaliputta Tissa Arhan, (2) Kosikputta Arhan and Gotiputta Arhan; the second those of (1) Maha Vanaya Arhan (2) Apagira Arhan and (3) Kodiniputta Arhan ; and the third, those of Vachiya Savijayata and others. These relics were brought on the 5 February 1956 by Shrimati Vijaya Lakshmi Pandit, Indian High Commissioner in U.K. and were received at Palam Airport at a colourful function by Prime Minister Nehru. The first casket was presented by the Government of India to the Government of Ceylon. The other two caskets were presented to the Maha Bodhi Society of India who enshrined them in the Sanchi Vihara.

The most outstanding event of the 2500th Buddha Jayanti

Celebrations took place on October 14 of that year. On that day, Dr. Ambedkar took formal refuge in Buddha-Dhamma, alongwith half a million followers, at an impressive and historic ceremony held at Nagpur and gave a clarion call to his followers to take refuge in the Buddha, the Dhamma and the Sangha. With the Turning of the Wheel of Law by Dr. Ambedkar at Nagpur on 14 October 1956, the revival movement entered into an Era of intense activity which can be rightly called the 'Ambedkar Era' of Indian Buddhism. It is worth noting that within a period of five years (1956-1961) the population of Buddhists registered a spectacular increase of 1670.71% i.e. from 1,80,823 it rose to 32,50,227. This figure has further gone up by now as the mass conversions initiated by Dr. Ambedkar have been continuing unabated.

In 1964-65, the Maha Bodhi Society of India celebrated the Anagarika Dharmapala's Birth Centenary. During the year-long celebrations, a number of functions were held throughout the country in honour of the pioneer Dhammaduta. The most impressive celebrations were those held at Calcutta, New Delhi and Sarnath. As a part of the Dharmapala Centenary celebrations in the capital of India, a Bo-sapling was planted on 25 October 1964 in the Buddha Jayanti Park by Lal Bahadur Shastri, Prime Minister of India. The sapling, which was brought by Mrs. Sirimavo Bandaranaike, Prime Minister of Ceylon, from the Bodhi Tree at Anuradhapura, was planted amidst the chanting of sacred Suttas in the presence of a distinguished and colourful gathering. It may be noted that about 2300 years ago, Princess Sanghamitra (Asoka's daughter) had taken a sapling from the original Bo-Tree at Bodh Gaya to Anuradhapura. Immediately after the planting ceremony, a public meeting was held in the premises of the Buddha Vihara on Mandir Marg, New Delhi, under the Presidentship of Lal Bahadur Shastri. Mrs. Bandaranaike, Prime Minister of Ceylon, was the Chief Guest. Referring to the planting of the Bodhi-sapling in the Buddha Jayanti Park, Shri Shastri said that "every Indian regarded the tree as sacred and would draw inspiration from it". He further said, "When the Bodhi-sapling grew into a tree, it would be a symbol of Buddha's lofty philosophy". The Bodhi Tree in the Buddha Jayanti Park is growing steadily. Because of its sanctity it has already become an object of veneration for the Buddhists who visit it on the Buddha-Purnima and other sacred days.

In November-December 1964, India was once again swept by

the Buddha-spirit. The occasion was provided by the Seventh Conference of the World Fellowship of Buddhits which was held at Sarnath, the Holy Isipatna, from November 29 to December 4. This being the first Conference of the W.F.B. to be held in India, the Indian Buddhists were naturally excited and they came in full strength to meet, and exchange ideas with their brethren from foreign lands. Out of 68 delegates and 75 observers drawn from 23 countries, the Indian delegation was the largest. They came from Assam, Delhi, Kashmir (Ladakh), Madras, Maharashtra, Mysore, Rajasthan, Tripura, Uttar Pradesh and West Bengal. The Conference was inaugurated by Dr. Sarvapalli Radhakrishnan, President of India, on the evening of 29 November. Among the notable personalities present were : His Holiness, the Dalai Lama, His Highness, the Maharaja of Sikkim, Mrs. Sucheta Kriplani, Chief Minister of U.P., the Maharaja of Varanasi (Benaras), Mrs. Lakshmi N. Menon, Minister of State in the Ministry of External Affairs, Mayor of Varanasi, Diplomats and a number of high ranking Mahatheras. A significant feature of the Conference was the presence of a large number of Dr. Ambedkar's followers who came in thousands from all parts of India.

The inaugural address of Dr. Radhakrishnan was the best speech on Buddhism heard in recent times. It was hailed by one and all for sublimity of thought and nobility of sentiment. Concluding the illustrious philosopher—President of India exhorted the audience "to follow sincerely the teachings of the Great Master not merely, in letter, but in spirit". The thanks-giving speech was delivered by Dr. G.P. Malalsekara of Ceylon due to whose vision, zeal and initiative the W.F.B. came into existence in 1950. The Conference adopted a number of resolutions and came to an end on 4 December with the closing address of the President of the W.F.B., Her Serene Highness Princess Poon Pismal Diskul of Thailand.

The year 1966 saw the completion of the magnificent Thai Monastery at Buddha Gaya. Constructed at a cost of Rs. 16 lakhs by the Buddhists of Thailand it is one of the finest Viharas to be constructed in modern India.

Within 20 years (1947-1967) Buddhism seems to have run full circle in the post-Independence era. Two decades earlier, its pros and cons were discussed inside the Parliament House by the Constitution-makers who recognised its heritage as the national heritage and adopted its ancient symbols as the symbols of modern India. In 1967, the sacred Buddhist Suttas were for the first time recited in the courtyard of Parliament House by the Venerable monks led by Bhadant Anand Kausalyayan as if to bless the Parliamentarians. The occasion was provided by the unveiling ceremony of the life-size statue of Dr. Ambedkar, the greatest modern Buddhist leader and Father of the Indian Constitution. The statue, which was prepared by Brahmesh V. Wagh, a well-known sculptor of Bombay, and presented to the Speaker of the Lok Sabha by the Dr. Babasaheb Ambedkar Memorial Committee headed by Y.B. Chavan, Minister of Home Affairs, Govt. of India, was unveiled by Dr. S. Radhakrishnan, President of India, in the presence of a distinguished gathering on Sunday, the 2nd April 1967. The large number of Buddhists, who had especially come to witness this historic ceremony from every nook and corner of the country, added solemnity to the function by taking Panch Sheel standing in front of the statue of their leader who had shown them the path of liberation.

In 1968, the Ambedkar Era of Indian Buddhism completed twelve years. To take stock of the socio-religious conditions of the neo-Buddhists who had followed in the footsteps of Dr. Ambedkar during the last 12 years and to discuss the ways and means to give further impetus to the revival movement, two Conferences were held at All India level in Bombay in the months of October and November. The first Conference was held on the 23 and 24 October under the auspices of the Bhartiya Bauddha Maha Sangha. Shrimati Indira Gandhi, Prime Minister of India, inaugurated this Conference and Prof. R.D. Bhandare, M.P. presided.

The second Conference, which was a more bigger affair, was held on the 23 and 24 November under the auspices and aegis of the Buddhist Society of India. It was inaugurated by His Holiness, the Dalai. Lama. Bhayyasaheb Y.B. Ambedkar, the only son of Dr. B.R. Ambedkar, presided over the deliberations of this Conference. Among the other Buddhist leaders present on the occasion were : Ven. Kushak Bakula, the Head Lama of Ladakh and Ven. Bhadant Anand Kausalyayan.

On the occasion of this Conference, the Memorial at the Chaitya Bhoomi (the ground where Dr. Ambedkar was cremated on December 7, 1956). Shivaji Park, Bombay was unveiled by the

Chief Minister of Maharashtra, V.P. Naik. The unveiling ceremony of the Memorial stupa took place on November 24.

The opening of the Vishwa Shanti Stupa (World Peace Pagoda) atop Ratnagiri hill at Rajgir (Bihar) by the President of India, V.V. Giri, on October 25 was the most significant event of the year 1969. Artistically designed by Prof. Minoru Ohoka of Japan and the noted Indian artist, Upendra Maharathi, the 160 ft. high, gold topped pagoda, almost double the dimensions of the Sanchi stupa, was built by the Venerable Nichidatsu Fuji, President of the Japan Buddha Sangha. In the top chamber of this Stupa, the sacred Relics of Lord Buddha, presented by India to Japan in 1952 have also been enshrined. The foundation stone of the Peace Pagoda was laid in March 1965 by Dr. S. Radhakrishnan, the then President of India. Another Peace Pagoda built by Ven. Fuji Guruji is atop the Dhauli hills, about 16 km from Bhuvaneshwar (Orissa). Dhauli is the place where Emperor Asoka is said to have been converted to Buddhism after the historic Kalinga War. The Kalinga Peace Pagoda was inaugurated on 8 November 1972.

The Royal Government of Thailand constructed the Wat Thai (Thai Buddhist Temple) at Bodh Gaya during the period 1970-72. Built in typical Thai style and almost a copy of the Marble Temple in Bangkok, this temple is quite impressive. The huge golden Buddha image in the Main shrine is its primary attraction.

Another beautiful Buddhist temple built at Bodh Gaya about the same time is the Japanese Buddhist Temple (Indosan Nipponji Temple). Built by the International Buddhist Brotherhood Association of Japan, it was inaugurated on 8 December 1973.

The first ever All India Bengali Buddhist Conference was held at Calcutta from 23 to 25 December 1973. Thousands of Bengali Buddhists participated in this 3 day conference. A number of Buddhist monks from Thailand, Laos, Cambodia, Japan, Sri Lanka, and Bangladesh provided added lustre and significance to this socio-cultural conglomeration. The object of this conference was to bring about unity and cohesion among the 1,50,000 Bengali Buddhists scattered all over India.

The first All India and Himalayan Region Buddhist Leaders' Conference for promoting peace, non-violence, and national integration was held at Darjeeling, West Bengal on May 24 and 25, 1975. The conference was attended by over 200 delegates scholars and political leaders from all over India,. Nepal and Bhutan. Those present included H.H. Dalai Lama, Kazi Lendup Dorji. Chief Minister of Sikkim, Siddhartha Sankar Ray, Chief Minister of West Bengal, Dupchan Rimpochhe, monks and lamas.

The Third Asian Buddhist Conference was held in New Delhi from 1-3 November 1975. It was attended by delegates from various Buddhist countries including those from Russia, Mongolia, Vietnam, Japan, Sri Lanka, Nepal, Korea, Malaya and India. The proceedings of the Conference started with a solemn religious ceremony headed by H.H. Dalai Lama. The closing session was presided over by Y.B. Chavan, Minister for External Affairs, Government of India.

A convention known as All India Buddhist Dhamma Convention was held at Nagpur from 6 to 10 December 1975. Some 300 delegates from various parts of the country participated in it.

The proceedings of the convention started with the Administration of Five Precepts and chanting of the suttas by the Ven'ble Bhikkhus headed by Ven. Dharmadhar Mahasthavir of Calcutta. It was followed by a memorial service to Dr. B.R. Ambedkar as the day coincided with his death anniversary, and it was presided over by the Ven. Bhadant Anand Kausalyayan. To mark this occasion a colourful procession of about 30,000 Buddhists with the image of Lord Buddha and a casket of the remains of Late Dr. B.R. Ambedkar was taken out. After parading the Main streets of Nagpur it returned to the venue of the convention at Ambedkar Park.

On the last day there was an open sesion of the convention in the form of an All India Buddhist Rally, which was inaugurated by His Excellency Prof. R.D. Bhandare, Governor of Bihar. It was attended by some four lakhs of Buddhists. Among others B.D. Khobragade and other Buddhist leaders addressed the vast gathering. Several resolutions were also adopted at the convention.

In 1976, the Buddhist world celebrated the 2600th Birth Anniversary of the Buddha. In India, as part of the year-long celebrations of this historic event an International Buddhist Seminar on 'Contribution of Buddhism to World Civilization and Culture' was held in the Vigyan Bhavan, New Delhi from 27 to 29 March, 1977. This Seminar was organised by the Maha Bodhi Society of India in co-operation with the Ministry of Education and Social Welfare, Government of India, who gave financial assistance for this purpose. Thirty foreign participants from Bhutan, Canada, Federal Republic of Germany, German Democratic Republic, Hong Kong, Republic of Korea, Mongolia, Nepal, Sri Lanka, Taiwan, Thailand, United Kingdom, United States of America, U.S.S.R. and five different organisations from Japan as well as fifty participants from different parts of India attended the Seminar. In addition, 18 persons participated as observers.

The Seminar was inaugurated by B.D. Jatti, the then Acting President of the Republic of India. The welcome address was read by Ven. L. Ariyawansa Maha Thera, Joint Secretary of the Celebration Committee. The inaugural ceremony concluded with a vote of thanks by Ven. N. Jinaratana Nayaka Thera, General Secretary of the Celebration Committee. Dr. Ananda W.P. Guruge was appointed as the Secretary General of the Seminar. In all, 36 papers were presented, and discussed and deliberated on by the delegates. Out of the papers, 26 most important pieces of research were later published in the form of a book by the Maha Bodhi Society of India. This volume was edited by Ananda Guruge and D.C. Ahir.

Meditation plays a very significant role in Buddhism. There are two forms of meditation. One from is Samatha, Calm or development of mental concentration. The other form is Vipassana, Insight, which was discovered by the Buddha at the time of His Enlightenment. Vipassana means to see things as they really are. It aims at "exposing the truth of impermanency, suffering, and the unsubstantial nature of all material and mental phenomena of existence". (Anicca, dukkha, anatta). Vipassana ultimately leads to the complete liberation of mind, to the realisation of the Ultimate Truth, Nirvana.

With the down-fall of Buddhism in India, the Vipassana technique also vanished. Luckily, it was preserved in Burma where Buddhism was introduced during the time of Asoka in B.C. third century. The greatest exponent of the Vipassana meditation in modern Burma was Sayagyi U Ba Khin (1898-1971), who retired as Accountant General of Burma. S.N. Goenka, an Indian born in Burma, joined a Vipassana course under U Ba Khin for the first time in 1955. For nearly 14 years he took training under U Ba Khin, and was named as 'teacher' by his illustrious Master. Sayagyi wished that the technique of Vipassana should go back to India, and help the suffering humanity in the land of its birth.

Goenka took this as the mission of his life and, leaving behind his flourishing business in Burma, he came back to India in 1969 with the Vipassana technique as his proud possession. In 1971, a trust was formed in order to propagate the Vipassana meditation in India. Soon the search began for a suitable site for the first Vipassana Centre in the land of the Buddha. Finally, such a site was identified and a twenty-acre hill-top, near Igatpuri (ancient Sugatpuri) about 140 km from Bombay, on the Bombay-Nasik Road (N.H. No. 3) was purchased. The auspicious hill-top was named as 'Dhammagiri' the Hill of Dhamma, and the Vipassana International Academy was established there in 1976. The Vipassana Research Institute since established there looks after research and teaching of Pali.

Dhammagiri-a modern prototype of ancient caves—now offers all the facilities for exclusive meditation, in cogenial environment, for over 400 persons—men and women. The complex of cells, hall, and Teachers' residence constitutes a unique meditation facility, offering each person the opportunity to meditate in the needed seclusion and also in close contact with the Teacher. Besides Dhammagiri, the Vipassana Centres have since been established at Hyderabad in Andhra Pradesh, and Jaipur in Rajasthan where at least one ten day course is held every month. There is absolutely no charge for the Vipassana course. The cost of all boarding and lodging is met by the organisers. At the end of the course, however, the meditator can offer donation in accordance with his means.

The All India Frontier Baudha Mahasabha, founded in January 1974, organised a two-day All India Buddhist Conference on 17-18 September 1978 at the Ladakh Buddha Vihara, New Delhi. This Conference was followed by an International Buddhist Conference on September 19 which was attended by a large number of delegates from abroad. At this Conference, discussions and deliberations were held on three important subjects; The development of Buddhist Education and Research in the world; promotion of Cultural contacts among world Buddhists, and the Role of Buddhism in the advancement of Human values.

A National Convention of Buddhists was held in New Delhi on 11-12 April 1981. P.K. Thungan, Union Deputy Minister for Supplies (formerly Chief Minister of Arunachal Pradesh) and T.S. Negi, Speaker, Himachal Pradesh Vidhan Sabha presided over the two main sessions of the Convention. The National Convention was organised by a Steering Committee under the Chairmanship of Ven. Kushak Bakula, Prof. N.C. Parashar, Member, Lok Sabha acted as Secretary-General of the Convention.

The Silver Jubilee of the unique event of the Great Conversion Ceremony in 1956 was celebrated with great reverence and enthusiasm all over the country in October 1981. The main celebrations at Deeksha Bhoomi, Nagpur were organised by the Param Poojya Dr. Babasaheb Ambedkar Smarak Samiti from 1-8 October, 1981. As a part of the programme, an All India convention of the eminent Buddhists, monks, leaders and scholars was also held. The main function to mark the occasion was held on October 8 (Vijaya Dashmi Day) when thousands of people embraced Buddhism standing at the very site where Dr. Ambedkar had embraced Buddhism.

The year 1981 also saw the completion and opening of the magnificent Japanese Buddhist Temple, known as, Nipponzan Myohoji Temple at Rajgir. Built by Fuji Guruji, this temple is also called Veluvana Vihara after the famous monastery built at Rajgir by King Bimbisara for the use of the Buddha.

In 1983, another beautiful Japanese Buddhist Temple came up at Bodh Gaya. The Daijokoyo Buddhist Temple has been built by the Daijokoyo Association of Japan. It was opened on 13 February 1983 by Giani Zail Singh, the President of India.

The First International Conference on Buddhism and National Cultures was held from 10-15 October 1984 in New Delhi. This august Conference was convened by the Indian Council for Cultural Relations, Indian Council for Historical Research, Indian Society for Art, Sangeet Natak Akademi, Lalit Kala Akademi, and Special Committee for Buddhist Studies under the Ministry of Education, Government of India. It was inaugurated by Smt. Indira Gandhi, Prime Minister of India, on

10 October 1984 in the Central Hall of Vigyan Bhavan. In her inaugural address, she highlighted "the unforgetful heritage to Indian culture that Buddhism has made and the Nation's indebtedness to the Buddha for His eternal message of peace and amity that He revealed to the world through forty-five years of his mission, pervading through the length and breadth of India".

At this unique Conference, scholars from 42 countries of varying disciplines deliberated, discussed, promulgated theories, urged methods of development of newer approaches to the propagation of Buddhism in the new world of the West where a steadfast interest is being evinced in the study of Buddhism and Buddhist Meditation.

On 8 February 1985, His Holiness the Dalai Lama inaugurated a magnificent Buddhist temple, called Santivana Buddha Vihara at Deulpara in district Hoogly, West Bengal. Built by a local businessman, Tarak Chandra Bairi and his wife, Snehalata, the temple cost about Rupees Sixteen Lakhs and it took nearly fourteen years to complete it.

Though most of the Buddhist ancient sites were discovered and excavated during the pre-Independence days, the post-Independence period from 1947 onward has also claimed some notable discoveries. To quote a few : at Kausambi, a capital city during the time of the Buddha, inscriptional evidence has been found identifying the spot, Ghoshitarama, where the Buddha had stayed during His visit to that place at the invitation of king Udyana. At Vaisali, the remains of the stupa built by the Licchavis over their share of the holy relics of the Buddha has been discovered. At Devnmori in Western India, the remains of the monastic establishment of the Buddhist monks and a relic-casket in the stupa have come to light. At Pauni in Vidarbha, inscriptions and sculptures of the Sunga-Satavahana period (2nd century B.C.) have been found. At Sannotha, on the left bank of the Bhima river in Gulbarga District, Karnataka nearly 2000 pear old brick—built stupas and relics have been discovered. At Chaneti, near Jagadhri in Haryana, the remains of a Mauryan stupa have been found. Four more Asokan Rock Edits have also been discovered. These are at : Rajula-Mandagiri in Andhra Pradesh (1953). Gujarra in Madhya Pradesh (1954); Ahraura in Uttar Pradesh (1961) and Bahapur, New Delhi (1966). Further, the place where the Buddha had delivered the famous Kalama-Sutta has been discovered.

This discovery was made in 1969 by Venerable Dharmarakshīta of Sarnath. He has identified the village Kadwar, on the river Gomati, about 10 miles to the north of Sultanpur in Uttar Pradesh, as the well-known Kesaputta of the Kalamas. In 1970, a vast complex of votive stupas neatly carved on the surface of the living rocks in the Akkhanna and Madanna Hills at Vijayawada in Andhra Pradesh was discovered by Dr. N. Venkataramayya, India's Deputy Director of Epigraphy. In 1971, the site of the famous Vikramasila University in Bihar during the reign of the Palas (750-1162 A.D.) was fully exposed and identified by the Patna University team which excavated the Mahabodhi temple described by the Tibetan historian Taranatha as being in the centre of the University. Another discovery during 1971 was of an ancient Buddhist cave with inscriptions in Brahmi script and Prakrit language in the Chanda forest, 64 kms from Nagpur. This discovery was made by a team led by Dr. S.N. Deo, Head of the Department of Ancient Indian History, Culture and Archaeology of Nagpur University.

The location of Kapilavastu had been a matter of controversy for over hundred years. Tilaurakot in Nepal and Piprahwa in India have been the main claimants for the site of Kapilavastu. Fuhrer, a German archaeologist commissioned by the Government of Nepal in 1896 put forward for the first time the claim of Tilaurakot as Kapilavastu. However, the discovery in 1898 of a huge stone coffer containing five relic-caskets from the Piprahwa stupa indicated that Piprahwa was the likely site of ancient Kapilavastu. Yet the matter remained unresolved for the next 75 years.

In January 1971, K.M. Srivastava of the Patna Archaeological Circle started fresh excavations at Piprahwa. First excavations showed that the stupa, which had earlier yielded relic caskets, enclosed a mud stupa. When this mud stupa was carefully probed it yielded in March 1972, two soapstone relic caskets containing charred bones of the Buddha and three dishes containing ashes. The relic casket found in the northern chamber was intact and was 12 cm × 7 cm. The relic casket in the southern chamber was 16 cm × 9 cm. As it was broken, the bones were rather muddy.

During further excavations in 1973, Srivastava and his team found from the adjacent Eastern Monastery more than 40 terracotta sealings with the legends in Pali "Devaputra Vihara Kapilavastu Bhikkhu Sanghas" and "Maha Kapilavastu Bhikkhu Sanghas" in Brahmi script of A.D. first century. In 1974, some more similar sealings were discovered, and the identification of Kapilavastu was clinched when the archaeologists found the lid of a pot carrying the same inscription as the first group of sealings.

The excavations revealed that the Piprahwa Stupa was built in three phases : the earliest mud stupa was built by the Sakyas in the fifth century B.C. over their share of the corporeal relics of the Buddha; it was enclosed by an enlarged stupa in the third century B.C. from which W.C. Peppe had discovered five relic caskets, and finally it was enlarged in the first century AD when the Eastern monastery was also built. According to inscriptions, the Eastern Monastery was built by the Kushana King, Kanishka (AD 78-101) for the Bhikkhu-Sangha of Kapilavastu. The archaeologists also exposed three other monasteries. The remains of the ancient town have been found at the nearby Ganwaria site where large scale excavations exposed two massive brick structures. These are believed to be the residential complex of the Sakya chief, king Suddhoddhana, father of the Buddha.

Piprahwa, the ancient Kapilavastu, is 22 km from Naugarh, a railway station on the Gorakhpur-Gonda loop line of North-Eastern Railway, and 9 km from Birdpur on the road to Lumbini from Naugarh.

The relics of the Buddha discovered from Kapilavastu are presently with the National Museum, New Delhi.

An ancient Buddhist Stupa was discovered in 1974 at Bharatpur on the left bank of Damodar river, 7 km South-West of Panagarh railway station on Eastern Railway in Durgapur sub-division of Burdwan district in West Bengal. This brick-built stupa of 8th-9th century AD was exposed upto its platform; and a few Buddha images in bhumisparsa-mudra recovered from the debris around the edifice. The excavations were conducted under the auspices of the Archaeological Survey of India and Museum and Art Gallery of the University of Burdwan under the over-all supervision of its Curator, S.N. Samanta; and Dr. S.C. Roy and S.K. Mukherji, Archaeologists of Government of India.

The year 1975 saw an outstanding discovery of a set of Asokan rock edicts containing some phrases noticed elsewhere in other versions of the King's edicts at Panguraria, Budhni Tehsil in Sehor district of Madhya Pradesh. The discovery was made by B.P. Bopardikar of the pre-history branch of the Archaeological Survey of India assisted by P.R.K. Prasad and Nambi Raju while the party was exploring pre-historic caves and other sites on the southern fringes of the Vindhyan hills, overlooking the Narmada river. The site is located about 30 km west of Hoshangabad on the Hoshangabad-Budhni-Rheti Road. The site is also associated with extensive rubble-built Buddhist remains of chaityas and stupas, in a dilapidated condition. It appears, therefore, to be a monastic site.

The Andhra Government Department of Archaeology excavated in 1976 a new stupa enclosed by a brick wall on all four sides, at Desanapalli village in Guntur district. Surrounded on three sides by steep rocky hills and enclosed by the swift flowing Krishna, Desanapalli is situated in this gorge amidst verdant jungle growth.

Among the items excavated from the site was a slab with the footprints of the Buddha on it. According to N. Ramesan, Director of the State Department of Archaeology, the footprints, unlike those on the gateways of Sanchi and Bharhut, contain symbols like Triratana, Swastika, Srivatsa and Ankusa. Another panel in marble in the shape of a crescent shows a vase carved on the model of a Srivatsa with sprouting lotus flowers, it contains an inscription in the early Brahmi script. The most important discovery at the site is a fragment of an Ayaka Stambha, Octagonal in shape, containing four lines of writing in early Brahmi script. The inscription gives the name of king Vasisthiputra Sri Santamula, who is known as the founder of the Ikshvaku dynasty, which ruled Andhra around the third century A.D. The object of the inscription was to record the consecration of a Buddhist Stambha (pillar) at Mahachaitya, belonging to the Mulavasi Vihara of the Bahusrutiya sect. Several decorative panels have also been discovered from this site. The slabs are elegantly carved in early Amaravati style and are modelled on a conceptual plane.

Hiuen Tsang's travelogue mentions Parimaiagiri, the monastery of Acharya Nagarjuna in Orissa, but an equally majestic Buddhist Vihara, Muchalinda, about 45 km. away towards the north, which escaped his attention, has been discovered recently.

The Muchalinda Vihara, located near the confluence of the Ang (or Ong) and Nagar rivers at Ganiapali in Sambalpur district was not only the earliest of its kind in Orissa, but even in India a structural monastery of this magnitude was rare during the fourth-fifth century A.D , says a report on the archaeological excavation of the ruins at Ganiapali, submitted by Dr. K.N. Sahu, Vice-Chancellor of the Sambalpur University.

The Muchalinda monastery, which covers an area of 1.5 acres, was a multi-storeyed structure of well-burnt bricks. The extensive floors paved with bricks suggest that there were big halls or dormitories in the north while the Site south of the Chaitya Hall appeared to have been the residential establishment.

The most significant discovery of the year 1976 was made at Mathura when more than 100 rare and valuable sculptures and other art pieces of the Kushana and Gupta periods were found near the Mathura water works and Bhuteshwar railway station in the western outskirts of the Mathura city. These were unearthed while levelling a large mound for construction of houses for the Govindnagar Housing Society. The antiquities include valuable sculptures of the Kushana and Gupta periods, fragments of railings, pillars, cross-bars, coping-stones, lintel beams and architraves—the remains of the famous 'Viradatta Vihara' which once stood there. One of the sculptures represents the standing Buddha with lovely curly hair, elongated ear-lobes and a very subtle and serene expression of the face. On the transparent drappery with beautiful rippling folds of the sculpture there is an inscription on the pedestal dated the 125th of the Gupta era (corresponding to A.D. 434) furnishing important information. It gives the name of the sculpture as Dinna. The date on this sculpture falls in the reign of King Kumaragupta Mahendraditya. Another remarkable specimen is a large-size image of the Buddha in the "abhaya" posture. The upper half of this piece is in an excellent state of preservation. There are also a number of other pieces depicting Buddha and Bodhisattvas in different forms and attitudes. A small fragment portrays beautifully the great event of the Buddha's renunciation when the hoofs of his horse were supported by the celestials.

A new set of Asoka rock edicts were discovered in Karnataka

on 24 August 1977 by K.V. Rao of the Archaeological Survey and a team of the Karnataka University scholars. The edicts discovered are on two boulders on the Sukrudatta Hill near Nittur in the Bellary district, and the site is to the north of the old discovery of edicts at Brahmagiri in Chitradurga district in Karnataka.

An important Buddhist settlement, which might have flourished from the first century BC to first century AD was discovered in 1983 at Bavikonda Hill, about 15 km from Visakhapatnam in Andhra Pradesh. In the light of the excavations, Bavikonda appears to have been not only a place of religious importance, but also an important education and medical centre. The excavations have revealed one Mahastupa, seven minor stupas and a Vihara consisting of 51 rooms. The Vihara had huge congregation hall, measuring 11 metres by 5.20 metres, a library and some rock-cut troughs. A small grinding stone, apparently used for preparing some herbal medicines was also discovered.

The Archaeology Department of Andhra Pradesh also found a huge Buddhist stupa, one of the biggest in South India, in Nelakondapalli in Khammam district. The stupa was wholly built of large-size burnt bricks.

The recent excavations at Sanghol in Tehsil Samrala, district Ludhiana have brought to light the rich heritage of Buddhism in Puujab. The name Sanghol has originated from Sanghpur—town of Buddhist monastic nature. Sanghol is 65 km from Ludhiana and 40 km from Chandigarh on the Ludhiana Chandigarh road. Sanghol is 16 km by road from Sirhind railway station. Another nearby railway station is Morinda, 9 km from Sirhind on Sirhind-Nangal loop line.

The most important monument uneathed in February 1985 at Sanghol by the experts of the Department of Archaeology and Museums, Punjab, is the stupa and the monastery complex. The Stupa, which appears to have been first built by Asoka in the third century B.C., is on the pattern of Dharma-Chakra (Wheel of Law). The cylindrical stupa is of 16 metre diameter on a 17 metre square platform—the pradakashina or circumambulation of the stupa raised at height. There is also a surkhi or murram pathway about 5.34 m in width all around the stupa. In the east is paved pathway along which a number of votive stupas of solid mud were erected by the devotees.

From the central portion of the stupa were recovered a tooth, ashes, and some bones as also the bottom portion of a relic casket—most probably the body relics of the Buddha. The excavations also yielded a lid with a Kharosthi legend of 1st-2nd century B.C. Upasaka Ayabhadra mentioned in the legend may have been responsible for enshrining the relics in the stupa.

The priceless find at Sanghol, which has put it prominently on the archaeological map of India, is the discovery of 117 sculptures of the Kushana period from the railing around the stupa on the square platform, These railing pillars were found in a pit between the monastery and the stupa on 2 February 1985. The valuable parts of the railing include 4 corner pillars, 58 upright pillars, 7 double-sided pillars, 35 cross bars and 13 coping stones.

Of the four corner pillars. one is with Dharma-chakradhvaja, two with Simhadhvaja and the last with stupa and devotees. The upright pillars have beautiful carvings of Yakshis, an Upasaka (a lay devotee), a Chakravartin (a royal devotee). The coping stones mounted on the railing pillars are decorated with a series of arched windows containing Buddhist symbols like dharmachakra, lotus, worship of the relic casket, worship of Buddha's bowl and other auspicious symbols. The cross bars which join the two pillars are decorated with lotus medallions. The Sanghol sculptures are considered as the best specimen of the Mathura school of art of AD second century.

During the excavations in the adjoining areas, a broken portion of stone from a gateway of the stupa, depicting Jataka stories, in redstone, was also recovered. Coins of all the kings of the Kushana dynasty and also seals and sealings in Kharosthi and Brahmi scripts have been discovered. A large citadel with internal and external moats has also been unearthed. The monastery is yet to be fully excavated.

How significant it is that the discovery of the Buddhist remains, which began in the 18th century is still going on unabated. Besides shedding light on the Buddha-Dhamma in the bye-gone days, each such discovery naturally gives vitality to the revival movement.

Turning to modern times again, we record with pride the erection of the tallest Buddha Image at Bodh Gaya, the land where the Buddha attaited Enlightenment.

Bodh Gaya, the sacred land of Englightenment, now has the honour of having the tallest Buddha Statue in India. Erected by the Daijokyo Sect, Japan, the Great Buddha Statue measures 80 feet in height, and it is 60 feet in width. It has been erected on a 2 acres of land acquired from the Government of Bihar adjacent to the Daijokyo Buddhist Temple premises. Built of pink Chunar Stone seated on a lotus built of yellow Chunar Stone, the Buddha Statue is in the meditation pose with eyes half-closed. Erected on a solid concrete hollow pedestal, the Statue is hollow-type with a spiral stair-case from the ground floor to the chest of the statue-which makes four storeys. Wooden shelves have been provided in the interior walls in the three storeys of the Statue wherein 16,300 small Buddha images made of bronze sent from Japan have been enshrined. The construction of the Statue took more than five years from 1984 onwards. The Great Buddha Statue was unveiled on 18 November 1989, in the presence of a distinguished gathering, by His Holiness the Dalai Lama (of Tibet). Rev. Y. Sugisaki President of the Diojokyo Sect, Japan welcomed the guests. The colourful unveiling ceremony, in which hundreds of Buddhist monks drawn from all disciplines performed Puja, concluded on 20 November 1989.

The Unveiling Ceremony of the Great Buddha Statue at Bodh Gaya marks a major landmark in the history of the revival movement. A century earlier, the Buddhists had no right to worship in the sacred Maha Bodhi Temple, and in fact, in 1895, Anagarika Dharmapala was not permitted to install, on the upper floor of the Maha Bodhi Temple, a small Buddha image, which was presented to him by the Buddhists of Japan. And now, besides having control over the Maha Bodhi Temple, the Buddhists have constructed a number of magnificent shrines, and the tallest Buddha Image at Bodh Gaya. This shows the prestige regained by Buddhism in India during the last hundred years.

Summing up

Nearly a century has rolled by since the Buddhist revival

movement began with the darkest possible conditions in the background. By now, the religion of the Buddha has made tremendous progress in all directions. India now has about five million Buddhists. And to cater to the spiritual and religious needs of the ever-increasing Buddhist population, a large number of Viharas have come up; the number of Bhikkhus has increased; and a good number of Buddhist Societies are now engaged in the propagation and preservation of the Dhamma. The position of this great religion is likely to improve further as the revival movement is still on the march.

CHAPTER II

Historic Sites and Shrines

THE Principal shrines in anicent India were the eight sacred spots (atthamahathanani), namely, Lumbini, Bodh Gaya, Sarnath, Kushinagar—the scenes of Birth, Enlightenment, First Sermon, and Mahaparinirvana of the Buddha; and Rajgir, Sankasya, Sravasti and Vaisali—the places sanctified by the Buddha. Asoka the Great, who calls a visit to these eight sacred spots 'dharmayatra' or a pilgrimage of piety, is said to have built nearly 84000 stupas, viharas etc. at these and other places, which though not directly connected with the life and legend of the Blessed One, rose into prominence with the spread of Buddhism in India. Asoka's example was emulated by succeeding Buddhist kings, queens and other wealthy men and women. Thus, India in due course became studded with Buddhist monuments, shrines and stupas.

In addition to the eight sacred spots, some of the other important centres of Buddhism in ancient India were : Amaravati, Bhattiprolu, Ghantasala, Goli, Gudivada, Guntupali, Jaggayyapeta, Nagarjunakonda, and Sankaram in Andhra Pradesh; Salkusa in Assam; Nalanda, Odantapuri, Pataliputra and Vikramasila in Bihar; Junagadh, Kampilya, Sanah, Siddhasar, Talaja and Valabhi in Gujarat; Sugh and Thanesar in Haryana; Kulu, Mandi and Nurpur in Himachal Pradesh; Srinagar and its outskirts like Saursa, Simpor in Kashmir; Srimulavasam in Kerala; Bagh, Bharhut and Sanchi in Madhya Pradesh; Ajanta, Bedsa, Bhaja, Ellora, Junner, Kanheri, Karle, Karhad, Kondane, Kondivite, Nasik and Śopara in Maharashtra; Baudh, Choudwara near Cuttack, Dhaulgiri, Jaugarh, Ratnagiri and Udayagiri in Orissa; Jalandhar, Patti and Sanghol in Punjab; Bairat near Jaipur, Dhamner, Hathigor, Kholvi, and Nagar near Udaipur in Rajasthan; Buddhavedu, Kanchipuram and Nagapattam in Tamil Nadu, Kanauj, Kausambi, Mathura and Prayag in Uttar Pradesh; Jugddala and Somapuri in West Bengal.

With the down-fall of Buddhism, all the Buddhist shrines fell into disuse. They were either destroyed and plundered or just ignored and neglected. The Buddhist shrines in Western India being mostly in the shape of rock-cut caves were covered with natural growth and were lucky to escape destruction, and even desecration.

Most of the anicent Buddhist places of interest unearthed by the archaeologists, antiquarians and explorers have since been restored and developed as religious-cum-tourist centres. The discovery of these historic sites and shrines of which 32 have been treated here in detail, has helped immensely the revival of Buddhism in modern India. Apart from adding historicity to Indian Buddhism, their discovery has also thrown valuable light on the bye-gone glory of the Buddhist art and architecture.

Besides the sacred shrines, the discovery of the Edicts of Asoka, which began in 1750, and is still continuing has also played a significant role in the Buddhist revival in India. The Asokan Edicts have since been discovered at 32 places within the boundaries of modern India. The discovered ones are in the states of Andhra Pradesh, Bihar, Delhi, Gujarat, Karnataka, Madhya Pradesh, Maharashtra, Rajasthan and Uttar Pradesh. The language of the Edicts inscribed on the Rocks and Pillars is Prakrit written in the Brahmi alphabet. In all the Edicts, except the two at Maski (Andhra Pradesh) and at Gujarra (Madhya Pradesh), the King is styled as "Devanampiya Piyadasi Laja", that is, "King Priyadarsi, Beloved of the Gods". In the Maski and Gujarra version, however, the name of Asoka is specifically mentioned.

I. HISTORIC SHRINES

1. Lumbini (Rummindei)

(a) Location : In Nepal. *10 km from the Indian border.

(b) Approach : 20 km by road from Nautanwa on the North-Eastern Railway in Gorakhpur District, U.P.

(ii) 35 km by road from Nowgarh on the North-Eastern Railway in Basti District, U.P.

*1 mile = 1.6 kilometres

(c) Importance : Lumbini, the birth place of the Buddha, was originally a grove of Sala trees near Kapilavastu. Mother Mahamaya gave birth to Śiddhartha in this grove while on her way to her ancestral home, Devadaha. Emperor Ashoka visited this place in about 250 B.C. as a pilgrim and erected a monolithic pillar to commemorate his visit.

(d) Monuments : *Asoka Pillar*

The pillar erected by Asoka at Lumbini still stands majestically proclaiming that here the Buddha was born. The royal incription clearly says :

* "Twenty years after his Coronation, King Priyadarsi, Beloved of the Gods, visited this spot in person and offered worship at this place, because the Buddha, the Sage of the Sakyas, was born here. He caused to be built a stone wall around the place and also erected this stone pillar to commemorate his visit. Because the Lord Buddha was born here, he made the village of Lumbini free from taxes and subject to pay only one-eighth of the produce as land revenue instead of the usual rate."

Mayadevi Temple

The historic Mayadevi temple, once again a living shrine, has a stone relic depicting the nativity of the Buddha. It shows queen Mahamaya holding on to a branch of the Sal tree and the newly born infant standing upright on lotus pedestal. It also shows Prajapati, sister of Mahamaya, and the maids. Another important remnant is the

Sakyan bathing tank where Siddhartha was given his first purification bath.

2. Bodh Gaya

(a) Location : Gaya Distt., Bihar.

(b) Approach : 12 km by road from Gaya railway station.

(c) Importance : Bodh Gaya or Buddha Gaya is the place where Siddhartha attained Enlightenment (Supreme Bodhi) and became Buddha while meditating under a pipal tree, now called Bodhi Tree.

(d) Monuments : *Maha Bodhi Temple*

The Maha Bodhi Temple, as it now stands, is approximately 170 feet high, while its base is 50 feet square. It consists of a straight pyramidal tower surmounted by a stupa. Its entrance porch, comparatively later than the original Temple, is on the east. Each of the four sides of the tower presents several tiers of niches, while the front face has a tall lancet opening for the admission of light into the sanctum and at the base of the tower there rises a turret at each of the four corners—a miniature replica of the main spire. The Temple is built of bluish bricks. with a coating of plaster. In front of the main entrance, there is an imposing gateway decorated with delicate carvings. The Gateway presents on the front an elegant stone votive stupa of small proportions. The niches on both sides of the main entrance to the Temple contain images of the Buddha. The central shrine room of the Temple, which is situated at the ground floor is reached after passing through a vaulted passage. The pillars and the main door are made of stone.

The great gilded image of the Buddha, in the earth touching attitude symbolising the supreme event of Enlightenment, is enshrined in the main sanctum at the base.

The upper storey of the Temple has two steep stone staircases on either side of the outer hall near the entrance. On the first floor one can walk right round the main tower as there is a wide and open promenade. At the four corners of this floor, there are four smaller towers which add much to the symmetry and grandeur of the whole structure. The two towers on the West side have small shrines containing images of the Bodhisattvas, while the other two shrines in the East contain the landings of the staircases. On the two landings, there are two large images of the Buddha. The parapet along the passage contains numerous votive stupas, some of which are exquisitely carved and those in the East are the best. Under the main tower on the first floor is a fairly large shrine with a Bodhisattva image installed on the altar.

Bodhi Tree

The sacred Bodhi Tree sitting under which Siddhartha had attained Supreme Enlightenment is situated to the west of the Temple. In the course of excavation work in 1870 the old Bodhi Tree fell down and a sapling from it was planted by Cunningham in its original place. This is the Bodhi Tree which we see today.

Vajrasana

The Vajrasana (Diamond Throne) seen between the Bodhi Tree and the Temple marks the actual spot sitting where Siddhartha attained supreme enlightenment. The holy seat is now marked by a red sandstone slab.

3. **Sarnath**

(a) Location : Varanasi (Banaras) District, Uttar Pradesh.

(b) Approach : (i) 10 km by road from Varanasi.

(ii) 1.6 km from Sarnath railway station on the North-Eastern Railway.

(c) Importance : Sarnath (Isipatana) marks the birth of Buddhism. Here in the Deer Park, Lord Buddha preached His First Sermon and set the Wheel of Law in motion before His five former ascetic companions. The place where the Buddha preached to the Panchvargiya Bhikkhus is marked by the Dhamek Stupa.

(d) Monuments : *Dhamek Stupa*

The Dhamek Stupa, the sole surviving symbol of the ancient glory of Sarnath, is now generally regarded to mark the original spot where Lord Buddha first encountered the five Parivrajikas and where He delivered the first sermon. As indicated by the inscription of Mahipala 1 of the Pala dynasty dated 1026 A.D., the Dhamek Stupa was earlier known as Dharmachakra Stupa.

The Dhamek Stupa originally built by Asoka is a solid cylindrical tower, 28.50 m in diameter at the base and 33.53 m in height or 42-06 m including the foundations. The structure consists of a circular stone drum to a height of 11.20 m resting on the ground without the usual rectangular basement. Above this drum rises the cylindrical mass of brickwork. Halfway up the base are eight niches which must have held images; immediately below them runs a broad course of beautifully carved yet elaborate ornament with geometrical and floral patterns with a combination of human figures and birds.

Dharmarajika Stupa

The ruins of the Dharmarajika Stupa are a bit further to the north. The original stupa built [by Asoka was 13.49 m in diameter. The first addition was made during the Kushana period. The second enlargement came in A.D. 500 or A.D. 600, with the addition of circumambulatory path (pradakshina-patha), nearly 4.88 m wide around the stupa and encompassed by a solid outer wall, 1.35 m high, pierced by four doorways in four directions. The last encasing of the Dharmarajika stupa took place in A.D. twelfth century. The Dharmarajika stupa was demolished in 1794 by Jagat Singh of Varanasi.

Mulagandhakuti (Main Shrine)

Towards the north of the Dharmarajika Stupa are the ruins of the Main Shrine. The building is square on plan, 18.29 m along each side, and faces the east. The Mulagandhakuti, according to Hiuen-Tsang, was about 61 m high. The ruins of the Dharmarajika Stupa and the Mulagandhakuti mark the place where Lord Buddha lived during His stay at Sarnath.

Asokan Pillar

The Asokan Pillar stands towards the west of the Main Shrine. This pillar appears to have been put up by Asoka at the spot where the Buddha first established the Sangha. The original pillar was 15-25 m high and was surmounted by the famous lion-capital with a crowning dharmachakra fitted above the heads of four lions. The stump standing in situ is 2.03 m high.

The Museum

The Museum, which was established in 1910 houses the antiquities discovered at Sarnath from 1904 onwards. The four most important sculptures in this Museum are :

The Lion Capital (modern India's National Emblem), The Bodhisattva, The Preaching Buddha and Buddha's life panels.

4. **Kushinara (Kushinagar)**

(a) Location : Deoria District, Uttar Pradesh.

(b) Approach : 55 km by road from Gorakhpur on the North-Eastern Railway.

(c) Importance : At Kushinara, the Buddha in His 80th year attained Mahaparinirvana under the twin-Sala trees. This site is marked by the Mahaparinirvana Stupa and a temple with a huge reclining stone image of the Buddha.

(d) Monuments : *Nirvana Temple*

The present Nirvana Temple at Kushinagar was built by the Government of India in 1956, as part of the

2500th Buddha Jayanti Celebrations, on the request of the Buddhists as the ancient temple restored by Carlleyle in 1876 offered practically no space for the pilgrims to circumambulate the shrine.

The 1500 year old Nirvana statue, which is again being worshipped, is 20 feet (6.1 m) in length and is executed out of one block of sandstone of mixed reddish colour probably from Chuner. It represents the Dying Buddha reclining on his right side with his face turned towards the west. It is placed on a 24 feet long brick throne with stone posts at the corners and once faced with stone slabs on all sides. The western side of the pedestal facing the entrance bears sculptures representing three human figures, each carved in a shallow niche cut into a solid block of stone. It is difficult to identify the figures; however, the central figure may be that of the donor, Haribala himself. Right below him an inscription of A.D. fifth century records that the statue was the appropriate religious gift of the Mahavihara-Svamin Haribala and that it was fashioned by 'Dinna'. The reclining Buddha image is believed to be on the very spot where Lord Buddha breathed his last.

Main Stupa

The Main Stupa, as repaired and restored in 1927, by Ven. U Chandramani, is 75 feet high.

Matha Kuar

The Matha-Kuar-temple, is just about two furlongs south-west of the Parinirvana shrine. The colossal statue installed in the shrine is 3.05 m in height and is carved out of the blue stone of the Gaya region and represents Buddha seated under the Bodhi tree in the "earth-touching attitude" (bhumisparsamudra) which symbolises the supreme event of His Enlightenment. The statue is about 1000 years old, having been installed in A.D. 10th century. The present temple was built in 1927.

Cremation Stupa

About 1.61 km to the east of the Matha-Kuar shrine on the road from Kasia to Deoria stands the Cremation Stupa or the Makutabandhana Chaitya of Buddhist tradition near the Ramabhar Jhil or pond which dries up in summer. The Cremation Stupa has a large circular drum 34.14 m in diameter, resting on circular plinth, and is 47.24 m in diameter at the base.

5. **Rajagaha (Rajgir)**

(a) Location : Patna district, Bihar.

(b) Approach : (i) 102 km by road from Patna.
(ii) 65 km by road from Gaya.

(c) Importance : Rajgir was the capital of the Magdha in the days of the Buddha. Lord Buddha had His favourite retreat here on the Griddhakuta Hill (Vulture Peak). It was at Rajgir that Lord Buddha performed the miracle of subduing by the power of His love the intoxicated elephant set upon Him by Devadatta. The first Buddhist Council was also held here immediately after the Mahaparinirvana of the Buddha.

(d) Mounments : Hot Springs.

Most of the hot water springs at Rajgir are at the foot of the Vaibhara Hill. These hot springs find mention in the sermons of the Buddha.

Saptaparni Cave

The Saptaparni Cave where the First Buddhist Council was held after the demise of the Buddha is situated on the top of the Vaibhara hill beyond the modern Jaina temple of Adinatha. The terrace in front of the caves is about 36.57 metres long and 10.36 metres wide at the east and 3.65 metres at the west.

Maniyar Math

About 1 km. from the north gate, to the right of the road, is a cylindrical brick-structure. It appears the site of an ancient monastery located between Rajgir and Bodh Gaya. Excavations have revealed successive shrines and structures.

Swarna Bhandar Cave

Towards the north-west of the Maniyar Math stands the Swarna-bhandar Cave. According to legend, this was Bimbisara's treasury.

Gridhakuta (Vulture Peak)

The Gridhakuta Hill was the favourite resort of the Buddha and the scene of many of His important sermons. Atop the Gridhakuta Hill there are two natural caves with steps approaching them, which, in all probability, represent the 'caves' mentioned by Hiuen Tsang.

6. Sankasya (Sankisa)

(a) Location : Farrukhabad District, Uttar Pradesh.

(b) Approach : (i) 11 km by road from Pakhna on the Northern Railway.

(ii) 64 km by road from Farukhabad on the Northern Railway.

(c) Importance : Lord Buddha is believed to have descended at Sankasya from the heaven of thirty-three gods (Trayastrimsa heaven) which He visited to preach the Dhamma to His mother and the gods.

(d) Monuments : An important relic of the past at Sankisa is the stump of the broken Asokan pillar surmounted by the elephant capital. It has beautiful carvings of lotus and leaves of Bodhi tree. About 20 yards to the south of the Asokan pillar, there is a high mound of solid brick work. It is believed that the Buddha had descended from heaven at this place.

7. Sravasti (Saheth-Maheth)

(a) Location : Border of Gonda and Bahraich District, Uttar Pradesh.

(b) Approach : 21 km by road from Balrampur on the North-Eastern Railway.

(c) Importance : At Sravasti, the capital of Kosala, the Buddha is said to have performed His greatest miracle. It is said that in a contest with the teachers of rival sects He created multiple representations of Himself from a thousand petalled lotus and showed water and fire coming out simultaneously from His body. Lord Buddha spent 24 rainy seasons at Sravasti, most of them in the Jetavana monastery which was built by the wealthy merchant Anathapindika in the large park bought for the purpose at a fabulous price.

(d) Monuments : *Jetavana*

The shrines at Jetavana as we see to-day are 19 Temples and Monasteries. Of these, the most important ones are : *Temple 2* marks the site of the original temple called Gandhakuti built by Anathapindika as part of the Jetavana monastery. Gandhakuti is one of the most sacred Temples in Jetavana, having been hallowed by the personal use of the Buddha. The present structure is a late renovation. *Temple 3*, is believed to mark the very spot where stood the original Kosambakuti built by Anathapindika and hallowed by the personal use of the Buddha. In front of the temple are two brick terraces erected on the original promenade (chankama) used by the Buddha for His walks.

Sravasti City

Leaving Jetavana by the north the visitor can go to the site of the ancient city by taking the road which enters it by the Sobhnatha Gate, one of the openings made in recent past in the high rampart that encompasses the city. The notable Buddhist monuments in this area are : the Angulimala Stupa, and the Sudatta (Anathapindika) Stupa, locally called Pakki Kuti and Kachchi Kuti.

8. **Vaisali**

(a) Location : Muzaffarpur District, Bihar.

(b) Approach : (i) 36 km from Muzaffarpur Railway Station.

(ii) 55 km from Patna across the Ganga.

(c) Importance : Vaisali was the capital of the powerful Licchavi clan in the days of the Buddha. Lord Buddha visited this place atleast thrice, and performed here one of His miracles, namely, the offering to Him of a bowl of honey by some monkeys. The second Buddhist Council was held at Vaisali about a century after the Mahaparinirvana of the Buddha.

(d) Monuments : The ancient city of Vaisali is now represented by the ruins of Raja Bishal Ka Garh at Basrah and the adjoining areas. At Koluha, 3 km to the north-west of this site, there stands an uninscribed Asokan pillar to a height of 40 feet, including lion capital. Nearby this pillar, to the south, there is a small tank now called Ramakund, which has been identified with the ancient monkeys' tank (Markata-hrada) believed to have been dug by a band of monkeys for the use of the Buddha. The ruins of the Asokan stupa are to the north-west of the tank. The ruined mound is 15 feet high and has a diameter of about 65 feet at the base.

9. Nalanda

(a) Location : Patna district, Bihar.

(b) Approach : (i) 12 km by road from Rajgir.
(ii) 90 km from Patna.

(c) Importance : Lord Buddha had visited Nalanda several times and delivered some important sermons there. Sariputta as well as Moggallana, the two chief disciples of the Budhha, were born somewhere near Nalanda. Sariputta also attained Parinirvana at Nalanda.

The University of Nalanda was one of the most celebrated centres of Buddhist learning in ancient India. In the seventh century A.D., it had more than ten thousand students from India and abroad.

(d) Monuments : The ruins of Nalanda extend over a vast area. The Stupa site No. 3 is a huge structure standing in the middle of the court surrounded by a number of stupas. The antiquities discovered from the vast ruins are preserved in the site Archaeological Museum.

10. Amaravati

(a) Location : In Andhra Pradesh.

(b) Approach : (i) 32 km by road from Guntur.
(ii) 75 km from Vijayawada.

(c) Importance : Amaravati was a flourishing centre of Buddhism for about thousand years from the second century B.C. onward. Its Great Stupa, which was famous as containing the body-relics of the Buddha, had an ornamental railing which was 4 metres high and measured about 54 m in diameter, pierced on all the four sides by gateways.

(d) Monuments : The Amaravati Stupa was dismantled by a local chieftain in 1797 for the sake of building material. Nothing much remains now of the grandest stupa except a small mound which consists of just the drum of the brick built stupa, the paved circumambulatory path and few uprights and pillars.

Majority of the surviving Amaravati sculptures are in the Government Museum, Madras. The site Museum at Amaravati also has good collection of sculptures.

11. Nagarjunakonda

(a) Location : In Andhra Pradesh.

(b) Approach : (i) 25 km from Macherala.
(ii) 150 km by road from Hyderabad.

(c) Importance : Nagarjunakonda, the older name of which was Sri-Parvata, is associated with the famous Buddhist saint and scholar, Bodhisattva Nagarjuna, who was the founder of the Madhyamika school and flourished in the reign of the Satavahana King, Gautamiputra Yajnasri, in the 2nd century A.D.

(d) Monuments : The sites of more than a hundred Buddhist monuments at Nagarjunakonda now stand submerged by the gigantic multipurpose Nagarjunasagar Dam. Hundreds of beautiful sculptures which would have been submerged by the construction of the dam have been lifted to the top of a hill, which stands right in the midst of the reservoir. The island museum, which is unique and first of its kind in the world, can be reached by a launch from Anuppu, the jetty point, about 14 km from Nagarjunakonda. A few monuments have been faithfully reconstituted out of ancient materials on the Nagarjunakonda and on the east bank of resorvoir. Important monuments which can be seen at Nagarjunakonda are: Maha Stupa-Site 1; Monastery-Site 4; Apsidal shrine-Site 43; and Stupa with swastika inset-Site 59.

12. Junagadh

(a) Location : In Gujarat.

(b) Approach : From Ahmedabad via Rajkot.

(c) Importance : Junagadh's association with Buddhism goes back to the time of Asoka. At Girnar, just 1 mile east of Junagadh, there is an Asokan Rock Edict, the text of which contains the Fourteen Rock Edicts.

(d) Monuments : 50 rock-cut caves. Some of the caves at Junagadh have two or three storeys. At Uparkot, the old fort of Junagadh, is a 'two storey hall' which is interesting and impressive on account of its plan and decorative motifs and sculptures. The largest cave at Khaprakhodia is locally known at Khajar Mahal. It measures 250 ft. by 80 ft.

13. Sanah

(a) Location : In Gujarat.

(b) Approach : 25 km south of Una railway station.

(c) Importance : 62 caves of the second century B.C.

(d) Monuments : These caves are of a plain type but have a good number of tanks for water. The largest of them is locally known as Ebhal- mandap and measures 68½ ft. × 61 ft. × 16½ feet.

14. Talaja

(a) Location : In Gujarat.

(b) Approach : 48 km south of Bhavnagar.

(c) Importance : 36 caves probably excavated in the second century B.C.

(d) Monuments : These caves are rather plain. The largest cave is 75 feet × 67½ feet and 17½ feet high.

15. Valabhi

(a) Location : In Gujarat.

(b) Approach : 37 km to the north-west of Bhavnagar.

(c) Importance : In ancient days Valabhi was an important centre of Buddhist learning, being next only to Nalanda. Hiuen Tsang visited it in 640 A.D. and was full of praise. According to Copper-plate inscriptions, the Madraka rulers of Valabhi gave grants to atleast 15 monasteries built there between the 7th and 8th centuries A.D.

(d) Monuments : Ruins of the University and monasteries.

16. Bagh Caves

(a) Location : In Madhya Pradesh.

(b) Approach : 7 km from Bagh town which is 176 km from Indore.

(c) Importance : Apart from their architectural or sculptural value, the Bagh Caves contain the beautiful examples of ancient Indian wall paintings. Besides Ajanta, it is only at Bagh that such priceless art treasures have survived.

(d) Monuments : Of the nine caves, only four have survived in a tolerable condition. The finest paintings at Bagh are in cave no. 4, which is locally known as 'Rang Mahal or the painted mansion. This cave is the largest excavation; its portico being about 220 feet long. In the three sides are 27 cells with one double and one triple cell. Within the pillard hall, there is a secondary group of 10 masonary pillars. They are so placed as to form three ornamental porches leading to the aisles formed by the 28 rock-cut pillars. This design is repeated on the other two sides also. All the capitals are sculptured and some of the capitals are painted. There are numerous sculptured Buddha figures and the chaitya arches. There are a series of mural paintings of varying narratives. The walls, ceilings and pillars of the hall have a variety of floral and animal paintings. The Bagh paintings, though inspired by religion, are secular in outlook.

17. **Bharhut**

(a) Location : In Madhya Pradesh.

(b) Approach : (i) 10 km from Uchahara and 15 km from Satna Station on the Central Railway.
(ii) About 152 km from Jabalpur.

(c) Importance : The Stupa and its magnificent gateways

and railings were created sometime between B.C. 250-150. The discovery of the Bharhut Stupa has added much historicity to Indian Buddhism. The historic scenes include : Mother Maya Devi's dream; Jetavana Monastery's presentation by Anathapindika; Visit of Ajatasatru to Buddha; and Visit of Prasenajit to Buddha. Most of the sculpture pieces have inscriptions below them which are in the same characters as those of the Sanchi Stupa. Thus the scene depicting Jetavana Monastery is described as 'Jetavana Anadhapediko-deti koti Santhatena Keta' i.e Anatha-pindika presents Jetavana (having become) its purchaser for a layer of Kotis.

(d) Monuments : Nothing much remains of the Mahastupa of Bharhut which was discovered by Cunningham in 1873. Majority of the surviving Bharhut sculptures are now preserved in the Indian Museum, Calcutta. The Bharhut sculptures pertain to Superhuman beings, Human beings, Animals, Trees and Fruits, Objects of worship, Decorative Ornaments; Buddhist Buildings etc. The objects of worship include stupas, dharmachakras, bodhi trees, Buddha-padas (footprints) and Triratana. But there is no Buddha as in the third century B.C. the Buddha had not been personified, and was depicted by various symbols.

18. **Sanchi**

(a) Location : In Madhya Pradesh.

(b) Approach : (i) Sanchi Station on the main Central Railway line.

(ii) 44 km from Bhopal.

(c) Importance : Sanchi is famous for its stupas, the Great Stupa constructed by Asoka and later on expanded by his successors being the most imposing one. The Gateways (Torans) to the stupas are particularly impressive and they depict many scenes from the life of the Buddha. Sanchi has the honour of preserving the relics of Sariputta and Moggallana, the two chief disciples of of the Buddha. The relics were housed in a new Vihara in 1952, after their return from London, where they were taken in 1851.

(d) Monuments : Stupas, Sculptured Gateways, Memorial Pillars, Monasteries. Of all the monuments, the Great Stupa is the grandest. The diameter of the Great Stupa, as it stands today, is about 120 feet and its height, excluding the railing and umbrella, is about 50 feet. It consists of an almost hemispherical dome, truncated near the top and crowned by a triple umbrella set at the centre of a heavy masonary pedestal, within a square railing. A high circular battered terrace approached by a double stairway on the South and meant for circumambulation is built against the base. At the ground level, the balustrade made of stone encloses the dome and the terrace; it has access from the cardinal directions through four gateways.

In the bas-reliefs on the gateways of the Sanchi Stupa, scenes from the life of the Buddha find a prominent place. Here the Buddha is not represented in human form; only certain symbols such as horse without a rider but with an umbrella held above, throne, wheel, foot-prints, trees commemorate His presence. On the summit of the gateway stands the emblem of Buddhism, viz., the Wheel of Law (Dharmachakra), supported on elephants flanked on either side by a guardian yaksha and at the end by Triratna-trinity of Buddhism-the Buddha, the Dhamma and the Sangha.

While the greatness of Stupa I is on account of the marvellous sculpture on the gateways, the stupas 2 and 3 are important because of the body-relics of some distinguished disciples of the Buddha discovered therein. According to the inscriptions on the four relic-caskets discovered from stupa 2, the bone-relics enshrined therein were of 10 Buddhist saints, who lived in the third century B.C.

Stupa 3, situated just near the Great Stupa, yielded the relics of Sariputta and Maha-Moggallana, the two chief disciples of the Buddha. The excavations in 1851 revealed a stone slab about five feet long lying from north to south. Beneath it were found two large boxes of grey sand stone, each with a short inscription in Brahmi characters on its lid. The box to the south bore the inscription Sariputasa and that to the north was inscribed Moggalanasa.

19. **Ajanta**

(a) Location : In Maharashtra.

(b) Approach : (i) 106 km by road from Aurangabad.
(ii) 60 km by road from Jalgaon.

(c) Importance : The Ajanta Caves belong to the glorious era of Buddhism i.e. the period from 200 B.C. to 800 A.D. They are unique in that they combine three forms of art : architecture, sculpture, and painting. The rock-cut Viharas are remarkable for the spaciousness of their halls and the great variety and beauty of their sculptures and paintings.

(d) Monuments : The Ajanta Caves are the product of both the Theravada (Hinayana) and Mahayana Buddhists. Of the 30 caves at Ajanta, five (Nos. 9, 10, 19, 26 and 29) are Chaitya halls. The remaining are Viharas. The oldest caves created by the early Buddhists belong to the period from second century B.C. to second century A.D. In this group are two Chaityas (Nos. 9 and 10) and four Viharas (Nos 8, 12, 13 and 30). The remaining 24 caves were added by the Buddhist devotees after a long interval during the period from the fifth to seventh centuries.

Cave 1 is one of the finest examples of Vihara architecture evolved towards the end of A.D. fifth century. The facade is lavishly ornamented; its beauty is enhanced by six richly carved columns in the verandah. The ornate doorway leads into a big hall, 64 feet square. Beyond the ante-chamber facing the entrance is a huge Buddha image grouped with the Master's five disciples and a wheel between two deer.

The wall of the back corridor, contains two majestic Bodhisattvas which are among the Ajanta masterpieces. The one to the left is Padampani with flower in hands. His eyes are lowered meditatively, his face has depth of spiritual calm born of compassion for all living beings. The other

Bodhisattva, Vajrapani, is richly bejewelled. The Jatakas illustrated in Cave I are: Sibi Jataka No. 499, Sankhapala Jataka No. 524, Mahajanaka Jataka No. 539 and Campeyya Jataka No. 506.

Cave 2, also a Vihara, is somewhat alike in the plan to cave I. The verandah, which is 46 ft. by 7 ft. 9 in., has a lovely painted ceiling. Among the excellent murals, one on the left wall of the hall, dramatizes the legend of the Buddha's birth with some vivid panels. The Jatakas illustrated in Cave 2 are: Hamsa Jataka No. 502, Vidurpandita Jataka No. 545, Khanti Jataka No. 313 and Ruru Jataka No. 482.

Cave 4 is the largest Vihara at Ajanta. The decorated main entrance leads to a hall with twenty eight pillars. The shrine has a large image of the Buddha in the company of Vajrapani and Padampani.

Cave 6 is a two-storeyed Vihara, the only Vihara of its kind at Ajanta. The door frame of the shrine is lavishly carved. There are a number of Buddha figures in various attitudes. In the shrine room, the Buddha is sitting cross-legged in the abhaya mudra. He is seated on a lion throne. Below is a dharmachakra wlth two small deer, one on each side. In the shrine room on the second floor, the Buddha is sitting cross-legged on a lion throne. Below are a dharmachakra and two deer.

Cave 7 is also a Vihara. In the shrine room is a seated Buddha. He is sitting cross-legged on a lion throne. On his two sides are Bodhisattvas holding chauries. The 'Miracle of Sravasti' is carved on the walls of the ante-chamber.

Cave 10, an apsidal Chaitya, is the largest excavation at Ajanta, and the second largest in India, the first being at Karla. This cave is 369 sq. metres in area (29.5 metres in length and 12.5 metres wide) with 39 pillars.

This chaitya hall is the earliest excavation at Ajanta. An inscription on its front indicates date as an early decade of second century B.C. Of special interest in this cave are the examples of the ancient painting. Cave 10 has paintings illustrating only two Jatakas: Sama Jataka and Chhaddanta Jataka.

Cave 16 is one of the most beautiful caves at Ajanta. An inscription of late sixth century A.D. gives its history: a Minister of the royal court had it excavated as a gift for the "best of ascetics". The nativity story of the Buddha started in cave 2 is continued here on the right wall. The masterpiece in this cave is a painting on the left wall, famed as "The Dying Princess". In Cave 16, there are paintings illustrating three Jatakas. They are: Hasti Jataka, Maha-Ummaga Jataka No. 546, and Sutosoma Jataka No. 537.

Cave 17 also belongs to the sixth century A.D. Its entrance, with the decorative panels and the corner projections, is considered to be "a thing of supreme artistic value". A mural on the portico's right wall illustrates the subjugation of a rogue elephant, Nalagiri, at Rajgir, one of the eight great miracles attributed to the Buddha.

Inside the cave, there are paintings depicting Jataka stories, scenes from the life of the Buddha and some historic incidents. The back wall of the ante-chamber contains the excellent "Mother and Child before Buddha". The occasion is the Buddha's return to his palace door with a begging bowl in his hand. At his mother's bidding Rahula begs of the Buddha his rightful inheritance as a son.

The Jataka paintings in cave 17 are: Chhaddanta Jataka No. 514, Vessantara Jataka No. 547, Mahakapi Jataka I, No. 407, Hamsa Jataka No. 502, Mahakapi Jataka II, No. 516, Sutosoma Jataka No. 537, Sarbhamiga Jataka No. 483, Matiposaka Jataka No. 455, Maccha Jataka No. 75, Mahisha Jataka, Nigrodhamiga Jataka No. 12, Sibi Jataka No. 499 and Sama Jataka No. 540.

Cave 19, a Chaitya-hall of the late Mahayana period, has an exquisitely carved facade (with many large Buddha figures in relief. The great arched window adds to its grandeur The interior has number of Buddha images. Boldly conceived and superbly executed in minute detail, this chapel is regarded as one of the best examples of Buddhist art. With its large number of stone figures, it has aptly been called "the sculptor's treasure-chest". The walls are painted with the figures of the Buddha in panels.

Cave 26 is a Chaitya excavated during the seventh century A.D. It is almost as crowded with sculpture as

Cave 19 but its chaitya hall is larger in size. It is 67 ft. 10 in deep x 36 ft. 3 in. wide x 31 ft. 3 in. It has a colossal Reclining Buddha figure-representing Mahaparinirvana. The Buddha is lying on his right side with his right hand under his head. The Reclining Buddha is 23 ft. 3 inches in length. Ananda and Kashyapa are shown standing mourning his passing. In front of the bed are other disciples and bhikkhus in grief. Above panel has devas scattering flowers.

20. **Bedsa**

(a) Location : In Maharashtra.

(b) Approach : 7 km from Kamshet, off Bombay-Poona Road, and about 18 km south of Karla.

(c) Importance : These caves may have been excavated in the second century B.C.

(d) Monuments : Of the 12 caves at Bedsa, the Chaitya Cave 11 is the most important one. It is provided with very artistic front columns on the corners of which are carved horses and elephants with male and female riders. To the north of the Chaitya is a Vihara which is considered unique in design. The Mahayana Buddhists occupied these caves in the fifth century A.D. and added some paintings of the Buddha.

21. **Bhaja**

(a) Location : In Maharashtra.

(b) Approach : About 9 km by road from Lonavla, and 3 km from Malavli railway station.

(e) Importance : These caves date back to the second century B.C. and are one of the earliest in India.

(d) Monuments : The use of timber in the rock-cut architecture is a special feature of these caves. The Chaitya-hall, (cave No. 12) which is 18 metres in length, 8.2 m wide and 3-4 m. in height with 27 plain pillars is a fine example of early Hinayana temple. The stupa is 11 feet in diameter at the floor level, the cylinder is 4 feet high and the dome 6 feet high, surmounted by a two-tiered box with place for relics and shaft of the umbrella. The roof is arched and ribbed inside with teak girders. Bhaja has also a number of stupas standing in the open.

22. Ellora

(a) Location : In Maharashtra.

(b) Approach : 30 km by road from Aurangabad.

(c) Importance : The caves at Ellora are a combination of three religious systems; Buddhism, Hinduism and Jainism and the first 12 caves at Ellora are the earliest and were excavated by the Buddhists over a period of 200 years from 550 A.D. to about-750 A.D. Unlike the paintings at Ajanta, sculptures, massive in size and superb in execution, dominate the Ellora Caves. They portray chiefly the Buddha, Bodhisattvas and other divinities and follow the accepted formulae of such representations.

(d) Monuments : Caves 2 has twelve massive colums with cushion capitals to support the roof. The entrance to the main shrine is flanked by the Bodhisattvas. The huge Buddha image at the rear is seated on a Lion Throne with Padmapani and Manjusri as chauribearers. The galleries, however, have Buddha figures seated on lotuses in the traditional postures of a preacher with Bodhisattvas in attendance.

Cave 5 is the largest Vihara, 35.66 metres by 17 metres, and has twenty-four pillars. There is a seated Buddha image in the main shrine attended by Avalokitesvara on one side and Maitreya on the other side. Cave 6 is notable for its ante-chamber which has several interesting sculptures.

Cave 10, known as Visvakarma, or the Carpenters' Cave, is the only proper Chaitya-hall at Ellora. Its facade, richly decorated has the semblance of masonary work. A porch surmounted by a gallery leads to another gallery inside the chapel. The Chaitya hall, third largest in India, measures 26 metres in length, 13.4 metres in width and 10.4 metres in height. In the far end is the stupa 8.2 metres high and 4.9 metres in diameter. On this is carved a large seated Buddha, attended by Avalokitesvara and Maitreya, under a Bodhi Tree. Beside the large number of seated and standing Buddhas, there are a number of images of the Bodhisattvas of the Vajrayana pantheon.

Caves 11 and 12 are large, three-storey Viharas alike in design and represent the peak of the earlier style at Ellora. Cave 12 is the bigger of the two and more impressive. Known as Teen Thal, it is a vast excavation. The facade nearly 50 ft. high plain and austere-looking has porches supported by pillars in each storey. Access to the ground floor is through a spacious verandah divided into three aisles by means of three rows of columns of eight each, making 24 pillars in all. At right angles to the verandah is another pillared hall having three aisles of three pillars each. At the far end is the shrine chamber having a seated image of the Buddha and other images on the walls.

The first storey of the Teen Thal is a large hall, 115 feet by 70 feet (35 metres by 21.33 metres) and 12 feet high divided by forty square pillars into five aisles. On the far side in the shrine room is the seated figure of the Buddha. There are figures of Bodhisattvas as well. The second storey is likewise a large hall. The shrine room is at the end of the central hall. Among the huge Buddha figures, with Avalokitesvara and Vajrapani in attendance, the one in the shrine room of top floor, arms folded and the face deeply meditative, is most impressive.

23. **Junnar**

(a) Location : In Maharashtra.

(b) Approach : 90 km by road from Pune and 140 km from Nasik.

(c) Importance : Junnar, the second Satavahana capital, was the largest Buddhist monastic establishment in India from B.C. 100 to A.D. 300.

(d) Monuments : There are 140 Buddhist caves at Junnar-131 Viharas and 9 Chaityas. The caves at Junnar are scattered in the three hills-Shivneri, Manmodi and Sulaiman-within a radius of 5 km around the old town. These caves include almost every variety of rock-cut temple but they are devoid of any human representation or Buddha images. The only ornamentation is by way of rail pattern, the chaitya-arch and animal figures on the pillar capitals.

The Shivneri hill, about 3 km to the north-west of the town, has the unique distinction of having Buddhist caves in the heart and an ancient fort on its top in which Chhatrapati Shivaji was born. Situated at a height of over 300 metres, the Shivneri fort is reached through seven gates, darwazas, built at different levels for security purposes. Sivabai's temple, which is at the level of initial fortification, is built in the hollow of a Buddhist cave.

The Manmodi hill, ancient, Manmukada, to the south-west of the town beyond Shivneri, has about 50 caves in three groups. These caves date back to the Ist-2nd centuries A.D. The central group of Buddhist caves at Manmodi is now known as Amba/ Ambika Lena as in one of the caves therein the Jains have added the figures of two Tirthankaras, and Ambika, the Sasanadevi of Neminath.

The Lenyadri or the Sulaiman range group of caves is 5 km. north-east of the town, off the Junnar-Udapur Road (Bombay Road). These caves were excavated towards the end of the first century A.D. Here the main group consisting of 30 caves is now called Ganesha Lena as one of the Viharas (No. 7) is now the abode of Ganesha, a Hindu deity. In this group, cave No. 4 is a small Chaityagriha. The next cave No. 5 is a simple Vihara with a large hall 26′ × 29′ and 8′ high. It has seven cells for resident monks. The adjacent cave No. 6 is the main Chaitya in this group. It is 40′ in length, 22′-5″ wide and 24′-2″ high. The

Ganesha Lena hall (cave No. 7) is the largest Vihara at Junnar. It is 50′-6″ by 56′-6″ and is 10′-2″ high with 3 doors and two windows in front and a stone seat round the inner three sides. It has 7 cells on each side and 5 at the back-central one having been altered for the 'rat-riding god' (Ganesha) whose large image is cut out of the rock probably from a dagoba (stupa) that may have been there. In front of the cave is a narrow verandah, with six pillars, and two attached ones rising from a bench as in cave 3 at Nasik.

24. **Kanheri**

(a) Location : In Maharashtra.

(b) Approach : (i) 42 km by road from Bombay.
(ii) 8 km from Borivli railway station.

(c) Importance : Kanheri had the second largest monastic establishment, and it was continuously occupied by Buddhist monks for about 1200 years from the second century B.C. onward.

(d) Monuments : There are 109 Buddhist caves at Kanheri. Majority of these caves are cells for the monks with a stone bench and verandah in front.

The main Chaitya (Cave No. 3) at Kanheri is 317 sq. mts. in area or 26.4 metres × 12 metres and is the fourth largest in India. It is 15.2 metres in height and has 34 pillars. The stupa is about 5 metres in height and has a series of relic caskets along the centre of the drum. It was excavated in about 180 A.D. and was used both by the Theravada and the Mahayana Buddhists. Among the sculptures added by some Mahayana followers sometime in the fifth century A.D. are colossal statues of the Buddha nearly seven metres high at each end of the verandah. There are also standing figures of the Bodhisattva Avalokitesvara and the Buddha on the front wall to the left of the verandah. The sculptures on the front screen are of the donor couples belonging to the second century A.D.

Cave No. 10 on the right side of the ravine is the largest Vihara at Kanheri. It is also known as the Darbar Hall as it was used as an assembly or convocation hall. It has 12 cells in its eastern and southern wall. The cell opposite the entrance is carved with a seated Buddha attended by Bodhisattvas on either side. The inner assembly hall is 22.3 metres in length and 9.8 metres in width. Cave 35 is one of the largest caves at Kanheri. It is about 14 metres x 12 metres, without pillars, with a bench or seat round three sides and with four cells. The Mahayana sculptures added later are on the inner walls of the cave and the verandah. The seated Buddha is on the lotus throne, His hands in the Dharmachakra mudra. Cave No. 41 has a representation of an eleven-headed Avalokitesvara, said to be the only relic of its kind in India. Cave No. 50 has a panel showing Buddha preaching. Cave No. 90 has the largest number of Buddha images. It also has a fine sculptured litany of Avalokitesvara in his role as the saviour of the Eight Great Perils.

An interesting feature of Kanheri caves is the number of steps and paths some with hand rails, leading from one cave to the next. Another important feature is the system of runnels, cisterns and reservoirs, which provided water to every cave.

Kanheri is the only place in India where monastic caves were continuously occupied by Buddhist monks from the second century B.C. to tenth century A.D.

25. **Karla**

(a) Location : In Maharashtra.

(a) Approach : 14 km by road from Lonavla. Lonavla is 114 km from Bombay on the Bombay-Poona Road.

(c) Importance : Excavated in the first century B.C., the arched Chaitya hall is the largest rock-cut temple in India.

(d) Monuments : The arched Chaitya-hall is the most magnificent cave at Karla. It belongs to the first century B.C. and is the largest rock-cut temple in India. It measures 525 sq. metres in area or 37.8 metres x 13,9 metres. It is 14 metres high and has two rows of 15 monolith pillars, the capitals of each are surmounted by well-sculptured men and women riders, seated on kneeling elephants, with their arms circling each other. At the further end of the temple is a huge dome-shaped stupa with places for relics and the beautifully carved umbrella. Its timber arches, which decorate the roof, are the finest example of the wood work of the early period. One of its own inscription tells us that the Karla Chaitya was regarded as the most excellent rock mansion in Jambudvipa (India).

The Mahayana Buddhists, who later occupied this Chaitya, added in the verandah a few images of the Buddha, attended by Padamapani and Manjusri and other imagery in the 5th-6th centuries A.D.

Originally on each side of the facade, a little ahead of the entrance were two pillars about 15 metres in height. The pillar on the left stands on a wide cylindrical base, surmounted by a bell shaped capital on which were four lions supporting a wheel (now damaged). The pillar on the right was destroyed due to land slide. The temple of Hindu goddess Ekvira now occupies the place where this pillar stood.

26. Nasik

(a) Location	:	In Maharashtra.
(b) Approach	:	10 km from Nasik on Bombay-Nasik Road.
(c) Importance	:	The earliest caves at Nasik were excavated in the second century B.C. and they appear to have been in continuous use upto A.D. seventh century. These caves have interesting inscriptions of Nahapana, Gautamiputra and Sriyajna Satakarni who ruled Nasik-Karla region in the second century A.D.
(d) Monuments	:	There are 23 Buddhist caves at Nasik. Locally, they are known as Pandavleni. The Nasik caves have a number of notable Viharas and three of them (Nos 3. 8 and 15) "have columned porticos and large central halls, without pillars, out of which open the usual range of cells containing in most instances stone beds".

Cave No. 10, is also a Vihara having a hall 12.5 metres wide and 14 metres deep with 16 cells and three plain doors. The pillars of the verandah contain bell-shaped capitals. The frontage of the shrine inside had once the Buddhist symbols: stupa and dharma-chakra, similar to those in cave No. 3. Later on, however, when the Brahmins occupied the caves, after the down-fall of Buddhism, the stupa and dharma-chakra were broken and superimposed by the image of Hindu God, Bhairon. The hall of the Vihara Cave No. 17 is 9.7 metres deep and 7 metres wide. On the back wall, there is a standing image of the Buddha. Cave No. 18 is a Chaitya and is probably the earlier excavation at Nasik. The Chaitya hall is 11.9 metres in length, 6.7 metres wide and 7 metres high. The dagoba (stupa) at the far end is 1.6 metres in diameter and 1.8 metre high. Cave No. 20 is the largest Vihara; the depth being 18.6 metres. The caves 17 and 20 appear to have been modified by the Mahayana Buddhists in the seventh century A.D. The shrine room of cave No. 20 has a large seated Buddha with Padmapani and Vajrapani Bodhisattvas in attendance.

27. Sopara

(a) Location : In Maharashtra.

(b) Approach : (i) About 70 km by road from Bombay, off the Bombay-Poona Road.

(ii) Nala Sopara is a small railway station on the Western Railway local line.

(c) Importance : Sopārā, a sea port in ancient days, was the earliest Buddhist centre in Maharashtra and continued to be so upto A.D. 10th century. Here, in 1882, were discovered, from the Stupa datable to A.D. 160, five relic-caskets, one of gold, and the others of silver, copper, jade crystal. In the caskets were found fragments of the Buddha's bowl, crystal, precious stone beads, gold flowers and a coin of Gautamiputra Satakarni, the twenty-third Satavahana king. Also found in the casket were eight bronze images of the seven Buddhas and the Bodhisattva Maitreya, the coming Buddha.

(d) Monuments : The remains of the Buddhist Stupa at Sopara are now locally known as 'Kot' or 'Kota'. The stupa mound is only a few metres high surrounded by fallen rail and few stones lying scattered here and there. Some of the carved stones have been piled up under a tree on the top of which a Buddha image has been placed in recent years.

28. **Sanghol**

(a) Location : In Ludhiana district, Punjab.

(b) Approach : (i) 60 km from Ludhiana and 40 km from Chandigarh on the Ludhiana-Chandigarh Road.

(ii) 16 km by road from Sirhind railway station.

(c) Importance : Sanghol was one of the largest Buddhist monastic establishments in ancient Punjab. Hiuen Tsang here saw as many as ten monasteries in the seventh century. At that time it was the capital of the Satadru kingdom.

(d) Monuments : The remains of the stupa and monastery complex. The stupa, which appears to have been first built by Asoka in the third century B.C., is on the pattern of Dharma-Chakra (Wheel of Law). The cylindrical stupa is of 16 meter diameter on a 17 meter square platform-the pradakashina or circumambulation of the stupa raised at height. There is also a surkhi or murram pathway about 5.34 m in width all around the stupa. In the east is paved pathway along which a number of votive stupas of solid mud were erected by the devotees.

The priceless find at Sanghol, which has put it prominently on the archaeological map of India, is the discovery of 117 sculptures of the Kushana period from the railing around the stupa on the square platform. These railing pillars were found in a pit between the monastery and the stupa on February 2, 1985.

29. **Dhamner**

(a) Location : In Mandasor district, Rajasthan.

(b) Approach ; 20 km west of Shamgarh railway station.

(c) Importance : A large group of 70 Buddhist caves excavated in about second century A.D.

(d) Monuments : In the Dhamner caves there is fine combination of the early Buddhist symbols of stupas with the reliefs of the Buddha images. For instance, in the Chaitya cave (No. 13), there is a large rock-cut stupa in the centre. Behind the stupa is a sanctuary containing a colossal seated Buddha with a processional path around it. The doors are also decorated with Buddha figures.

At Kholvi, which is 35 km from Dhamner, there are about 50 caves. Like Dhamner, the Chaitya shrines at Kholvi have images of the Buddha in various mudras but there are no images of the Bodhisattvas of the Mahayana Buddhists. The most impressive image is a 12 feet standing Buddha in a preaching posture in the main Chaitya hall.

30. **Nagapattam (Nagapattinam)**

(a) Location : In Tamil Nadu.

(b) Approach : Beyond Madras on the East Coast in Tanjore District.

(c) Importance : Nagapattam had a Buddhist settlement till the 11th century A.D. According to a Copper-plate inscription the Cola King Rajaraja gave the village of Anaimanglam for the maintenance of the Cula-manivarma Vihara. Another Vihara at Nagapattam was the Dharma-soka Vihara residing where Dhamma-pala composed the commentary on the Nettipakarana in the sixth century A.D.

(d) Monuments : The remains of monasteries.

31. **Kausambi (Kosam)**

(a) Location : In Uttar Pradesh.

(b) Approach : 56 km to the west of Allahabad.

(c) Importance : Kausambi, now known as Kosam, was the capital of Vatsa during the time of the Buddha. Lord Buddha visited this place at the invitation of King Udayana. In view of its historical importance Asoka raised here two Pillar Edicts which were removed to the Allahabad Fort by Akbar.

(d) Monuments : Ruins of the ancient city of Kausambi, Stupa and Monasteries. The spot

Ghoshitarama where Lord Buddha stayed during His visit to that place has since been identified.

32. **Mathura**

(a) Location : In Uttar Pradesh.

(b) Approach : (i) 146 km by road from Delhi.
(ii) 54 km by road from Agra.
(iii) Mathura is a railway station on the main Delhi-Bombay line.

(c) Importance : The historic city of Mathura was a stronghold of Buddhism for over 1000 years from the third century B.C. onward. Both Fahien and Hiuen Tsang who visited the city in the fifth and seventh century A.D. respectively speak of the flourishing condition of Buddhism in Mathura. In fact, Mathura stands immortalised in the history of Buddhism on account of the distinct school of art that originated there in the first century A.D. The excavations at Mathura during the last 200 years have brought to light a large number of Buddhist sculptures, viharas and stupas.

(d) Monuments : The glory of Mathura art can best be seen in the Mathura Museum. It has the richest collection of antiquities from third century B.C. to tenth century A.D. discovered during the excavations at various sites in Mathura. In particular, it is the richest Museum preserving the Buddhist art of Kushana period as well as the Gupta period.

One of the finest images is that of fifth century standing Buddha, rich nimbus, thin drapery, witn rippling folds, serene expression on face. A tall meditative Buddha representing same characteristics now adorns the Durbar Hall, Rashtrapati Bhavan, New Delhi.

The Mathura Museum has also a number of railing pillars, cross-bars of Buddhist railings, architectural fragments decorative motifs and terracotta objects.

II. EDICTS OF ASOKA

The Asokan Rock Edicts fall into three groups, viz. Major Rock Edicts, Minor Rock Edicts and Cave Inscriptions. The Pillar Edicts can also be classified into three categories, viz. Major Pillar Edicts, Minor Pillar Edicts and Pillar Inscriptions.

A. ROCK EDICTS

(i) Major Rock Edicts

Edict No.	*Year of issue*	*Subject*
I	257 B.C.	Prohibition of animal sacrifice for religious purposes and prohibition of Samaj festive gatherings.
II	257 B.C.	Provision of medical treatment, shade and water for men and animals throughout his dominion and also in the neighbouring countries.
III	257 B.C.	Institution of quinquennial tours of officials for the propagation of Dhamma.
IV	257 B.C.	Success attained by his propagation of the Dhamma is greater than that attained by conventional methods.
V	256 B.C.	Appointment of the Dhamma-Mahamatras, and their activities.
VI	256 B.C.	Asoka's tireless zeal in serving the interest of the public.

Edict No.	Year	Subject
VII	256 B.C	Asoka's impartiality towards all religious sects.
VIII	256 B.C.	Cammencement of the Dhamma-tours.
IX	256 B.C.	Futility of conventional auspicious ceremonies, and the superior merits of Dhamma-practices.
X	256 B.C.	The object of Asoka' exertions.
XI	256 B.C.	Superiority of the gift of Dhamma.
XII	256 B.C.	The desirability of inter-communal understanding and regard.
XIII	256 B.C.	The evils of conquest by war and the excellence of conquest by Dhamma.
XIV	256 B.C.	A review of the Rock Edicts.
XV	256 B.C.	Emphasis on need of integrity on the judicial officers in Kalinga in the administration of the Law.
XVI	256 B.C.	Assurance to the people of Kalinga and others of Asoka's goodwill towards them.

The Major Rock Edicts have been discovered at the following sites in Modern India :—

Site	Location	Contents	Year of Discovery
1. Girnar	Near Junagadh in Gujartat.	Edicts 1-XIV	1822
2. Dhauli	Near Bhuvaneshwar in Orissa.	Edicts I-X, XIV, XV & XVI.	1837
3. Jaugada	In the Ganjam District, Orissa.	Edicts I-X, XIV, XV and XVI.	1850
4. Kalsi	In the Dehra Dun District, U.P.	Edicts 1-XIV	1860

Site	*Location*	*Contents*	*Year of Discovery*
5. Sopara	In the Thana District Maharashtra.	Edicts VIII & IX (The inscription is now preserved in the Prince of Wales Museum, Bombay).	1882
6. Yerragudi	In the Kurnool District, Andhra Pradesh.	Edicts 1-XIV	1929

(ii) Separate Rock Edict

Siie	*Location*	*Year*	*Subject*	*Year of Discovery*
Bairat-Bhabru (The inscription is now preserved in the Museum of Asiatic Society, Calcutta).	Near Jaipur in Rajasthan.	Not known.	Buddhist Texts to be studied by the members of the Sangha.	1840

(iii) Minor Rock Edicts

Edict No.	*Year*	*Subject*
I	About 260 B.C.	The fruit of zeal in practising Dhamma.
II	Not known	The fruit of zeal in practising Dhamma. It is addressed to the Mahamatras.

These Edicts have been discovered at the following sites :-

Site	*Location*	*Contents*	*Year of Discovery*
1. Sahsaram	In the Shahbad District, Bihar.	Edict I	1839
2. Bairat	40 miles to the north of Jaipur in Rajasthan.	Edict I	1840

Site	Location	Contents	Year of Discovery.
3. Rupnath	In the Jabalpur District, Madhya Pradesh.	Edict I	1871
4. Brahmagiri	In the Chitaldurg District, Karnataka.	Edicts I & II	1892
5. Jaitinga-Ramesvara.	In the Chitaldurg District, Karnataka.	Edicts I & II	1892
6. Siddapura	-do-	Edicts I & II	1892
7. Maski	In the Raichur District, Andhra Pradesh.	Edict I	1915
8. Yerragudi	In the Kurnool District, Andhra Pradesh.	Edicts I & II	1929
9. Gavimath	Near Kopbal in the Raichur District, Andhra Pradesh.	Edict I	1931
10. Palkigundu	Near Gavimath in the Raichur District, Andhra Pradesh.	Edict I	1931
11. Rajula-Mandagiri.	-do-	Edicts I & II	1953
12. Gujarra.	In the Datia District, Madhya Pradesh.	Edict I	1954
13. Ahraura	Near Chunar in Uttar Pradesh.	Edict I	1961
14. Bahapur	Near Srinivaspuri, New Delhi-14.	Edict I	1966
15. Panguraria	District Sehore, Madhya Pradesh	Edict I	1975

(iv) **Cave Inscriptions**

Site	*Location*	*Year*	*Subject*	*Year of Discovery*
Barabar Hills :	15 miles to the north of Gaya in Bihar		Records gift by Asoka of the caves to the Ajivikas.	1785
(i) Nyagrodha Cave		(i) 257 B.C.		
(ii) Khalatika Hills Cave No. 1		(ii) 257 B.C.		
(iii) Khalatika Hills Cave No. 2		(iii) 250 B.C.		

B. PILLAR EDICTS

(i) **Major Pillar Edicts**

Edict No.	*Year*	*Subject*
I	243 B.C.	Exhortation of the practice of Dhamma.
II	243 B.C.	What constitutes the practice of Dhamma.
III	243 B.C.	Exhortation on vigilance against sin.
IV	243 B.C.	The duties of the Rajjukas.
V	243 B.C.	Prohibition of the killing of and infliction of pain on animals.
VI	243 B.C.	Asoka's object in writing the Dhamma rescripts.
VII	243 B.C.	Review of Asoka's life-long activities.

These Edicts have been discovered at the following sites :—

Site	*Location*	*Contents*	*Year of Discovery*
1. Kausambi (Allahabad-Kosam).	Kosam, a village in the Allahabad District, U.P. Removed to Allahabad Fort by Akbar.	Edicts I-VI	1750

Site	Location	Contents	Year of Discovery.
2. Mirath (Delhi-Meerut).	Mirath, a village near Meerut, U.P. Removed and re-erected on the Ridge, Delhi by Feroz Shah Tughlak in 1360.	Edicts-I-VI	1750
3. Lauriya-Araraj.	Near Radhia in the Champaran District, Bihar.	Edicts I-VI	1784
4. Topra (Delhi-Topra).	Topra, a village in the Ambala District, Haryana, Removed to Delhi and re-erected at Kotla Feroz Shah, Delhi by Feroz Shah Tughlak in 1356.	Edicts I-VII	1785
5. Lauriya Nandangarh.	Near Mathia in the Champaran District, Bihar.	Edicts I-VI	1834
6. Rampurva.	In the Champaran, District, Bihar.	Edicts I-VI	1902

(ii) **Minor Pillar Edicts**

Edict	Year	Subject.
I	Not known.	Punishment for Schism in the Buddhist Sangha.
II	Not known.	Asking the followers to assemble near the above Edict on every fasting day.
III	Not known.	Registration of Queen Charuvaki's gifts in State Documents.

These Edicts have been discovered at the following sites :

Site	*Location*	*Contents*	*Year of Discovery.*
1. Kausambi (Allahabad-Kosam).	Kosam, a village in the Allahabad District, U.P. Removed to Allahabad Fort by Akbar.	Edict I	1750
2. Kausambi (Allahabad-Kosam).	-do-	Edict III	1750
3. Sanchi	Sanchi near Bhopal in Madhya Pradesh.	Edict I	1863
4. Sarnath	Sarnath, U.P.	Edicts I & II	1904

(iii) **Pillar Inscriptions.**

Site	*Location*	*Year*	*Subject*	*Year of Discovery*
1. Lumbini (Rummindei)	In Nepal, 6 miles from the Indian Border.	249 B.C.	Asoka's visit to the birth-place of Lord Buddha.	1896
2. Nigliva	In Nepal. 13 miles north-west of Lumbini.	249 B.C.	Asoka's visit to the Stupa of Buddha Kanakamuni.	1895

CHAPTER III

The Himalayan Buddhists

Introductory

WHILE Buddhism declined and disappeared from the mainland of India, it continued to be professed by the people living in the high Himalayan valleys, such as, Ladakh, Lahul, Spiti, Kinnaur, Sikkim and Arunachal Pradesh. This happened largely due to their proximity to Tibet, the mysterious mountainous kingdom, where Buddhism had penetrated in the seventh century A.D., and continued to flourish thereafter in all its glory till the Chinese occupied Tibet in 1959 and forced the 14th Dalai Lama, the spiritual and temporal head of Tibet, to flee to India. Before we turn to the story of Buddhism in the Himalayan region, it would be worthwhile to have a look at the growth and development of Buddhism in Tibet itself.

Though Buddhism was first introduced into Tibet in the fourth century A.D. yet it was only in the seventh century that it gained roots there through the strenuous efforts of the first great ruler of Tibet, Stron-btsan-sgam-pa (Sronsen Gampo) who ruled from 620-650 A.D. At that time, no writing existed in Tibet The King deputed his Minister and linguistic genious, Thombi Sambhota, to India to study the art of writing. He reached Nalanda University and studied Sanskrit, Buddhist philosophy and literature. On return to Tibet, he designed Tibetan alphabets on the basis of the Indian script. From then onward, all literature in Tibet was translated and written down in this script. During his lifetime, Stronsen Gampo built the famous temples of Rimpoche and Jokhang in Lhasa. He also promulgated laws to harmonize with the Ten Virtues prescribed by the Buddha. A century later, Thisong Detson or Khri-sron-ide-btsan (775-797), the fifth ruler of Tibet invited Santarakshita of Nalanda to Tibet to spread the true teachings of the Buddha. As he failed to impress the masses, who were still under the influence of the Bon religion, Santarakshita suggested that Padmasambhava, the powerful apostle of Tantrism be invited from Urgyan in the Swat Valley to tackle the situation. Accordingly, Padmasambhava was invited by the King and he reached Tibet in A.D. 747. Devoting himself to the task of soldifying the hold of Buddhism in Tibet, Padmasambhava introduced the new form of Buddhism, the Lamaism, in which certain Bon practices were retained. For his splendid services to the cause of Buddhism, the Tibetans call Padmasambhava, Guru Rinpoche or the precious Guru. In 749, the king, on the advice of Padmasambhava, established a monastery near Samye, and appointed Santarakshita as its head. The next most powerful Indian teacher to go to Tibet and propagate Buddhism there was the great Acharya Atisa, also called Dipankara Srijnana, of the Vikramasila monastery in Bihar. He reached Tibet in 1038 A.D. and died there in 1054 A.D. As a result of his efforts, Buddhism struck roots in Tibet and thereafter flourished there as an indigenuous mode of religious and philosophical thought.

Since scriptures were introduced by different scholars—both Indian and Tibetan—at different times, different sects and sub-sects came to be founded in Tibet, all having the same basic tenets. The four main schools of Tibetan Buddhism are Nying-ma-pa, Kar-gyu-pa, Sakya-pa and Ge-lug-pa. The oldest sect is the Nying-ma-pa which is directly based on the teachings of Padmasambhava who introduced Buddhism in Tibet in the eighth century A.D., and is called Guru Rinpoche by the Tibetans. The Kar-gyu-pa sect or School of Oral Tradition is said to have been founded in 1050 A.D. by the Tibetan Lama Marpa, a friend of Atisa (Dipankara Srijnana), and disciple of the Indian Tantrist, Naropa, head of the Nalanda University in Bihar in the 11th century. Another great exponent of this sect was Mila-re-pa, the famous poet-saint of Tibet. The third sect Sakya-pa or Saskya-pa derived its name from the colour of the soil where their first monastery was located in Tibet. Founded in 1071 A.D., this sect became powerful in the 13th century, but later declined. These sects are also known as 'Red Hat' sects. The fourth sect, called the Ge-lug-pa (School of the Virtuous) or 'Yellow Hat' sect is the reformed sect founded by the saint Tson-kha-pa around 1400 A.D. His Holiness the Dalai Lama belongs to this sect.

The rise of the hierarchy of the Dalai Lamas marks the most important chapter in the later history of Tibet. The line of the Dalai

Lamas, starting from Gedun Trupa (14th century) right upto the present fourteenth Dalai Lama, who sought asylum in India in 1959 has been the most conspicuous promoter of Buddhism in Tibet. Prior to 1959, there were more than five thousand monasteries scattered all over Tibet, of which the vast majority were Gelugpa monasteries, the sect to which the Dalai Lama belongs. The monasteries of Drepung, Sera and Ganden used to be the largest in Tibet having a teeming population of over twenty thousand monks.

The Tibetans not only practised the Buddha-Dhamma through the ages, they also preserved a large number of Indian Buddhist texts, either in original or in translations. The Tibetans have more than 4566 Indian Buddhist texts. They are divided into two groups, namely, the Kang-gyur (Kanjur) or sayings of Lord Buddha, consisting of 1108 texts, and the Tang-gyur (Tanjur) or a collection of the writings of Indian scholars on philosophy, religion, grammer and history, consisting of 3458 texts.

With this brief introductory note on Tibetan Buddhism, we proceed further to unfold the story of Buddhism in the high Himalayan valleys of India.

LADAKH

Ladakh now forms part of Jammu and Kashmir, the northern most state of India. Asoka is said to have built 500 monasteries in Kashmir and later given the Valley itself as a gift to the Buddhist Sangha. Like Asoka, Kanishka too is said to have made a gift of Kashmir to the Sangha. Thus Kashmir was a strong-hold of Buddhism for many centuries. The Buddhists were, however, mercilessly persecuted by Mihirkula, a Huna, who came to power in 515 A.D. On Mihirkula's death, Kashmir was fortunate to have a staunch local Buddhist as its ruler. He was Meghavahana. He undertook the propagation of Buddhism with great zeal and built many Viharas. His wives too vied with each other in erecting Viharas. Famous among these was Amritabhavana, which was got built by the queen Amritaprabha. As the queen was a Ladakhi lady and her guru was also from Ladakh, she dedicated this Vihara to Amitayu, the river of long life. This place is now known as Antbhavan and lies in the vicinity of Vicharnag, Srinagar. Though the rulers following Meghavahana were not Buddhists but Buddhist sacred buildings continued to be put up in their time. In the time of Pravarsena II who ruled towards the later part of the sixth century

A.D. a big Vihara was constructed in Srinagar by the king's maternal uncle, Jayendra. It was called Jayendravihara and Hiuen Tsang stayed there when he visited Kashmir. Similarly Skanda, founded an imposing Vihara called Skanda-bhavanvihara which has left its name Skandabhavan to a locality in Srinagar. Lalitaditya, a great indigenous ruler of Kashmir though not a Buddhist, had keen interest in Buddhism. He built a huge Vihara—the Rajavihara in Parihasapora. Its ruins have been excavated at Paraspore. Chankuna, the Chief Minister of Lalitaditya, was a Buddhist and he too constructed a Vihara named after him as Chankuna-Vihara.

While Buddhism declined in the Kashmir Valley after the twelfth century for the reasons into which we need not go here, it has been a living faith in Ladakh through the ages. This is a very significant achievement of the people of Ladakh. Behind this lies a long story of their bravery and sacrifice.

A vast region of arid tracts and bare mountain ridges, Ladakh lies to the east of the Kashmir Valley at a height of 12,000 to 18,000 feet above the sea level. It is bounded by China (Sinkiang), Gilgit and Tibet. It has an area of 97,872 square kilometres. It is composed of various regions known as Kargil, Zanskar, Rupshu, Nubra, Aksaichen, Rong, Tanktse and Leh. Leh, the district headquarters of Ladakh, is now linked with Srinagar by a metalled road (434 kilometres) which passes through the Zozila pass and the Fotela pass, at a height of 13,400 feet. Two other routes to Leh are via Kulu, and via Suru-Kargil. These routes are difficult and are used by trekkers only.

Buddhism seems to have entered Ladakh long before the beginning of the Christian era. In the first century A.D. Ladakh came under the imperial authority of the Buddhist emperor Kanishka (of the Kushana dynasty) who became the ruler of Kashmir. Upto the sixth century, Ladakh formed part of Kashmir and remained under the Kashmir rulers. Then in the middle of the seventh century, Stron-btsan-sgam-pa (Stronsen Gampo), the famous king of Tibet, conquered Ladakh. And in the beginning of the tenth century, it became part of the Western Tibetan Kingdom of Guge, founded by Kyide Nyimagon. Just before his death in 930 A.D., Nyimagon divided the Guge kingdom into three parts and gave one to each of his three sons. The eldest son, Palgyigon, got Ladakh proper. The Guge kings were devout Buddhists and great patrons of

Buddhist art and literature. This Buddhist dynasty ruled Ladakh for 540 years till it was replaced by another Buddhist dynasty in 1470.

During the reign of the Guge kings, a large number of Buddhist temples came up all over Ladakh, either directly or indirectly with their help. The most important monasteries founded during this period were the Alchi monastery and the Lamayuru monastery These monasteries were founded by a devout Buddhist, Rinchen Zang-po in the tenth century. The beautiful paintings in the Alchi monastery, which have survived, are the earliest examples of paintings in Kashmir.

The rise of Islam in Kashmir had an impact on Ladakh also. The Muslims started penetrating beyond the Zojila pass in the mid-fourteenth century. The most fierest attack on Ladakh was by Zainful Abidun who invaded Ladakh and plundered its monasteries during the reign of the Ladakhi king, Lodo Chodan (1440-70). Taking advantage of the weakening position of the king, Bhagan Namgyal, a cousin of Lodo Ghodan, deposed and imprisoned the king and founded the second Ladakhi dynasty in 1470. During the next 350 years, Ladakh had to suffer serious invasions both at the hands of the Muslims from Central Asia as well as at the hands of the Muslim rulers of Kashmir. One of the Ladakhi kings, Deldan Namgyal (1640-75), forced by the circumstances, not only accepted Mughal sovereignty and promised to pay tribute to the Mughal Emperor but, under the influence of an envoy from Kashmir, even accepted Islam in 1664 and assumed the name of Aqabat Khan. Luckily, however, his successors reverted to Buddhism.

The last independent Buddhist king of Ladakh, Tse-pal Namgyal (C. 1790-1834, 1840-42) proved a weak and indolent ruler. He failed to maintain the integrity and sovereignty of Ladakh. During his reign, Ladakh was invaded and plundered many a time. In 1821, a strong Balti force entered Ladakh, plundered the villages and escaped with booty. In 1825, the powerful Hindu ruler of Chamba invaded Zanskar, and devastated it. The worst thing happened to Ladakh in 1834 when Raja Gulab Singh, the Dogra ruler of Jammu, turned his eyes towards Ladakh. Zorawar Singh Kahluria, Raja Gulab Singh's Governor in Kishtwar, invaded Ladakh four times between 1834-39. The Ladakhis put strong opposition and fought valiantly many a pictched battle but were ultimately defeated. When the people of the Suru valley revolted in 1836, Zorawar Singh rushed there with his troops and after putting down the rebellion hanged thirteen men. He also offered fifty rupees for each 'traitor' captured. Two hundred prisoners were produced before him and all of them were beheaded. Leaving behind this trail of blood, he marched on to Leh where the Ladakhis had rebelled. Two years later, after recapturing the fort of Chatargarh, Zorawar Singh is said to have cut off the ears and noses of all the prisoners. In 1840, Zorawar Singh invaded Baltistan Then becoming ambitious, he invaded Tibet in 1841 but this time Dogras suffered a crushing defeat. Most of them were slain. Zorawar Singh was also shot dead on 14 December 1841. Taking advantage of this opportunity, the king of Ladakh, Tse-pal Namgyal, declared his independence; presumably at the instance of the Tibetans. However, the Dogras soon rallied, and put down the rebellion. The Dogra troops even pursued the Tibetans into their country. Ultimately, the Dogras and the Tibetans signed a peace treaty on 24 September 1842, reaffirming the historical boundary between Ladakh and Tibet and also stipulating non-interference by either of them in the affairs of each other. Thus came to an end the second Buddhist kingdom of Ladakh after a reign of 372 years.

After the first Anglo-Sikh War of 1845, the British Government confirmed Gulab Singh's title to Ladakh. While doing so, however, in 1846, the British detached from Ladakh the valleys of Lahul and Spiti, and added them to the British possessions of Kangra, Kulu and Mandi. That is how, the Lahul and Spiti now form a part of Himachal Pradesh.

At one time, Ladakh was almost wholly Buddhist but now Kargil area is Muslim dominated. According to 1981 Census, there are 69706 Buddhists out of which 64,944 live in the villages and the remaining 4,962 in the towns. Thus, Buddhism in Ladakh is largely village based. The most important monasteries or gompas in Ladakh are : the Lakhang monastery at Leh; Sankar gompa, just 3 km from Leh; Hemis gompa, the largest and the most sacred monastery, 45 km from Leh, on the Ladakh-Tibet Road; and Thiksey and Shey gompas, on the way to Hemis gompa. The monastery of Lama-yuru, 96 km from Leh on the Leh-Kargil Road, and the Alchi monastery, beyond Lama-yuru, and about 10 km off the highway Other important monasteries in Ladakh are : Likir, Spituk, Nimaun, Skara, Phiong, Stana, Saspal, Rizong, Chimrey, Mathoo and Sakte.

Because of its proximity to Tibet, and consequently more

frequent contacts with Tibet than with India, Ladakh follows the Tibetan form of Buddhism, which is also called Lamaism. As in Tibet, all the four sects of Lamas are prevalent in Ladakh. These are : Nying-ma-pa, Kar-gyu-pa, Saskya-pa and Ge-lug-pa. Besides the gompas which dot the whole of Ladakh, there is always a chorten at the entrance of every village. The famous Mahayana mantra 'Om Mani Padme Hum' (Hail though possessor of Jewel Lotus) is almost continuously recited by the devout Buddhists. Not only that, it is often written on a piece of cloth or inscribed on a stone and left on the spot where it is pronounced by the devotee. Such monuments are called Mani walls and can be seen every where near the villages, on tops of passess, near fordes and on the banks of rivers. Though the religion followed by the Ladakhi people is more ritualistic but its impact on the lives of the people has been very whole-some. By nature, the Ladakhis are honest, kind, courteous and hospitable. Mahapandit Rahul Sankrityayan, the great Buddhist scholar and explorer, visited Ladakh in June-July 1933. He was so much over-whelmed by the courtesy and kindness of his hosts that while staying at Leh, he wrote three small books in Tibetan for the benefit of the Ladakhi children. In his travelogue on his visit to Ladakh 'Meri Ladakh Yatra', he speaks very highly of the devotion of the Ladakhi people to Buddhism.

Michel Peissel, a French scholar, who spent two weeks in 1978 in Zanskar also speaks highly about the qualities of tolerance, mercy and compassion of the Ladakhi people. Says he :

"Mystery and magic are often, and rightly so, associated with Tibetan Buddhism; yet if this is true at the level of ritual, in general the Buddhists of the Himalayas have mostly retained the better aspects of Buddhist teachings : tolerance, kindness and moderation. Too much is written and said of the world's religions in terms of their dogmas, and rituals, and too little said about what actually filters down to the common man.

Of course, there is always a considerable difference between practice and theory, and while Lamaist theory is most complex, in fact shatteringly so with literally one hundred thousand divinities and many magic rituals : tolerance, kindness and compassion are practised by all.

It is a great lesson to see how the naturally turbulent inhabitants of the Himalayas, who are soldiers by nature and have a rugged disposition, moderate their impulses to become tolerant and kind even to the most objectionable people, animal or insect that they encounter".

LAHUL, SPITI AND KINNAUR

The valleys of Lahul and Spiti in Himachal Pradesh ie at a height and 10,000 to 16,000 feet above sea level and are separated from the Kulu valley by the famous Rohtang Pass, which is also known as the Pass of the Dead. The Lahul valley lies beyond the Rohtang Pass towards the North comprising the watersheds of the Chandra and the Bhaga rivers which later on join to form the Chenab. In area, it is 2200 sq. miles and has an average altitude of 12000 ft. Spiti, which lies to the east of Kulu in the extreme north-east corner, beyond the Rohtang Pass, is 2,931 sq. miles in area. Spiti, locally pronounced Piti, is a Tibetan word meaning middle province. It is bounded on three sides by Ladakh, Tibet and Bushahar (Rampur). The valley of Kinnaur lies on both the banks of river Sutlej around its uppermost region bordering Tibet.

Buddhism is said to have entered Lahul and Spiti sometime in the early centuries of the Christian Era even though it was introduced into the country of Himalayas in the third century B.C. by the missionaries led by Ven. Majjhima who were deputed by Asoka to convert the people of the Himalayan region as a part of his Dhamma-Vijaya campaign. Their bonds with Buddhism became stronger when the famous Padmasambhava sojourned in these valleys on his way to Tibet in 747-48 A.D. One of the greatest preachers of Buddhism in this area was Rin-chen-bZang-po (Rathabhadra, 958-1055 A.D.) who is said to have been born at Sumra in Kinnaur. The ancient monasteries in this region go back to the 11th century and are believed to have been founded by him.

The Buddhists of Lahul, Spiti and Kinnaur follow the Tibetan form of Buddhism, and their monks are called Lamas. Owing to proximity to Tibet, the impact of the Tibetan culture on the people of this region is quite significant and is visible in many ways. Their temples, gompas, monasteries have Tibetan names. The main shrine in each monastery is called Lha-khang, and images of the Buddha,

Badhisattvas and other divinities are installed there. Each monastery has also a hall for teaching purposes. It is called Du-khang, the assembly hall. Some of the monasteries have beautiful paintings depicting scenes from the Jatakas and the life of the Buddha. At the entrance to every village, there is always a chorten, a replica of ancient stupa. The erection of these chortens is considered an act of piety; hence their number is large and they can be seen every where. In Kinnaur as well as in Lahul and Spiti, the famous Mahayana mantra 'Om Mani Padme Hum' (Hail thou possessor of Jewel Lotus) is considered by the Buddhists as saviour from all dangers, and is almost continuously recited by the devout persons. Not only that, it is often written on a piece of cloth or inscribed in Tibetan script on stone and left on the spot where it is pronounced by the devotee. Such monuments are called mani walls and can be seen every where near villages, on tops of passes, near fordes and on the banks of rivers.

At present, there are about 30 monasteries each in Lahul, Spiti and Kinnaur. The important monasteries in Lahul are at Kyelang, Kardang, Gurmrang, Gemur, Jholing, Shashin and Tupchilling; in Spiti the important monasteries are at Dhankar, Gungri, Hansa, Ki, Kibar, Losar and Tabo; and in Kinnaur they are at Chini, Kanum, Lipa, Nako and Poo. Apart from the monasteries, many families have a chapel of their own.

In Himachal Pradesh, the Kargyupa and the Gelugpa sects are the most popular sects. The sectwise distribution of monasteries in Lahul, Spiti and Kinnaur is somewhat as under : Kargyupa-Dugpa 40 (28 in Lahul and 12 in Kinnaur) : Gelugpa 37 (1 in Lahul, 21 in Spiti and 15 in Kinnaur); Nyingmapa 12 (7 in Spiti and 5 in Kinnaur); and Sakyapa 2 (in Spiti). In 1981, the Buddhist population in Himachal Pradesh was 52,629. Out of them, approximately 70 per cent live in Lahul, Spiti and Kinnaur.

SIKKIM

Sikkim also known as Densong (rice-country) is the most fascinating state of the Himalayan region. It lies on the southern slopes of the western half of the eastern Himalaya. It is bounded by Tibet on the north, Bhutan on the east and Nepal on the west, From Gangtok, the capital of Sikkim, the nearest rail-heads are Siligiri and New Jalpaiguri, at a distance of 114 km and 125 km respectively. Gadgtok is also connected by road with Darjeeling and Kalimpong.

The people of Sikkim now consist of three different ethnic groups, namely, the Lepchas, the Bhotiyas, and the Nepalese.

The Lepchas are the original inhabitants, while the Bhotiyas and the Nepalese are immigrants from Tibet, Bhutan and Nepal. Not much is known about the history of the Lepchas prior to their conversion to Buddhism by the Tibetan missionaries around 1640. Sikkim became a separate political entity in 1642 A.D. when three Lamas—Gyalwa Lhastsun Chhempo, Sempa Chempo Chhempo and Rigzim Chhempo of Tibet of the Nyingmapa sect, consecrated Phuntshog Namgyal (1604-1670), of the Bhotiya tribe, as the King of the Lepcha land with the title of Chogyal (King who rules according to Chho—righteous law, and enforces respect for it) at Yaksam in western Sikkim. After this, several waves of immigrants came from Tibet and Bhutan. The three aforesaid Lamas of Tibet were also responsible for laying the foundations of first Buddhist monasteries in Sikkim and replacing the Bon religion with Buddhism. The Namgyal dynasty ruled Sikkim for 333 years, till 1975, when Sikkim became a part of India.

Phuntshog Namgyal was succeeded by his son, Tensung Namgyal, in 1670. Soon after ascending the throne, he shifted the seat of government from Yaksam in western Sikkim to Rabdentse, also in western Sikkim. Tensung Namgyal was in turn succeeded by his son, Chhagdor Namgyal, in 1700. Chhagdor proved a great benefactor of Buddhism. He expanded the monastic system; rebuilt or restored a number of monasteries, the most important monastery rebuilt by him was the great Pemayangtse Monastery. This was rebuilt in 1715. He also built the Tashiding Monastery. The most learned Lama in Sikkim at that time was Jigmi Pawo of the Labrang Monastery. Under Jigmi Pawo's advice, Chhadgor Namgyal also devised a script for the Lepcha language. Jigmi Pawo compiled the first chronicle of Sikkim, known as Bras Ljongs Rgyal Rabs. The next ruler of Sikkim, Gyrumi Namgyal (1707-33) built the first Karmapa monastery in Sikkim at Ralang in 1730. Several other Karmapa monasteries, such as, Phodang and Rumtek in Sikkim were built in 1740, during the reign of the next Chogyal, namely, Namgyal Phuntshog Namgyal (1733-1780). During his reign, Sikkim fell on bad days. Bhutan attacked Sikkim in 1770 and occupied the entire country east of the Tista river. Nepal also invaded Sikkim during 1774-75 and took most of its territory west of the Singli ridge. The Nepalese invasion on Sikkim proved more disastrous as wave after wave of Nepalese started settling down in south Sikkim. Now the Nepalese constitute the majority of the Sikkimese population. The Lepchas and the Bhotiyas, the original inhabitants of Sikkim are now in a minority in their own homeland.

Compelled by the circumstances, the Government of Sikkim had to turn to the British Government in India for help. For securing security against aggression of the Gorkhas of Nepal, in particular, the Chogyal of Sikkim, Tsugphu Namgyal (1785-1863) presented the Darjeeling and Kalimpong area to the British Government on 1 February 1835 in lieu of which the British sanctioned an annual subsidy of Rs. 3,000 as compensation to Sikkim in 1841. It was increased to Rs. 6,000 in 1846. Ultimately, in 1861 Sikkim became a protectorate of the British Government India. In accordance with the treaty signed by the Sidkyong Tulku, the then Chogyal of Sikkim, on 28 March 1861, Sikkim agreed to give right to the Government of India to construct roads through Sikkim to the Tibet frontier, and also to shift the seat of Government from Tumlong in north Sikkim (where it had been shifted in 1914 as the earlier capital of Sikkim, Rabentse, was too close to the Nepal border) to Gangtok in east Sikkim. The treaty also established free intercourse between the subjects of British India and Sikkim, and permitted the Government of India to survey the country. From then onward, the British Government treated Sikkim like all other princely states in India.

With the attainment of independence by India in 1947 and merger of the princely states with the rest of India, things began to change in Sikkim also. The people of the Nepalese origin, largely Hindus, who formed the bulk of Sikkim's population began demanding democratisation of the administration. In the wake of this political turmoil, the Government of India annexed Sikkim on 14 May 1975. With this, the institution of Chogyal was also abolished. The last Chogyal of Sikkim, Palden Thondup Namgyal died broken hearted in New York in 1932.

There are about 70 Buddhist monasteries or gompas in Sikkim. The most important monasteries are: Pemayangtse, Tashiding and Rumtek. Other important monasteries are : Enche (at Gangtok), Phensang, Phedong, Tholang (in North Sikkim), Ralong, Sang-Choilng, Khachod Palri, Dabdi, Sinon (in West Sikkim). Of the four sects of Tibetan Buddhism, two sects are more popular in Sikkim. These are : Nyingmapa and Kargyupa. In 1981 the Buddhist population in Sikkim was 90,848 as against the total population of 3,16,385.

ARUNACHAL PRADESH

Arunachal Pradesh (the land of Sunrise) was earlier known as the North-Eastern Frontier Agency-NEFA. It is bordered by Tibet and China on the north, Bhutan on the west, Burma on the east and the Brahmaputra Valley of Assam on the south. Arunachal Pradesh has an area of 18,426 square kilometres. It is inhabited by as many as 30 tribes which are further divided into many sub-tribes. Of them, the Monpas and Sherdukpas of Kameng district; the Khamptis and Singhpos of Lohit district; and some Tongas of Tirap district profess Buddhism.

Buddhism was introduced into Arunachal Pradesh by the great Indian saint Padmasambhava (c. 717-762), who is revered as the great Guru, Rinpoche, in Tibet. It was however, sustained thereafter as a result of constant inter-action between Arunachal Pradesh (Tawang area in particular) and Tibet. There is evidence to show that Karmapa missionaries from Tibet had visited the Tawang area in the 12th and 13th centuries and founded some monasteries there. The most prominent one among them was Rangchung Dorjee (c. 1109-1192), founder of the Karmapa sub-sect of the Kargyupa sect of Tibetan Buddhism. He is said to have established monasteries at Domzang, Garam (Jangda), Jang and Bangajanga in the Tawang area. Some prominent Lamas of the Nyingmapa sect also visited Arunachal Pradesh during the 13th and 14th centuries and propagated Dhamma there. In the 17th century, the Fifth Dalai Lama also helped the cause of Buddhism in Arunachal Pradesh. He is said to have donated a "Thanka" (scroll painting) to the great Tawang monastery which was constructed during his reign, and completed in 1680. Two other important monasteries in Arunachal Pradesh are at Dirang and Dhong. With a population of 86,483, out of 6,31,839 in 1981, the Buddhists in Arunachal Pradesh form 13.69 per cent of the total population of the state.

CHAPTER IV

Bhikkhus and Viharas

THE monks and monasteries play an important role in any religious movement. It is more so in the case of Buddhism as Sangha is one of the three pillars (Triple Gem) on which this great religion stands. When the revival movement began in 1891, there were neither any Bhikkhus nor any Viharas in India, excepting a few in the hilly tracts. Even the Great Maha Bodhi Temple at Bodh Gaya, the sole surviving symbol of the past glory of Buddhism, was, in the absence of any Buddhist monk, being sacrileged by a Hindu Mahant.

The first Hindu to become a Buddhist monk in modern times was Mahavira. He was nephew of Babu Kunwar Singh of Jagdishpur in Bihar who had taken part in India's Revolt in 1857 against the British rule. Later in life, Mahavira took to wrestling, and while taking part in the wrestling matches, he went to Sri Lanka via Madras. There, he embraced Buddhism and became a Bhikkhu in 1890. He returned to India by way of Burma in 1891, and started living at Kushinara, the site of Buddha's Mahaparinirvana. In 1901, he constructed there a Dharmashala for the convenience of the pilgrims. And in 1902, he constructed a modern Buddha Vihara at Kushinagar, which was in fact the first modern Vihara to be constructed any where in India.

Ven. Mahavira, or Mahavir Swami as he was known, was followed by Dharmananda Kosambi. Kosambi was born in Goa in 1876. One day, in 1897, he read Lord Buddha's life-sketch in a Marathi monthly for the children published from Bombay. He was so much impressed by the sublime story of the Buddha that he immediately resolved to make a thorough study of Buddhism. Thus prompted, he left his home in December 1899, and to begin with he studied Sanskrit for a couple of years at Poona and Varanasi.

Not satisfied with the knowledge of mere Sanskrit language, he went to Nepal in search of Buddhism. Disappointed at what he saw at Kathmandu in Nepal, Kosambi came back and went to Bodh Gaya, the Seat of Buddha's Enlightenment. There, a Buddhist monk advised him to go to Sri Lanka where he could see and experience the living Buddhism. Accordingly, he set off for Sri Lanka and reached Colombo in March 1902. Soon thereafter, he embraced Buddhism and was ordained as a monk; thus becoming the second Indian to don the robes of a Buddhist monk in modern times. Dharmananda Kosambi was the first scholar of Pali to introduce Pali in Devanagari script in India. He also wrote a number of books on Buddhism in Marathi and Gujarati. In 1937, he built a small Vihara at Parel. Bombay, and called it 'Bahujana Vihara' or 'the Buddhist temple of the masses'. He passed away in 1947.

Dharmananda Kosambi was followed by Bodhananda. He was born in a Bengali family in Mirzapur district of Uttar Pradesh. His parents passed away when he was just a child. So he came to live with his widow aunt who was residing at Varanasi (Banaras), where he became a Sadhu and was given the name of Nij Bodhananda. In 1896, he met per chance some Buddhist monks from Sri Lanka who were on a pilgrimage to Sarnath. Impressed by their serenity, dignity and way of life, he was attracted to Buddhism. He became a Buddhist monk in 1914, and was the first monk to be ordained in India. As at that time there was no consecrated Seema in India for the ordination of monks, Ven. Bodhananda was ordained in 1914 by Ven. Kripasaran Maha Thera and others in a boat in the Ganges near Calcutta. According to the Vinaya, a Bhikkhu can be ordained on water in the absence of a consecrated land Seema. It is a matter of pride that consecrated Seemas for the Upasampada (ordination) of the monks now exist at Sarnath, the Holy Isipatana, and Kushinagar in U.P. : Dharmankur Vihara, Calcutta and Siliguri in West Bengal, Asoka Mission Vihara, New Delhi, and at a few other places in Assam and Tripura.

In 1916, Ven. Bodhananda founded the Indian Buddhist Society, with headquarters at Lucknow, in order to preach and propagate Buddhism in North India. In 1925, he constructed a beautiful Buddha Vihara at Risaldar Park, Lucknow. He also established a Buddhist Library to which he added a large number of books in Pali, Sanskrit, Bengali, Hindi Urdu, Persian and English. With the establishment of this Vihara and the Library, Lucknow became a good centre of Buddhism. And over the years, he inspired many persons to come to the refuge of the Buddha. Ven. Bodhananda passed away in 1952.

Ven. Bodhananda was followed by Bhadant Anand Kausalyayan. Born on 5 January 1905 in a Punjabi family at Sohana near Chandigarh, he graduated from the National College, Lahore in 1924. Soon thereafter, he left home. While wandering hither and thither in search of inner peace, he per chance met Rahul Sankrityayan in 1926. Following the latter's example, he also became an Arya Samaji Parivrajik, and changed his name from Harnamdas to Brhmachari Vishvanath. In 1927, Rahul Sankrityayan joined the Vidyalankara Pirivena, Kelaniya, Sri Lanka (Ceylon) as a Sanskrit teacher. In response to his invitation, Vishvanath also went to Sri Lanka and joined the Pirivena. There, he embraced Buddhism and was ordained as a monk on 10 February 1928, with the new name of Anand Kausalyayan.

Rahul Sankrityayan was born on 9 April 1892 in Azamgarh district, Uttar Pradesh. He was restless from the very beginning, and left home at the age of 13 when he was still in the school. While leading a life of aimless wanderer, he was picked up by the Mahant of Parasa in district Chhapra, Bihar to succeed him, and given the name of Sadhu Ramodardas. But the 'hunger' of knowledge and 'lust' of travel prompted Rahul to leave Parasa. So he again took to the road in July 1913. While touring the country, he came under the influence of the Arya Samaj, and was recruited as an Arya Samaj preacher. During one such preaching tour of Lucknow in 1971, he came in contact with Ven. Bodhananda and learnt his first lessons of Buddhism from him. In 1927, he joined the Vidyalankara Pirivena, Kelaniya in Sri Lanka as Sanskrit teacher. There, he became a Buddhist monk in 1930.

Rahul Sankrityayan was followed by Ven. Jagdish Kashyap. He was born at Ranchi in Bihar in 1908. After graduating from Patna in 1929, he went to Varanasi and did his Master of Arts in Philosophy from the Banaras Hindu University in 1931. Under the influence of his grandfather, Jagdish Kashyap was drawn to the Arya Samaj, and was appointed as the Principal of the Gurukula at Baidyanathdham in Bihar during the years 1931-33. Gradually, he became disenchanted with the organisation of the Gurukula and became very much concerned with the gap between the precepts and the practice of the Arya Samaj, particularly as it related to the functioning of the caste system. Then in November 1933, he met Rahul Sankrityayan in Patna at the residence of K.P. Jaiswal. Impressed by the manuscripts brought by Rahulji from Tibet, he resolved to study Buddhism, and expressed his desire to go to Sri Lanka. Arrangements were accordingly made by Rahul Sankrityayan, and Jagdish Kashyap joined the Vidyalankara Pirivena soon thereafter. In 1934, he was ordained as a Bhikkhu.

Rahul Sankrityayan, Bhadant Anand Kausalyayan and Ven. Jagdish Kashyap became life-long friends and worked in unison for the Buddhist revival in India. On return from Sri Lanka the 'Trio' were together for some time in 1936 at Allahabad. There, it is said that one day they expressed their individual programmes for the future like this : "Rahul Sankrityayan said that he would write as many books as possible. Anand Kausalyayan said that he would love to undertake lecture tours and do journalistic work of writing articles, and serving the cause of Hindi literature. Jagdish Kashyap expressed his desire to spend his time in study, research and teaching, and in founding educational institutions".

By and large, they adhered to their programmes of action indicated above. Mahapandit Rahul Sankrityayan will always be remembered for enriching Hindi literature, and creating enormous Buddhist literature when there was practically none. He also made a major contribution to Indian Buddhism by bringing to light a large number of Sanskrit Buddhist texts preserved in the monasteries of Tibet. Bhadant Anand Kausalyayan, apart from creating a vast literature on Buddhism in Hindi, did a yeoman's service to the neo-Buddhist movement, after the sudden demise of Dr. Ambedkar in 1956 The credit for making Deeksha Bhoomi, Nagpur, a living Buddhist shrine goes to him. He came to live there in 1968, and during the next 20 years, he established there a Buddha Vihara, and a Bhikkhu Niwas for the training of monks. He also translated Dr. Ambedkar's monumental work 'The Buddha and His Dhamma' into Hindi and Punjabi. The notable contribution of Ven. Jagdish Kashyap was the founding of the Nava Nalanda Mahavihara at Nalanda in Bihar which is now a reputable Pali Research Institute. He also accomplished the most difficult task of editing and publishing the entire Pali Tripitaka in Devnagari script.

The seventh prominent Indian monk was Ven. K.

Dharmarakshita. He was born in 1923 near Kushinagar in Uttar Pradesh. Coming under the influence of Venerable U Chandramani Maha Thera, he embraced Buddhism and was ordained as a monk in July 1942. He also studied Pali in Sri Lanka and was awarded the degree of Tripitakacharya. After joining the Maha Bodhi Society, he spent most of his time at Sarnath. For a number of years, he was Editor of Dharmaduta, the Hindi monthly published from Sarnath. He was also a great scholar of Pali and authored a large number of books on Buddhism. He was also an eminent educationist. In 1959, he became Principal of the Maha Bodhi College, Sarnath and held that post, with distinction, for more than 15 years.

The first great Bhikkhu born in modern times amongst the old Buddhist communities was Ven. Kripasaran Maha Thera. He was born in 1865 in a Barua Buddhist family in Chittagong district (now in Bangladesh). At the age of 16, he became a Sramanera, and received his Upasampada in 1885. In 1886, he came to Calcutta and began organising the Barua Buddhists living there. He founded the Bengal Buddhist Association in 1892, and in 1903 he constructed the Dharmankur Vihara in Calcutta which became the focal point for all religious and cultural activities for the Bengali Buddhists.

Inspired by the missionary spirit of Anagarika Dharmapala, a number of Buddhist monks came from Sri Lanka and devoted their lives to the cause of Buddhism in India. Ven. K. Sriniwasa was the first monk to come from Sri Lanka and take up missionary work in India. He came in 1920, at the invitation of Anagarika Dharmapala, and joined the Maha Bodhi Society as a Dhammaduta worker, After serving the Dhamma for more than 48 years, he passed away at Sarnath in 1968. The second Sri Lankan monk to come to India was Ven. D. Sasanasiri. On a request from Anagarika Dharmapala, he came to India in 1929 and began training the Sramaneras brought from Sri Lanka for missionary work in India. Later, he served as Bhikkhu-in-charge of almost all the centres of the Maha Bodhi Society. He breathed his last at Sarnath in 1966. Ven. N. Jinaratana was the third notable Sri Lankan monk who devoted his whole life to the cause of Buddhism in India. He came to India in 1936 and joined the Maha Bodhi Society as a Dhammaduta worker. Soon he became an important functionary of the Society. In 1968, he became General Secretary of the Society following the demise of Devapriya Valisinha.

Ven. M. Sangharatana and Ven. Dr. U. Dhammaratana were among the ten Sramaneras brought by Anagarika Dharmapala in 1930 to work for the Buddhist revival in India. After completing education, Ven. Sangharatana devoted himself to the affairs of the Society at Sarnath and was chiefly responsible for making the Holy Isipatana a living shrine. In 1969, he came to live at Sravasti where he established a school, a rest house and a Buddha Vihara. He passed away in 1984. Ven Dr. U. Dhammaratana was a great educationist and scholar of Pali and Buddhism. For a number of years, he was Professor of Pali and Philosophy at the Nava Nalanda Mahavihara, Nalanda. He was also associated with the editorial team of the Maha Bodhi journal. In 1983, he was appointed as General Secretary of the Maha Bodhi Society but could not continue for long due to his failing health. He died in a London hospital in 1985.

Three other prominent Buddhist monks to come from Sri Lanka and devote themselves to the Dhamma work in India were Venerables H. Dhammananda, N. Somananda and H. Punnatissa.

The Bhikkhus who came from other Buddhist countries and took up missionary work in the land of the Buddha were : Ven. U Chandramani, Ven. U Zayanta, Ven. Dr. Revata and Ven. Kittima (Burma), Ven. V. Dhammavara (Cambodia) and Rev. Fujii Guruji (Japan). Of them, the contribution of Ven. Chandramani Maha Thera was the greatest. Born in a devout Buddhist family of district Akyab, Burma in 1876, he started his education as a monk at the age of seven. In 1888, he was ordained as a Sramanera and given the name of Chanda. When in 1891, Anagarika Dharmapala requested Ven. U Chandima of Akyab to send some Dhammadutas for missionary work in India, he sent two Sramaneras : Chanda and Surya to Calcutta. On arrival in India, Chanda or U Chandramani as he later became famous, came to Bodh Gaya and started staying in the Burmese Rest House. In 1895, he per chance met Ven. Mahavira at the residence of a Burmese Buddhist in Calcutta. Impressed by the keenness of the young Sramanera, Mahavira made arrangements for his studies in a Sanskrit Paathshala in Bihar. On completion of his studies there, he went back to Burma for pursuing Pali studies. He received his higher ordination (Upasampada) in Burma in 1903. Then he returned to India and started living with Ven. Mahavira at Kushinagar.

The first thing Ven. Chandramani did at Kushinagar was to take possession of the historic Nirvana Temple from the Archaeological Survey of India and to make it a living shrine. He also repaired and restored the Main Stupa, and the Mathakuar Temple. Then he turned his attention to education. He established at Kushinagar two schools and a college. Extending his activities to the other shrines around Kushinagar he constructed a Buddha Vihara at Sravasti, Dharmashalas at Balrampur, and Sarnath and a Buddha Vihara at Lumbini. Being a great saint and scholar, Ven. Chandramani inspired many Indians and foreigners to seek refuge in the Buddha-Dhamma and ordained a large number of Buddhist monks. He had also the honour of being the Dhamma-Guru of Dr. B.R. Ambedkar who embraced Buddhism at his hands on 14 October 1956. After serving the Dhamma for seventy years in India, Ven. Chandramani passed away at Kushinagar, at the ripe age of 96, in 1972.

The Bhikkhu Sangha in modern India embraces both the Theravada and Mahayana forms of Buddhism. Since Buddhism came back to India from Sri Lanka (Ceylon) where the Theravada Buddhism has flourished in its pristine glory ever since its introduction there in the third century B.C., the neo-Buddhists follow the Theravada tradition. The traditional Buddhists of Assam, Bengal and Tripura also follow the Theravada tradition. The Himalayan Buddhists, however, are Mahayanists and follow the Tibetan form of Buddhism. To-day, India has over 500 Theravada monks and about 5000 Mahayana monks or Lamas. The Theravada monks are scattered all over India. The Mahayana monks or Lamas live mainly in Ladakh, Himachal Pradesh, Sikkim and Arunachal Pradesh. The district of Ladakh in Kashmir has the largest number of Lamas. It has about 2500 monks and nuns. About 1000 monks are under training in various centres in India.

The Theravada monks have since formed an All India Bhikkhu Sangha with headquarters at Sarnath. The first Sangha Nayaka of India was the late Bhadant Anand Kausalyayan (1905-1988). At present, Ven. Ananda Mitra Maha Thera of Calcutta is the Sangha Nayaka.

The Himalayan monks look forward for guidance to Ven. Kushak Bakula, the Head Lama of Ladakh.

Turning to the Viharas, we find that the first Vihara to be constructed in modern times was at Kushinagar in 1902 by Ven. Mahavira. Next was the Dharmankur Vihara which was established at Calcutta by Ven. Kripasaran Mahasthavir in 1903. The Vihara constructed at Perambur, Madras in 1906 by the South India Buddhist Association was the third one. Then comes the magnificent Sri Dharmarajika Vihara, Calcutta which was founded by Anagarika Dharmapala in 1920. Ven. Bodhananda established the fifth Vihara at Risaldar Park, Lucknow in 1925. In 1927, a Buddha Vihara was constructad at Calicut, Quilon (Kerala). In 1931, the famous Mulagandhakuti Vihara constructed at Sarnath by the Maha Bodhi Society was opened. The opening of this Vihara marked an important milestone in the history of modern Buddhism. Same year, the Ananda Vihara was established at Bombay by Dr. Anandrao L. Nair. Some of the notable Viharas constructed thereafter are : Bahujana Vihara, Bombay (1937) Buddha Vihara, New Delhi (1939), Desangpani Vihara, Assam (1939), Buddha Vihara, Bangalore (1940). Venuvan Vihara, Agartala (1946). Madras (Kennet Lane) Vihara (1947), Asoka Mission Vihara, New Delhi (1950) and New Cetiyagiri Vihara, Sanchi (1952). Most of the other modern Viharas have come up after the Buddhist renaissance of 1956 started by Dr. Ambedkar. In Maharashtra, almost every Buddhist colony, whether in towns or villages, has a Vihara of its own. The largest number of Viharas are in Nagpur, the Deeksha Bhoomi. Delhi, the Capital of India, has the second largest concentration of Buddha Viharas. It now has more than twenty-five Viharas as against two prior to 1956. A significant feature of the post—1956 era is the construction of magnificent Buddhist Temples by the foreign Buddhists. These include : The Wat Thai (The Buddhist Temple) at Bodh Gaya built by the Royal Government of Thailand in 1970-1972; Indosan Nipponji (Japanese Temple) at Bodh Gaya built by the International Buddhist Brotherhood Association of Japan in 1973; Daijokoyo Temple (Japanese Temple) built by the Daijokoyo Association of Japan in 1983; World Peace Stupa (Vishwa Shanti Stupa) atop the Vulture Peak at Rajgir built by Fujii Guruji of Japan in 1969; Kalinga Peace Pagoda at Bhuveneshwar built by Fujji Guruji in 1972; and Veulvana Vihara (Nipponzan Myohoji Temple) at Rajgir built by Fujii Guruji in 1981.

As there is shortage of qualified Buddhist monks, some of the newly built Viharas do not have resident Bhikkhus. The movement has further suffered a set back with the passing away of some eminent Buddhist monks, namely, Ven. D. Sasanasiri (1966), Ven. K. Sriniwasa (1968), Ven. U Chandramani (1972), Ven. Jagdish Kashyap (1976), Ven. Dharamarakshita (1977), Ven. N. Jinaratana (1983), Ven. M. Sangharatana (1985), Ven. U. Dhammaratana (1985), and Ven. Dr. Bhadant Anand Kausalyayan (19 8).

With this brief introduction, we proceed further to describe the position of Bhikkhus and Viharas in each State. While doing so, the population of Buddhists in each State/Union Territory has also been given. The figures are based on the 1981 Census. In terms of population, Maharashtra tops the list. As many as 84 per cent Indian Buddhists live in this State.

ANDAMAN AND NICOBAR ISLANDS

The Union Territory of Andaman and Nicobar Islands has only 127 Buddhists Mainly, they are the Burmese settlers. The Buddha Viharas in the A & N Islands are at Port Blair, Maimyo and Mayabunder. Ven. U Ginawonsa of Vishwashanti Vihara, Phongyi Kyaung, Port Blair, is the Chief Bhikkhu in these Islands.

ANDHRA PRADESH

As against 230 Buddhists in 1951, Andhra now has 12,830 Buddhists. The pioneer Bhikkhu to propagate Buddhism in Andhra was Ven. Sumedha Vimalaksha. Born in Bengal, he came to Guntur as a Sramanera in 1960s and established an organisation by name "Buddha Vihara Saraswati Samithi at Guntur" and began propagating Teachings of the Buddha in Andhra, the land of renowned Buddhist shrines of Amaravati and Nagarjunakonda. Ven. Sumedha also established another Vihara known as "Nagarjuna Buddha Vihara" at Hindupur, Rayalseema. He also published scores of books and pamphlets on Buddha-Dhamma. Notable among them being : Dhammapada (Telugu), Dhammapada (English with Pali original), Ashok Samrat (Telugu) and Buddhani Jeevita Kathaly (Telugu).

Two other Bhikkhus now engaged in missionary work in Andhra Pradesh are : Ven. Sariputta Bhikkhu, and Venerable U. Ratanapala, Bhikkhu-in-charge of the Maha Bodhi Society, Madras. The Buddha Viharas have since been established at Hyderabad, Secunderabad and Visakhapatnam. A major landmark in modern Andhra will be the erection of a giant statue of Lord Buddha by the Government of Andhra Pradesh. This 60 feet high statue of the Buddha is proposed to be installed on the Gibraltor Rock in the picturesque Hussainsagar lake situated in the heart of the twin cities of Hyderabad and Secunderabad.

ARUNACHAL PRADESH

Arunachal Pradesh (the land of Sunrise) was earlier known as the North-Eastern Frontier Agency – NEFA. It has as many as 86,483 Buddhists. They are mainly concentrated in the districts of Tawang, Lohit and Tirap. The most sacred Buddhist shrine in Arunachal Pradesh is the Tawang Monastery.

The Tawang monastery was built by Mera Lama, a local Buddhist leader, about the middle of the seventeenth century. It is situated on a 3048 metres high plateau, and looks like a fortress with a commanding view. The main shrine is in the central hall of the sprawling Gompa. The holy and mysterious "Thanka" (scroll painting) donated by the fifth Dalai Lama, during whose reign this Gompa was completed, is kept cloistered behind a curtain in a separate recess. The Tawang monastery has more than 700 scriptures, of which eight large volumes of Getama are its prized possession.

The origin of the Tawang Gompa is shrouded in mystery. It is said that on completion of his studies in the yellow sect monasteries of Tashi Mympo and Derbung in Tibet, the young Mera Lama returned to his native place and constructed a small Gompa. Soon he became popular in the area. The Lamas of the rival sect became jealous, and one night set fire to his Gompa. Mera Lama fled for his life into the mountains. Exhausted and hungery, he fell off to sleep in the jungle. During the night, he dreamt of a beautiful white horse sleeping peacefully on a grassy knoll. He considered it an auspicious sign, and decided to build the new Gompa at this particular spot. In northern Monpa, 'Ta' means a horse; and 'wang' is 'to flourish'. Another interpretation is that Tawang is a place where 'horses' (Ta') were in excellent condition'. Yet another view is that 'Ta' means Buddha, and 'ong' means blessing Hence, 'Taong' or 'Tawang' means blessing of the Buddha.

The Tawang monastery is now a major religious and cultural centre in Arunachal Pradesh. It is also a great seat of learning and training of Lamas. Presently, the monastery has about 350 monks under training. According to tradition, the Buddhists in the Tawang area generally offer their second son to the monastery. The present Rinpoche, the Head Lama, was appointed in 1981 when His Holiness the 14th Dalai Lama visited the Tawang monastery.

The other important monasteries in Arunachal Pradesh are at Diran, Dzong, Domzang, Jagda, Jangda, Jang, Bangajanga and Karpotsang. An important modern Vihara is Chowkham Raj Vihara, Chowkham.

ASSAM

There are about 55,000 Buddhists in Assam. The Buddhists of Assam trace their origin to the Thais of Thailand and the Shans of Burma. The Buddhists of Central and Eastern Assam are a branch of the Ahomas, a tribe allied to the 'Shan' race of Upper Burma who penetrated into Assam in the 13th century and founded a kingdom there. There are about 100 Viharas and 150 Bhikkhus in Assam.

The pioneer missionary monk in modern Assam was Ven. Nandabansa. He was born in a Hindu family in 1909 in the Sibasagar district. He was drawn to religion after the sudden death of his parents. To begin with, he studied the Hindu suriptures but not finding satisfaction therein, he turned to Buddhism in 1930. In 1937, he took his Upasampada at the Rahanpather Buddhist Temple at the hands of Ven. Usumangala Mahasthavir, Ven. Uttamananda Mahasthavir and Ven. Tejabhanta Bhikshu. In 1939, he established a Buddhist Temple at Desangpani Same year, he founded the All Assam Buddhist Association. Apart from bringing the Buddhists of Assam on one platform, Ven. Nandabansa also founded schools and colleges. He also published more than 25 books on the Buddha-Dhamma in Assamese which helped a lot in the propagation of Buddhism in Assam. Some other notable Bhikkhus in Assam are : Ven. Shilabansha Mahasthavir, Ven. Buddhnanda Mahasthavir, Ven. Sasanabangsha, Ven. Prajnananda, Ven. Devpriya, Ven. Rahul, Ven. Sanjaya Nanda, Ven. Dr. Dharamavansa, Ven. Gunachara, Ven. Sangharakhit, and Ven. Kondinya.

Of the numerous Buddhist temples in Assam, the important ones are at : Desangpani, distt. Sibsagar; Chalapather, distt. Sibsagar; Grahambazar., Dibrugarh; Digboi; Jorhat; Naharkatia: Tipam, Dibrugarh; Duliajan; Guwahati; Tinsukia; Borkhamati. North Lakhimpur; Rajapukhuri, Golaghat.

BIHAR

The population of Buddhists in Bihar, the ancient land of Viharas, is now 3,003. There are about 50 Bhikkhus in this state. Notable among them are : Ven. Dr. Dharmavanso Maha Thera, Ven. B. Pannarama Maha Thera, Ven. Jnanajagat Maha Thera, Ven. Dr. Rashtrapal, Ven. U Zayanta, Ven. Tensho Yagi, Ven. Deva Visuddhi Moli, Ven. Vipassi, Ven. D. Vimla, Ven. B.M. Prajna Nandasri.

The most sacred shrine in Bihar is the Maha Bodhi Temple at Bodhi Gaya where Lord Buddha had attained Enlightenment. The historic Mahabodhi Temple appears to have been built in the second century A.D. Thereafter, additions, alterations and repairs were carried out by the Buddhists from time to time. When Buddhism declined in India, Bodh Gaya was deserted by the Buddhists. Taking advantage of the situation, a Hindu Mahant established his Math at Bodh Gaya in 1590 A.D. With the coming of the Mahant, the holy Buddhist shrine passed into the hands of Hindus and the phase of its sacrilege began. In 1861, Cunningham found the Mahant and his followers indulging in all sorts of un-Buddhistic ceremonies in the main shrine of the Mahabodhi Temple. Further, though the Mahant claimed the Temple and land around it as his own property yet he took no steps to repair the decaying historic temple.

In 1875, King Mindan Min of Burma, sought and obtained the permission of the Government of India and the Mahant, to repair the decaying Maha Bodhi Temple. As the repairs initiated by the Burmese were not proceeding on right lines, the Government of India appointed in 1880 J.D. Beglar to make thorough repairs of the building. General Cunningham and Dr. Rajendra Lal Mitra were also deputed to supervise the repairs. The restoration was done on the basis of a small model in stone found among the ruins from which the whole design of the building as it existed in medieval times could be traced with tolerable completeness. The restoration and renovation of the Maha Bodhi Temple to its present condition, almost an exact replica of the original shrine, was a lengthy affair but was accomplished with rare devotion and dedication.

The Maha Bodhi Temple, as it now stands, is approximately 170 feet high, while its base is 50 feet square. It consists of a straight pyramidal tower surmounted by a stupa. Inside the Temple is a great gilded figure of the Buddha touching the earth which symbolizes the supreme event of Enlightenment. To the west of the Temple stands the Bodhi Tree. The holy seat of Enlightenment, Vajrasana, is marked by a red sandstone slab.

The movement for regaining the control of the Holy Maha Bodhi shrine began in January 1891 when Anagarika Dharmapala visited Bodh Gaya. Visibly moved by the neglect of the Seat of Buddha's, Enlightenment, he resolved then and there to take steps to stop further desecretion of the holy shrine. As a first step, the far—sighted Dharmapala founded the Buddha Gaya Maha Bodhi Society on May 31, 1891. Then he persuaded four Buddhist monks from Sri Lanka to come and stay at Bodh Gaya. Venerables Duanuarla Chandajoti, Matale Sumangala, Anuradhapura Pemmananda and Galle Sudassana reached Bodh Gaya in July 1891 and took up their residence in the Burmese Rest House, constructed a few years earlier. As the Mahant had ownewship right on the entire property at Bodh Gaya, he objected to the presence of the Bhikkhus. And in February 1893, two of the monks were severely beaten up by his men. Two years later in 1895, when Dharmapala attempted to install an image of the Buddha, presented to him by the people of Japan on the upper floor of the Temple, he was assaulted and prevented by Mahant's men to do so. The Buddha image was later kept in the Burmese Rest House.

In 1906, the Mahant filed a suit seeking ejection of the Buddhist monks from the Rest House. The Buddhists also filed a civil suit claiming control of the Maha Bodhi Temple. The legal war of nerves continued till, after independence, the Government of Bihar enacted the Buddha Gaya Temple Management Act in 1949 in accordance with which a Management Committee was constituted by the State Government in 1952 and entrusted with the management and control of the Temple land, and other property. As provided in the Buddha Gaya Management Act of 1949, the Committee consists of eight members, four Hindus and four Buddhists, with the Collector of Gaya as Chairman.

Ven. Jnanajagat is at present Superintendent of the Buddha Gaya Management Committee. The daily services in the Maha Bodhi Temple are looked after by Ven. B. Prnnarama, Bhikkhu-in-charge of the Maha Bodhi Rest House, and his assistant Ven. D. Vimla Thera.

The Great Maha Bodhi Temple is once again a living shrine

and is visited by thousands of pilgrims every year from all over the world. The prestige of this sole surviving symbol of ancient grandeur and glory has been enhanced by a number of modern temples and monasteries built at Bodh Gaya by the Buddhists of other countries. Chronologically, these are : the Burmese Monastery (1875), Chinese Temple (1935), Tibetan Temple (1938), Thai Buddhist Temple (1972), Japanese Temple, Indosan Nipponji, built by the International Buddhist Brotherhood Association of Japan (1973), Daijokyo Buddhist Temple, built by Daijokyo Association of Japan (1983), Bhutanese Monastery (1988), and the Great Buddha Statue by Daijokyo Association (1989).

Rajgir, ancient Rajagriha, the capital of Bimbisara during the time of the Buddha, is now well-known for the mighty Vishwa Shanti Stupa (World Peace Pagoda) atop the Ratnagiri hill adjacent to the Gridhrakuta or Vulture Peak at Rajgir. Artistically designed by Prof. Minoru Ohoka of Japan and the noted Indian artist, Upendra Maharathi, the 160 feet high, gold-topped pagoda, is almost double the dimensions of the Sanchi Stupa. It was built by Fujii Guruji, the founder of the Japan Buddha Sangha, and consecrated on 23 October 1969. In the top chamber of this stupa, the sacred relics of Lord Buddha, presented by India to Japan in 1952, have also been enshrined.

The Buddha Sangha of Japan, founded by Fujii Guruji, has also constructed at Rajgir a magnificent Vihara a model of the Venuvana Vihara where the Buddha had often stayed while at Rajgir. Built in an area of 32,400 sq. ft., this Vihara, also known as Nipponzan Myohoji Temple, is the biggest Vihara in modern India. Its inaugural ceremony was performed on 24 October 1981.

The modern Rajgir has also a Burmese Buddhist Temple. Ven. U Zayanta is the Bhikkhu-in-charge of this Vihara.

At Nalanda, the Nava Nalanda Mahavihara, founded by Bhikkhu Jagdish Kashyap, is the main Institute. The Buddhist temples at Nalanda are : the Chinese Buddhist Temple, Japanese Buddhist Temple, Thai monastery, and Tibetan Buddhist Temple.

Three other important Buddha Viharas in Bihar are: Pataliputra Vihara, Rajendra Nagar, Patna : Buddha Vihara, Gautam Dhara, Ranchi; and Buddha Vihara, Sakchi, Jamshedpur.

CHANDIGARH

The Union Territory of Chandigarh has 454 Buddhists. The only Buddha Vihara built recently is near the village Khuda Ali Sher, just 5 km from Chandigarh.

DADRA AND NAGAR HAVELI

There are only 189 Buddhists in the Union Territory of Dadra and Nagar Haveli.

DELHI

In 1981, Delhi, had 7,117 Buddhists as against 503 in 1951. Prior to 1950, Delhi had only one Buddha Vihara. Now there are over twenty five Buddha Viharas catering to the needs of the Buddhist devotees in the Capital of India. Of these, the important Viharas are : New Delhi Buddha Vihara, Asoka Mission Vihara, Ambedkar Bhavan Vihara, Ladakh Buddha Vihara, and Jagajjyoti Buddha Vihara.

The first Buddhist temple to be built in Delhi was the Buddha Vihara on Mandir Marg, New Delhi—110001. The foundation stone of the first Vihara in the capital of modern India was laid by K. Yonewaza, Consul General for Japan on 31 October 1936. Raja Seth Jugal Kishore Birla, on being approached by Devapriya Valisinha General Secretary of the Maha Bodhi Society of India, bore the entire cost of the Vihara and its buildings, and dedicated it to the sweet memory of his father, Raja Baldev Dass Birla. He donated the Vihara to the Maha Bodhi Society of India with the understanding that in the times to come the expenses of upkeep and maintenance will be borne by him, his heirs and executors. The Vihara was opened by Mahatma Gandhi on 18 March 1989. A replica of the historic preaching Buddha (Sarnath Museum) is enshrined in this Vihara. The walls have paintings depicting the major events from the life of the Buddha.

The first Bhikkhu-in-charge of this Vihara was Ven. Gyanasiri. He was followed by Ven. Mahanama; Ven. Dharamadhara; Bhadant D. Shasansiri; Ven. Y. Dhammaloka and Ven. Dr. H. Saddhatissa. Ven. L. Ariyawansa the present incumbent, took charge of the Vihara in November, 1950.

With the establishment of this Vihara, Buddhism can be said to have come to the Capital of India. The history of this Vihara is the history of the revival of Buddhism in the Capital. Delhi's first Buddha Jayanti celebrations were held in this Vihara in 1939. Since then the Buddha Jayanti is celebrated here every year. In 1950, Delhi witnessed the first Buddhist procession which was taken out from this Vihara at the instance and with the blessings of Dr. Ambedkar.

Since 1951, that is, after the arrival of Ven. Ariyawansa, present Bhikkhu-in-charge, the Buddha Jayanti celebrations, at the Vihara are being celebrated in a more organised manner. Every year a number of distinguished personalities, eminent scholars and Diplomats from the South-East Asian countries participate in this function. The interest shown by National leaders in the activities of this Vihara is more than evident from the list of the participants in the Buddha Purnima Day functions held from 1951 onward. They include : Dr. B.R. Ambedkar, Jawaharlal Nehru, Dr. Kailash Nath Katju, Govind Ballabh Pant, Morarji Desai, Dr. Rajendra Prasad, Lal Bahadur Shastri, Shrimati Indira Gandhi, Gopal Swarup Pathak and B.D. Jatti.

The Asoka Mission Vihara, P.O. Mehrauli, New Delhi-110030, was established in 1950 by Venerable V. Dhammavara Maha Thera, a Cambodian monk. This Vihara is situated in beautiful, seren and calm environments near Qutab Minar and caters to the needs of the rural population around. Ven. Lama Lobzang is now the President of Asoka Mission.

The foundation stone of the Ambedkar Bhavan, Rani Jhansi Road, New Delhi-110055, was laïd on 15 April, 1951 by Babasaheb Dr. B.R. Ambedkar himself. In 1956, one of its rooms was converted into a shrine room. This Vihara is managed by the Buddhist Society of India (Bhartiya Baudha Maha Sabha), an organisation founded by Dr. Ambedkar to work for the Buddhist revival in India. The Buddhist Society of India organises every year, on the occasion of the Buddha Jayanti, a huge, colourful procession which starts from the historic Red Fort and, after passing through the main bazars in the city, terminates at Ambedkar Bhavan, where a public meeting is held in the evening.

The Ladakh Buddha Vihara, Bela Road, Delhi-110054 is situated on the bank or river Yamuna, and is the most spacious Vihara in Delhi. It has over 40 furnished bed rooms, a meeting hall a temple and a library. This prestigious Institution of the Buddhists of Ladakh was founded by His Holiness Kushak Bakula who is also its President since its inception. It was constructed in 1963 under the kind patronage of Jawaharlal Nehru, the first Prime Minister of India, and was opened by him on 24 February, 1963.

The shrine room of the Ladakh Vihara has three beautiful statues of Lord Buddha, Sariputta and Moggallana. Six large size paintings, depicting the life of the Buddha, decorate the temple walls.

The Rest House, attached to this Vihara, was constructed by the Government of India at a cost of Rupees 5.50 lakhs for the use of Lamas and other pilgrims from border areas in response to a request made by Ven. Kushak Bakula to the Prime Minister of India. The temple was built with public donations.

In its library, the Ladakh Buddha Vihara has a rich collection of ancient Tibetan scriptures. These have been retrieved from the monasteries as well as private sources in Ladakh. The oldest manuscript at the Vihara is 1200 years old. It was written by King Songstsan Gampo of Tibet. The Vihara has also procured all the 16 volumes of the Boom scriptures, which are supplementary to the Tripitaka, and are most popular with the adherents of the Mahayana Buddhism.

The Jagajjyoti Buddha Vihara,—Sant Nagar, New Delhi 110016, is just near the newly discovered Rock Edict of Asoka at Bahpur. It was constructed in 1968 by the Bengali Buddhist community in the Capital, at the instance and under the guidance of Ven. L. Ariyawansa Nayaka Maha Thera.

Twenty other Viharas in Delhi are in: Ashok Vihar Baradpur, Baljit Nagar (West Patel Nagar), Bhogal, Dr. Ambedkar Nagar, Govindpuri (main), Govindpuri (DDA Flats), Goverdhan Bihari Colony (Bholanath Nagar), Laxminagar, beyond I.T.O. bridge, (1. established by Ven. Vishuddhananda, 2. Tibetan Temple, 3. Japanese Temple), Madangiri, Munirika, Pacchim Vihar, R.K. Puram, Sector III, Shahdra (1. in Vishwas Nagar, and 2. on Loni Road), Siddharth Colony, Sri Lanka Buddhist Pilgrims Rest, near New Delhi Railway Station, and Sultanpuri.

Most of the Buddha Viharas in Delhi have resident monks. The senior most Buddhist monk in Delhi is Ven. L. Ariyawansa Nayaka Maha Thera, and Chief Sangha Nayaka of Northern India. He was born in 1915 in a Barua Buddhist family in Chittagong (now in Bangladesh). He received his higher ordination (upasampada) in 1938 in Sri Lanka where he received his religious training for nine years. He joined the Maha Bodhi Society of India as a Dhnmmaduta worker in 1949 and came to Delhi in November 1950. Among the Mahayana monks, Venerable Kushak Bakula, the Head Lama of Laddakh is the senior most. He is an Ex-Minister of Jammu

& Kashmir and also an Ex-Member of Parliament. He was a member of the Minorities Commission of India. He has recently been appointed India's Ambassador in Mongolia.

Some other prominent Buddhist monks in Delhi are :

Ven. Lama Lobzang, Ven. Vishuddhananda Maha Thera, Ven. Mahanama Maha Thera, Ven. Silananda Maha Thera, Ven. Dr. Satyapal, Ven. Karunanand, Ven. Gyanratana, Ven. Satyasheel, Ven. Dr. Doboom Tulku (of Tibet), Ven. Mahaviro Maha Thera (of Thailand), Ven. Vijitadhamma Maha Thera (of Sri Lanka).

GOA

There are only 302 Buddhists in Goa, Daman and Diu.

GUJARAT

As against 198 in 1951, there are now 7,550 Buddhists in Gujarat The newly constructed Buddha Vinaras in Gujarat are in Ahmedabad, Baroda and Keshod, Junagarh.

HARYANA

The population of Buddhists in Haryana is 761 only.

HIMACHAL PRADESH

According to 1981 Census, there are as many as 52,629 Buddhists in Himachal Pradesh. They are mainly concentrated in the valleys of Lahul, Spiti, Kinnaur, Kulu and Kangra. To cater to their religious needs, there are a large number of Buddhist monks (lamas) and about one hundred monasteries in Himachal Pradesh.

LAHUL

The notable monasteries in Lahul are at Kyelang and Tupchiling. Kyelang, the district headquarters of Lahul, has an impressive Buddhist monastery. The Shashur gompa, here is said to have been founded by Lama Deva Gyasatsho of Ladakh in the 17th century A.D. The Guru Ghantal monastery at Tupchilling is said to be located on the site where Guru Padmasambhava meditated before going to Tibet in 747 A.D. Initially, this monastery was called Guru Gandhola. The word Gandhola in Tibetan means the

Untained (pure) House and refers to the holy site of Buddha's enlightenment at Bodh Gaya. This monastery believed to be the site of Padmasambhava's enlightenment came to be known as Guru Gandhola. In course of time, this was distorted by the foreigners and the monastery came to be known as Guru Ghantal. The monastery has a wooden image of the Buddha which is said to have been installed in the eleventh century by Lama Rin-chen-bZong-po of Kinnaur.

The other monasteries in Lahul are at : Lindur, Bokar, Gumrang, Tyul, Tinno, Kolong, Khangsar, Gemur, Jispa, Tingal, Darcha, Lepchang, Thola-Pyasu, Jholing, Piukar, Gajang, Kardang, Dalang, Gondhala, Khinang, Shashin, Jagdang, Labrang, Ghokhur' Teling, Damphung and Othang.

SPITI

The Tabo monastery, known as the Chos-hKhor, is the largest monastery in Spiti. It has as many as nine temples. Of these, atleast five temples are traced back to the 11th century A.D. Three most important temples are : the Golden Temple, the Large Temple of Drompton, and the Temple of Enlightened Gods. The Golden Temple has beautiful murals of the divinities and the protective deities on the walls. The ceiling of the temple is painted with Gandharvas, birds and flora motifs. The Large Temple of Drompton has a large painted figure of the Buddha flanked by Sariputta on the right and Maha Moggallana on the left. The side walls have figures of the Eight Medicine Buddhas. The Temple of Enlightened Gods has the largest number of images.

Another important monastery in Spiti is at Ki. The walls of the assembly hall (du-khang) of this monastery have beautiful murals. Yet another important monastery in this valley is at Gungri in Pin valley. It is believed to have been founded by Padmasambhava in the eighth century A.D.

The other monasteries in the Spiti valley are at : Losar, Hansa, Rangrik, Kibar, Kaza, Kaung, Keuling. Komik, Hikim, Langja, Lara, Lidang, Domal, Sanglung, Rama, Lha-lun, Dhankar, Mane Gogma, Mane Yogma, Giu, Kaurik Tangti, Phar, Sagnam, Todnam, Tiling and Mud.

KINNAUR

Of all the Buddhist temples in Himachal Pradesh, those at

Kanum, a tiny village in Kinnaur are most important, on account of their architecture, wall paintings and literary treasures. Situated in the lap of hills at an elevation of 9600 ft. Kanum is about 186 miles from Simla, the capital of Himachal Pradesh, and 33 miles beyond Kalpa, the district headquarters of Kinnaur. The Tehsil headquarters, Poo, is 16 miles farther away. Of the seven temples in Kanum, three most important are described here.

The Kangyur Monastery, the most ancient in Kanum, is situated in the heart of the village. Its two storey building houses a very fine library which contains 108 volumes of Kangyur (Kanjur) and 255, volumes of Tangyur (Tanjur) books written in Tibetan script; a rare collection indeed for a village library. According to Rahul Sankrityayan, the wooden stencils of these books were engraved in Narthang monastery in Central Tibet in the 16th century. The famous Hungarian-born Tibetan scholar, Alexander Csoma de Koros (1784-1842) had made use of this library in compiling his Tibetan English Dictionary. He stayed at Kanum for over three years in 1827-30; collected and arranged 40,000 Tibetan words and nearly completed the Tibetan-English Dictionary, which was later published by the Asiatic Society of Bengal, Calcutta.

Lundup Ganfel Gompa is the biggest monastery in Kanum and is situated on the top of the village. This monastery is also called Kache-lha-Khang, i e., the Kashmiri temple, by the local people. According to Rahul Sankrityayan, it was built by Maha Pandit Shakya Virbhadra of Kashmir, the last Sangharaja of India, who ran from India in about 1213 AD and lived for 10 years in Tibet. On his way back to his birth place in Kashmir, he stayed at Kanum and got constructed a Vihara. Shakya Virbhadra in Bhot is known as Kache-pan-chhen' (Kashmiri Pandit). Hence, the Vihara constructed by him came to be known as Khache-lha-Khang. This Gompa has on its walls the nicest and beautiful mural paintings depicting various phases of the life of the Buddha. The monastery has also good collection of religious books and Buddha statues made of clay, and sandalwood.

Lachao Labrang or Lha-Khang Lochalama monastery commemorates the visit of the Rinpoche Locha Lama of Tashilhunpo, Tibet who visited Kanum in 1897 AD when he came to consecrate the Buddhist temple built at Rampur by Tikka Raghunath Singh of Bushahr.

Some other monasteries in Kinnaur are at : Hango, Chuling, Leo, Chango, Nako Shalkhar (Kyahar), Sumra, Pilu, Ropa, Sunam, Shiasu, Poo, Namgia, Lipa Rarang, Ribba, Rispa, Morang, Tashigiang, Thangi, Charang, Chini, Pangi, Purbani, Poari, Baring, Kilba, Sapni, Barua and Sangla.

KULU-KANGRA

The important Buddha Viharas in the Kulu-Kangra valley are at Kulu and Dharamsala. A Tibetan Buddhist temple has recently come up at Manali also. Dharamsala, the headquarters of Kangra district, has a beautiful newly built Tibetan monastery. Being the permanent abode of His Holiness the Dalai Lama, who took asylum in India in 1959 under compelling circumstances, Dharamsala has now become a place of pilgrimage for the Buddnists. The Council of Religious Affairs of His Holiness the Dalai Lama which manages Tibetan institutions in India has also its headquarters at Dharamsala.

In Kangra district, a large Buddhist monastic complex has recently come up at Bir, a village in Tehsil Palampur. Built by the Tibetan settlers, the complex has five monasteries. These monasteries have giant images of the Buddha Padmasambhava, and other divinities. One of these monasteries, known as Sherab-ling, or "the land of wisdom", is located on a hill-top with forests all around. The main temple, a three storey building, faces a courtyard enclosed by classrooms and living cells for monks. The ornately carved throne of the Tai Situ, decorated with the traditional dharmachakra and dragons dominates the shrine room. Sherab-ling is a vast project designed to cater to the spiritual, cultural, medical, and educational needs of the people. The complex has furnished guest houses and retreat houses with meditation cells. Adequate educational facilities have also been provided. Bir is now attracting many visitors, from India and abroad, who come here for study and meditation.

Another Buddhist monastery in district Kangra is at Tilokpur, 32 km below Dharamsala, and on the straight way from Pathankot to Mandi. It is a Mahayana monastery for Nuns.

Rewalsar, 20 km from Mandi, is the most important Buddhist shrine in Mandi district. Here, a fair called Sichu takes place every year in the month of Phalguna (March-April) in the Mani-pani temple—an old shrine dedicated to Guru Padmasambhava who meditated here in 747 A.D. before going to Tibet. Since Padmasambhava, also known as Guru Rinpoche, was the first propagator of Buddhism in Tibet and is revered by all the followers of Lamaism, irrespective of sects, this fair is attended by a considerable number of Buddhists from all over Himachal Pradseh and even Ladakh.

There is only one ancient Buddhist Temple in Shimla district. It is at Rampur and was built by Tikka Raghunath Singh of Bushahr in 1897. Recently, a large Tibetan Buddhist monastery has been established at Sanjauli in Shimla, the capital of Himachal Pradesh.

JAMMU AND KASHMIR

There are 69706 Buddhists in the state of Jammu and Kashmir. Almost all of them are in the district of Leh and district of Kargil in Ladakh. The Ladakhis follow the Mahayana form of Buddhism and are one of the oldest groups in India. There are as many as 2,500 monks and nuns in Ladakh and about 1,000 monks are under education at different Buddhist centres in India, viz., Bangalore, Dharamsala, Mysore, Varanasi etc. There are seven Head Lamas in Ladakh. They are :

1. Ven. Kushak Bakula, Head Lama of Spituk Gompa.
2. Ven. Kushak Staksang Respa of Hemis Gompa.
3. Ven. Kushak Khanpo Rimpoche of Thiskey Gompa.
4. Ven. Kushak Stakna Rimpoche of Stakna Gompa.
5. Ven. Kushak Tokdan Rimpoche of Gaon Gompa.
6. Ven. Kushak Stras Rimpoche of Rizong Gompa.
7. Ven. Kushak Chhoje Rimpoche of Chumur Gompa.

These Venerabte Kushaks or Kushoks are incarnated. Ven. Kushak Bakula, the senior most Lama of Ladakh, is the most respected Buddhist leader of Ladakh. Padma Bhushuna awarded by the Government of India, Ven. Kushak Bakula has recently been appointed as India's Ambassador in Mongolia. Earlier, for 14 years he was a Minister in the J&K Government, and thereafter he was Member of Parliament. Prior to his appointment as Ambassador, he was a Member of the Minorities Commission of India

The whole of Ladakh is dotted with monasteries, known as 'Gompas'. A gompa means 'solitary place', and some of them are in fact solitary places. The most important monasteries in Ladakh are at : Leh, Hemis, Chemrey, Taktak, Shachukul, Nyoma Korzok, Anlay, Chumur, Thiksey, Matho, Stakna, Spituk, Gaon (Fiang), Likir, Rozong, Lamayuru, Linoshad, Doskit, Samstanlinn, Yarma, Gonbo, Zannpocholing in Leh, Nubra and Channthan Sub-Divisions; Karsha, Sani, Padam, Bardan, Muni, Phuktal, Stongde, Zanqkul in Zanskar; and Rangdum, Sharnol, Mulbek in Kargil.

In 1987, the Ladakh Buddhist Association, with the help of the local Buddhists, constructed a Historical Palace for His Holiness the Dalai Lama at Jiwa Tsal Shay at a cost of Rupees thirty-three lakhs. H.H. the Dalai Lama visits Ladakh every year during summer months.

A grand Shanti Stupa (Peace Pagoda) is presently under construction at Changspa Hill, Leh by the Japan Buddha Sangha, with the help of the local Buddhists.

Some of the important monasteries in Ladakh are described here :

The Hemis gompa, 45 kilometres from Leh on the Ladakh-Tibet Road, is the largest and the richest monastery in Ladakh. It was founded in 1630 by Lama Stag-tsang-ras pa under the royal patronage of Sengge Namgyal. The main shrine, the Du-khang, has some remains of the 17th century murals, though not in a very good condition. The Tsogs-khang temple has an enormous silver chorten said to have been dedicated by Lama Shambhunath, the third Kushok in line from the monastery's founder, some time in the first half of the eighteenth century. There is also a fine image of the Buddha.

Sankar gompa, just three kilometres from Leh, is a pleasing cluster of buildings and chorten nestling among trees on the edge of the village. It has a number of images of Lama Tsong-kha-pa, founder of the Gelug-pa or the Yellow sect.

Spituk gompa is about eight kilometres down the Indus from Leh. This monastery was founded in the fifteenth century, and was the first Gelug-pa monastery to be founded in Ladakh. Its name in Tibetan means 'Effective as an Example'. It has a number of small shrines.

Shey gompa is about fourteen kilometres from Leh and is on the way to Hemis gompa. Shey was the ancient capital of Ladakh till Sengge Namgyal built his palace at Leh in the seventeenth century. The palace temple has a giant copper gilt image of the Buddha. There are also a large number of images of deities and objects of worship. The lower storey has a library of sacred scriptures. Its walls are painted with representations of the Thousand Buddhas.

Thiksey, also on the way to Hemis gompa, is the largest and most impressive gompa in central Ladakh. It was established probably about the middle of the fifteenth century during the early epoch of Gelug-pa expansion in Ladakh. Its main attraction today is the new Maitreya temple which was dedicated by His Holiness the Dalai Lama in September 1980. This impressive gompa has an enormous image of Maitreya in an unusual manifestation sitting in the lotus position.

Fiang gompa, on the right bank of the Indus and about fifteen kilometres down-stream from Leh, was founded by king Tashi Namgyal in the second half of the sixteenth century. This gompa has a large number of images and paintings.

Chemrey gompa is about forty-five kilometres from Leh, just off the road to the Chang-La. It was completed in 1646. The main Du-khang has images of Stag tsang ras-pa and other Drug pa Lamas. The murals are mainly of the Buddha. There is also a fine silver chorten. Twenty-nine volumes of the scriptures have title pages whose lettering is in solid silver of exquisite craftsmanship; the rest in pure gold.

Thak-Thak gompa, a few kilometres beyond Chemrey, was founded in the second half of the sixteenth century. Nearby it is one of the caves where Padmasambhava is said to have stayed and meditated during his journey to Tibet in the eighth century. Stakna gompa is the earliest Drug-pa monastery established in Ladakh. The present temple was built in the first half of the seventeenth century. The Du khang has a number of images and mural paintings on the walls. A recent addition is a silver chorten of exquisite craftsmanship studded with flawless turquoises.

Likir gompa was first built in the eleventh century by the King of Ladakh. It was rebuilt by the Gelug-pa sect in the fifteenth century. The smaller Du-khang has an image of eleven-headed Avalokitesvara and paintings on the side walls, representing benevolent Bodhisattvas.

Lamayuru monastery, ninety-six killometres from Leh on the Leh-Kargil road is one of the oldest gompas in Ladakh. Its main attraction is a sixteenth century statue of Avalokitesvara with eleven heads and thousand arms.

The Alchi monastery, beyond Lamayuru, and about ten kilometres off the main Srinagar-Leh highway, has beautiful paintings from 9th century to 12th century. Alchi was founded by Rinchen Zang-po during the reign of the Guge kings (A.D. 970-1200) of Ladakh who were great patrons of Buddhism. The Alchi paintings have a great historical value as they preserve the art tradition which flourished in the Kashmir Valley during the hey day of Buddhism. There are five temples in the Alchi village. Of them, the Sum tsek is the most interesting physical structure of Alchi. The best and the better preserved paintings are also in this temple. The paintings are divided into two levels with the mandalas painted above and multiple images of Amitabha, Aksobhya, Manjusri and Sakyamuni at the lower level. Apart from the paintings, the temple has three statues in stucco of Avalokitesvara, Maitreya and Manjusri which stand twelve feet high. The second temple, Du-khang is the main assembly hall of the complex. The central image, painted in gold, is that of Vairocana, the Dhyani Buddha, attended to by thirty-six divinities. There are six large mandalas painted on the walls and a protective Mahakala image over the door. The mandalas illustrate the various cycles of Vairocana surrounded by four other Buddhas, Aksobhya, Ratna-sambhava, Amitabha and Amoghasiddhi, and their four saktis. The third temple. known as Lha-Khang Soma is the newest temple in the complex. The paintings in this temple are quite different from the other temples. The Lotsawa Lha-Khang and Manjusri Lha-Khang temples are located at the lower end of the complex. While the first temple is dedicated to the founder of the temples of Alchi, Rinchen Zang-po, the other temple is almost entirely filled with a massive stucco fourfold image of the deity Manjusri.

KARNATAKA

There are now 42,147 Buddhists in Karnataka as against 1707 in 1951. The chief Buddha Vihara in Karnataka is at 14, Kalidasa Road, Gandhinagar, Bangalore. Though founded in 1940 by the Maha Bodhi Society, it became a living centre of Buddhism only in 1956 after the arrival of Ven. Acharya Buddharakkhita. As a result of his single-minded devotion and dedication, this Vihara is now a flourishing Buddhist centre. It has an Institute of Buddhology, an International Meditation Centre, a Stupa and a Printing Press. Some other organisations founded by Acharya Buddharakkhita are : Mahabodhi Maitri Mandal, Bangalore and Mysore; Mahabodhi Arogya Hospital and Artificial Limb Centre, Bangalore; and Mahabodhi Vidyapeeth. Bangalore with branches at Mysore and Leh, Ladakh. Ven. Buddharakkhita is a meditator, psychologist, philosopher and educationist. He is also a prolific writer, and has published over fifty books and pamphlets on Buddha-Dhamma in English and Kannada. He is also Editor of the monthly journal 'Dhamma' which was founded by him in 1976. In the multifarious activities of the Buddha Vihara, Ven. Acharya Buddharakkhita is now being ably assisted by Ven. Sanghasena.

Two other Buddha Viharas in Karnataka are : Asoka Vihara, Asokapuram, Mysore city, and Buddha Vihara, Champion Reef, Kolar Gold Fields. Two Tibetan monasteries in the state are : Thegchay Ling Tibetan Monastery, Bylakuppe, and Namgoling Tibetan Monastery, Bylakuppe.

KERALA

There are only 223 Buddhists in Kerala. The only Vihara in this state is at Calicut, Quilon. It was founded by the Maha Bodhi Society of India in 1927 through the efforts of C. Krishnan, Editor of the 'Mitavadi' and M. Rama Iyer. Ven. Dharmakhanda was the first Malalyali to become a Bhikkhu and to give impetus to the revival of Buddhism in Malabar.

MADHYA PRADESH

There are as many as 75,312 Buddhists in Madhya Pradesh. The most important modern Buddha Vihara in this ancient land of Buddhism is the Cetiyagiri Vihara at Sanchi in which are preserved the sacred relics of Sariputta and Mahamoggallana. The foundation stone of the new Cetiyagiri Vihara, which is perched on the extremity of the northern facade of the famous Chetiya Giri Hills, was laid on 8 January 1946 by His Highness the Nawab of Bhopal. Col. Ryan and Swamy Rao designed this beautiful Vihara in which the sacred relics of the two great disciples of the Buddha Sariputta and Mahamoggallana were enshrined in

November, 1952, in the presence of the Prime Minister of India (Jawaharlal Nehru) and Burma (U Nu). These relics, which were discovered by General Cunningham in 1851 and taken to London the same year were returned to India in January 1949 at the request of the Maha Bodhi Society of India. The cost of the Vihara (about Rs. two lakhs) was borne jointly by the Maha Bodhi Societies of India and Ceylon (Sri Lanka). The Nawab of Bhopal also contributed Rupees 25,000 besides supplying some building materials and technical staff.

Venerable Punnatissa Maha Thera (of Sri Lanka) who was the first Bhikkhu-in-charge of the Cetiyagiri Vihara was primarily responsible for restoring Sanchi to its grandeur and glory of by-gone days.

The other Buddha Viharas in Madhya Pradesh are in Bhopal, Sagar, Bhilai, Mhow, Dongargad, Aamla, Kohkadeebar in district Balaghat, Sonagiri in district Datia, and Mathani in district Betul. The monks in Madhya Pradesh are Ven. Dharmasheel, Ven. Sugatanand, Ven. Dhammapiti and Ven. Yashas.

MAHARASHTRA

The state of Maharashtra with a population of as many as 39,46,149 Buddhists, or 84% of the total Buddhist population in India, is the pride of Buddhist India

The pioneers of the Buddhist revival movement in Maharashtra were Dr. Anandrao L. Nair and Dharmananda Kosambi. Dr. Nair was a medical practioner and well-known for his many charitable works. In 1922, he founded the Buddhist Society of Bombay in order to popularise Buddhism in Maharashtra. In 1931, he built a Buddha Vihara (Ananda Vihara) in the compound of his hospital in Bombay. Dharmananda Kosambi was the first Maharashtrian to become a Buddhist monk. He was ordained as a monk in Sri Lanka in 1902. From 1912 to 1918, Kosambi taught Pali at Fergussan College in Poona. In 1937, Kosambi built a small Buddha Vihara at Parel, a mill-workers area of Bombay, and called it 'Bahujana Vihara' or the Buddhist temple for the masses. He also wrote some thought-provoking books on Buddhism in Gujarat and Marathi; the most important being 'Bhagwan Buddha' published in 1940. But the effect of his efforts was not much. Then came Dr. B.R. Ambedkar who was a giant intellectual ever born amongst the down-trodden of India. He generated a new consciousness among his people; fought valiantly for a change in their status; and showed them the way to progress, to emancipation. When Dr. Ambedkar, gave a clarion call to his followers in 1956 to embrace Buddhism, the people of Maharashtra responded in a big way. And Buddhism came to life overnight in Maharashtra.

The most notable Buddhist monk who was instrumental in sustaining the Buddhist movement in Maharashtra, after the sudden demise of Babasaheb Ambedkar in December 1956, was Ven. Dr. Bhadant Anand Kausalyayan, a Punjabi Bhikkhu, who came to live at Deeksha Bhoomi, Nagpur after his return from Sri Lanka in 1968. He established at the sacred site a Buddha Vihara and the Bhikkhu Niwas to facilitate training of new monks. Ven. Anand Kausalyayan shifted in 1982 to the Buddha Bhoomi, Kamptee Road, Khairi, Nagpur which is also coming up as a good centre of Buddhism. Other eminent Buddhist monks in Maharashtra are : Ven. Dr. S. Medhankar, Ven. Shivli Bodhi, Ven. K. Ananda, Ven. Dharmakirti, Ven. Bodhanand, Ven. Sumedhha, Ven. Sadanand, Ven. Dharmasatan, Ven. Sheelaratana, Ven. Buddhghosh, Ven. Satsheel.

In Maharashtra, small Buddhist temples have sprung up in every Buddhist colony and Viharas in every town. The Buddha Vihara at Dehu Road, Pune, is the only Vihara where Dr. Ambedkar had himself installed an image of the Buddha, presented to him by the Burmese Buddhists in 1954. The Dehu Road Vihara was consecrated on 25 December 1955. In Bombay, the important Viharas are : 1. Ananda Vihara, Nair Hospital Compound, Dr. Anand Rao Nair Road, Bombay—8. Built by Dr. A.L. . Nair, it was taken over by the Maha Bodhi Society of India in 1953; 2. Bahujana Vihara, Parel, Bombay—12. This Vihara was established by Dharmananda Kosambi in 1937 with the help of Seth J.K. Birla. It was taken over by the Maha Bodhi Society in 1950: 3. Japanese Buddha Vihara (Nipponzan Myohoji Temple), Worli, Bombay. It was built by Fujii Guruji, with the help of Birla Brothers; 4. Nalanda Vihara, Ambedkar Colony, Khar, Bombay—29. It was built under the supervision of Dr. Ambedkar; 5. Siddharth Vihara, Wadala, Bombay. Built by the People's Education Society, it is attached to the Students Hostel; 6. Chaitya

Bhoomi Stupa, Shivaji Park, Bombay. Built on the site where Dr. Ambedkar was cremated on 7 December 1956, it was unveiled on 24 November 1968.

In Nagpur, where Dr. Ambedkar embraced Buddhism alongwith half a million followers on 14 October 1956, there are about forty Viharas. Some notable Viharas in Nagpur are : Deekhsha Bhoomi, Buddha Bhoomi (Kamptee Road), Sadar, Panch Sheel Nagar, Milind Nagar, Gitti Khan, Ward No. 62, Imambara, Samta Nagar, Bara Indora, Dharmpeth, Ambedkar Nagar, Bheem Nagar, Mahavihara, Ward No. 14, Basant Nagar, and Shanti Vihara.

The following are some of the Buddha Viharas at other places in Maharashtra : Nawab Medhi Khana, Poona—1; Nasik Road, Nasik; New Buddhwar Peth, Ambedkar Nagar Sholapur-2; Maney Gaon, district Bhandara; Bhusaval; Pulgaon; Kerjhar district Wardha; Shahpur, district Bhandara; Madgi, district Bhandara; Nandgaon, district Jalgaon; Balapur, district Akola.

MANIPUR

There are only 4/3 Buddhists in Manipur. They are mainly tribal.

MEGHALAYA

The Garo Hills, United Khasi and Jantia Hills, and Mikir Hills in the erstwhile state of Assam have now been formed into a separate state of Meghalaya. There are 2739 Buddhists in this state. The chief Vihara is at Shillong, the capital of Meghalaya. Ven. Jinaratana Maha Thera is the Bhikkhu in-charge of the Vihara.

MIZORAM

The newly formed Union territory of Mizoram (formerly) the district of Mizo Hills in Assam) had as many as 40,429 Buddhists in 1981. The Buddhists of Mizoram belong to the Chakma tribe and have a long history and tradition. In the centuries preceding the British they were the rulers of a vast area around Demagiri in the western Mizo Hills. They are very much attached to their religion and their land, western part of Mizoram, is replete with monks and monasteries. There are over 40 Buddha Viharas and

130 Buddhist monks in Mizoram. The Chief Bhikkhu is Ven. Rakha Bausho Bhikshu.

NAGALAND

There are only 517 Buddhists in Nagaland.

ORISSA

There are now 8,462 Buddhists in Orissa. The main Buddha Vihara at Plot 4-Unit 9, New Capital, Bhuvaneshwar. At present, Ven. Saddhananda is the Bhikkhu-in-charge of this Vihara.

A major Buddhist landmark in modern Orissa is the construction of a Peace Pagoda by Fujii Guruji, founder of the Japan Buddha Sangha, atop the historic Dhauli hill, where Emperor Asoka, after witnessing the large scale massacre in the Kalinga war, had sought refuge in the Buddha-Dhamma. The Kalinga Peace Pagoda is situated at a distance of 15 km from Bhuveneshwar, just near the Rock Edict of Asoka. The foundation stone of this Stupa was laid on 25 January 1971. Built wlth some financial assistance from the Government of Orissa, the Kalinga Peace Pagoda was inaugurated on 8 November 1972.

PONDICHERRY

There are only 75 Buddhists in Pondicherry.

PUNJAB

In the modern Punjab, which came into being on the Ist November 1966, after re-organisation, there are 799 Buddhists only. This figure does not include 454 Buddhists in Chandigarh. Recently, two modern Buddha Viharas have come up in Punjab; the first being at Siddharth Nagar, P.O. Model Town, Jalandhar city; and the second at Anandgarh (Mehlanwali) in district Hoshiarpur.

RAJASTHAN

There are 4,427 Buddhists in Rajasthan. The Maha Bodhi Ashoka Mission, Ajmer founded by Rahul Suman Chhawara is trying its best to revive the Dhamma amongst the Koliyas of Rajasthan. The Koliyas of today trace their origin to the Koliyas of Buddha's time. The ancient Koliyas had shared the sacred relics of the Buddha and erected a stupa at Ramagrama, their capital. The Buddha Viharas in Rajasthan are at : Dr. Ambedkar Marg, Mayo Link Road, Ajmer : Vadipur, Tehsil Kishanganj, district Kotah; and Bheem Nagar, Sarmathura, district Bharatpur.

SIKKIM

Sikkim became a separate political entity in 1642 A.D. when three lamas Gyalwa Lhatsun Chhempo, Sempa Chhempo and Rigzim Chhempo of Tibet of the Nyingmapa sect, consecrated Phuntshog Namgyal (1604-1670) as the King of the Lepcha land with the title of Chogyal (King who rules according to righteous law, and enforces respect for it) at Yaksam in western Sikkim. On 14 May 1975, Sikkim became a State of the Union of India. With this, the institution of Chogyal was abolished.

There are about 70 monasteries or gompas in Sikkim. Of these, the most important ones are described here.

The Pemayangtse monastery at Gyalshing in West Sikkim is the most important and the principal religious centre in Sikkim. It belongs to the Nyingmapa sect, and was founded in 1705 by Gyalwa Lhatsun Chhempo, the Chief Lama, who performed the consecration ceremony at Yaksam in 1642. The main images in this gompa are gold gilted huge statues of Guru Padmasambhava and Guru Tsengyat. There are also many other precious images and holy objects.

The Tashiding monastery, in the centre of Sikkim, is the most holy place in Sikkim, having been blessed first by the great Padmasambhava in the 8th century and later in the 17th century by Ngadak Sempa Chhempo, one of the Lamas who consecrated the first Chogyal at Yaksam in 1642.

The Rumtek monastery in East Sikkim was founded in the 18th century. It belongs to the Karma Kargyud sect. After the Chinese occupation of Tibet, His Holiness the Gyalwa Karmapa, the 16th incarnate of the original Gyalwe Karmapa of Tibet, came to Sikkim with a number of Lamas, monks and lay followers. The late Chogyal of Sikkim made a gift of 74 acres of land to His Holiness for building up a monastery in the vicinity of Rumtek monastery. The Prayer Hall of the new monastery is embellished with beautiful mural paintings, and 1001 miniature golden images of Lord Buddha enshrined in niches on the wall facing the wide front door besides other statues of Buddhist Pantheon.

The Phensang monastery is at a distance of 25 km from Gangtok, close to the North Sikkim Highway. It was built in 1721 by Lama Jigme Pawo, who was considered as the third incarnation of Gyalwa Lhatsun Chhempo, during the reign of the third Chogyal of Sikkim. The original building was destroyed in a fire in 1947 and it was rebuilt in 1948. It belongs to the Nyingmapa sect.

The Ralong monastery in West Sikkim was founded by the fourth Chogyal of Sikkim in the 18th century in fulfilment of the promise he had made to the Chief Lama of Tsorphu near Lhasa, the head of the Karma Kargyupa sect whom he had met during his visit to Tibet on pilgrimage.

The Phodang monastery, which is 35 km from Gangtok towards North Sikkim, belongs to the Kargyupa sect. It is famous for its old mural frescoes and paintings. It was also founded during the reign of the fourth Chogyal of Sikkim.

Some other important monasteries in Sikkim are: Sanga-Choling, Khachod Palri, Dubdi, and Sinon (all in West Sikkim), Tholung (North Sikkim), and Enchey at Gangtok.

TAMIL NADU

There are only 735 Buddhists in Tamil Nadu. The revival movement in Tamil Nadu was pioneered by Pandit Ayodhaya Dass, founder of the South India Buddhist Association, Professor P. Lakshmi Narasu, author of the famous Buddhist work, 'Essence of Buddhism', and Ven. Nilwakke Somananda Thera, a Tamil knowing monk, who was for a time in the thirtees representative of the Maha Bodhi Society in Madras.

Two important Buddha Viharas in this state are in Madras. The first one is at Kennet Lane, Egmore, Madras-8. It is managed by the Maha Bodhi Society of India. The spacious building for this Vihara was purchased in 1947 at a cost of Rupees 60,000. The present Bhikkhu-in-charge of this Vihara is Ven. Ratanapala.

The second Vihara, known as Mrs Mary Foster's Buddhist Hall, is at 41 Paddy Field Road, Perambur, Madras—11. The Hall, including Vihara, was purchased with the funds donated by Mrs.

Mary E. Foster of Honolulu, who collaborated with Anagarika Dharmapala and invested her enormous wealth for the purpose of reviving Buddha-Dhamma in India. The first Bhikkhu-in-charge of this Vihara was Bhikshu Nandarama of Sri Lanka who came in 1906 and preached Dhamma amongst the local people. The Buddhist Hall is also the headquarters of the South India Buddhist Association.

Two other Viharas in Tamil Nadu are at Buddhavedu, Distt. Madras and Rajapalyam, Distt. Ramnad.

TRIPURA

The number of Buddhists in Tripura is 54,306 Majority of the Buddhists belong to Chakma tribe, a tribe which is a survival from the Buddhist Period. There are about 100 Bhikkhus in Tripura. Mostly they are of tribal origin and they live in the interior areas of Tripura. Notable Bhikkhus in Tripura are: Ven. Khantivara Mahasthavir, Ven. U Teza Mahasthavir, Ven. U Zejinda Mahasthavir, Ven. U Nanda Mahasthavir, Ven. U Chandasara Mahasthavir, Ven. Sudarshan Bhikkhu and Ven. Khemasara Bhikkhu. There are about 14 important Viharas in Tripura. The most important Vihara is the Venuvan Vihara in Agartala, the capital of Tripura. This magnificent Buddhist temple was built in 1946 by His Highness the Maharaja Sri Bir Bikram Kishore Manikya Bahadur of Tripura State. The Maharaja of Tripura, had much love and devotion for Buddhism. So he got constructed this Buddhist Temple in his Capital at Agartala, near his Royal Palace and named it as "VENUVAN VIHAR" in holy commemoration of the old 'Veluvana' Vihara of ancient "RAJAGAHA" modern Rajgir in Bihar After the grand opening ceremony performed in 1946, the noble Maharaja dedicated the temple, and the entire land on which the temple was built, to the Bhikkhu Sangha and appointed Venerable Aryamitra as the Bhikkhu-in-charge of the Venuvan Vihara. As a result of his missionary zeal, the Vihara is now the Centre of all the Buddhist activities in Tripura.

UTTAR PRADESH

In Uttar Pradesh, there are now 54,542 Buddhists as against 3221 in 1951. Notable Bhikkhus in this state are : Ven. Pragyananda,

Ven. Kondinya, Ven. Gyaneshwar, Ven. D. Rewata, Ven. Tissa, Ven. Dhammapiti, Ven. Sanghpal, Ven. Pragaya Ratana, Ven. Dharmakirti, Ven. Bodhanand, Ven. A. Karuna, Ven. Sugatananda, Ven. Upali, Ven. Chandima, Ven. Mahavir, Ven. Sobhita, Ven. Sheelbhadra Ven. Achutanand, Ven. A. Amarawansa, Ven. U. Samidhi, Ven. D. Aryadeva, Ven. Dharmadarshi, Ven. Pragayajjyoti, Ven. Gyan Prabhakar, Ven. Dharmaloka, Ven. Sashanrashmi, Ven. Sumangal, Venerable Sheelratana.

There are over 40 Viharas in Uttar Pradesh. The most important Viharas are at Sarnath, Kushinagar and Lucknow.

Sarnath, the Holy Isipatana, was completely in ruins till the beginning of this century. When Anagarika Dharmapala visited this place in 1891, he resolved to save the decaying Dhamek Stupa, symbol of the First Sermon of the Buddha, and the carvings from the hands of the vandals. Some years thereafter he laid the foundation of a new Sarnath by purchasing a few bighas of land from a local Zamindar. In 1904, he purchased another 10 bighas of land. The foundation stone of Mulagandhakuti Vihara, the life of new Sarnath, was laid in November 1922 by Sir Harcourt Butler, the Governor of the United Provinces. The name 'Mulagandakuti' has a historic basis. This name was first used for the monastery in which Lord Buddha actually resided. During the archaeological excavations at Sarnath a piece of tablet was found on which this name was inscribed. This discovery prompted Anagarika Dharmapala to name the new Vihara as 'Mulagandhakuti Vihara'. The Mulagandhakuti Vihara cost about Rs. 1,20,000 and the Principal donor was Mrs. Mary E. Foster of Honolulu, who is generally called the modern Visakha of the Buddhists. This magnificent Vihara was opened on November 11, 1931 (Kartika Purnima). On the same day, the sacred relics of Lord Buddha, which were discovered from Taxila. Punjab, in 1913-14 by Sir John Marshal, were presented by the Director General of Archaeology to the Maha Bodhi Society on behalf of the Government of India, and enshrined in this Vihara.

The beautiful Ajanta-style Frescoes in the Mulagandhakuti Vihara were painted by the famous Japanese artist, Kosetsu Nosu who spent about three years in executing the work in 1932-35. B.L. Broughton, who donated Rs. 10,000 was the chief donor for this splendid work of beautifying the Mulagandhakuti Vihara.

The other Buddhist temples at Sarnath are: The Burmese, Chinese, Thai and Tibetan monasteries.

When in 1890 the late Ven. Mahavir Swami came to stay at Kushinagar site of the Mahaparinirvana of the Buddha, it was not only a deserted but a dreaded place also. Ven. Mahavira, whose first shelter was only a bamboo cottage, took steps to restore the Vihara and to provide accommodation for the visitors. Necessary funds for this purpose were raised by him from Burma with the help of Maung Khee Zarhee of Burma who had settled in Calcutta. Swamiji's work was continued in this direction by his worthy associate Ven. U Chandramani who came to stay with him in 1903 and made Kushinagar as his permanent residence. The present incumbent is Venerable Gyaneshwar Maha Thera

Ven. Bodhananda Mahasthvir was one of the pioneers of revival of Buddhism in North India To fulfil his mission he constructed a beautiful Vihara at Risaldar Park, Lucknow in 1925. Thus, Lucknow has the honour of having the first Vihara in modern Uttar Pradesh at a place not connected with Lord Buddha. After the death of Ven. Bodhananda in May, 1952, the management of this Vihara was taken over by the Maha Bodhi Society of India. The present incumbent is Venerable Pragyanand Maha Thera.

Some of the other important Viharas in U.P. are : 1. Buddha Vihara, Chakki Paat, Agra; 2. Buddha Vihara, Diggi, Shahganj, Agra; 3. Buddha Vihara,, Katra Wazir Khan, Agra; 4. Sakya, Religious Centre (Rajpur) Mussorie; 5. Buddha Vihara, Ambedkar Nagar, Fatehpur; 6. Buddha Vihara, Uncha Garhi, Rajapur (Allahabad); 7. Buddha Vihara, Anguri Bagh, Farrukhabad; 8. Buddha Vihara, Datia, District Jhansi; 9. Buddha Vihara, Etah.; 10. Buddh Math, Buddhapuri, Babupurwa, Kanpur; 11. Buddha Vihara, Madhoganj, Partapgarh; 12. Buddha Vihara, Sadar Bazar, Partapgarh; 13. Naujeevan Baudh Vihar, Meerut City; 14. New Jetavana Vihara, Sravasti; 15. Buddha Vihara, Ganga Darwaza, Amethi, District Farrukhabad; 16. Buddha Vihara Neemkroori, District Farrukhabad; 17. Buddha Vihara Bhartan, District Etawah; 18. Alvak Vihara, Vangarmau District Unnao; 19. Mahatma Buddha Vihara, Siddharth Nagar, Lakhimpur-Kheri; 20. Dr. Bhimrao Ambedkar Buddha Vihara, Rai Bareilly and 21. Maha Pragaya Buddha Vihara, Bhoor, Bulandshahr (founded by Ven. Bhikshu Pragaya Ratana.

WEST BENGAL

In West Bengal, there were 1,56,296 Buddhists in 1981. Thus

in population it is number two state in India. Majority of the Buddhists in West Bengal are Barua Buddhists, who have adhered to Buddhism throughout the past 2,000 years or so, and the Nepalese Buddhists, who have settled in and around Darjeeling. There are about 70 Bhikkhus and 480 Tibetan Lamas in West Bengal. Notable Bhikkhus in this state are : Ven. Dharmapal Maha Thera, Ven. Anandamitra Maha Thera, Ven. Dharmadhara Maha Thera, Ven. Dr. Prajnanand, Ven. Jinasen, Ven. Jinananda, Ven. L. Ariyawansa Maha Thera, New Delhi Ven. Buddharakkhita Maha Thera. Bangalore Ven Dr. Rastrapal Maha Thera, Bodh Gaya and Ven. Jinaratana Maha Thera, Shillong are four notable Bengali monks doing useful work outside West Bengal.

There are more than fifty Viharas in West Bengal. The most important of them are Sri Dharmarajika Vihara and Bauddha Dharmankur Vihara in Calcutta. The Dharmarajika Vihara, Bankim Chatterjee Street, Calcultta—73 was constructed by Anagarika Dharmapala chiefly by donations from Mrs. Mary E. Foster of Honolulu. It was in the year 1914 that the Anagarika secured a plot of land in the College Square at a cost of about Rs. 20.000. The foundation stone of the Vihara was laid in December 1918. The plan of this magnificent Vihara was prepared by Sir John Marshal on the model of the Ajanta Temple and M.M. Ganguly, the author of the Orissan Architecute, supervised the construction work. It cost more than Rs. 1,10,000. out of which Mrs Foster paid about Rs. 88,000. Its opening ceremony was performed on November 20, 1920 by H.E. Ronaldshay, the Governor of Bengal. On the same day, the sacred relics of the Buddha, discovered in a rock crystal casket during the excavations at Bhattiprolu in Andhra Pradesh, were enshrined in this Vihara. Since its constructi n, the Dharmarajika Vihara has served as a beacon light in the movement of reviving Buddhism in India.

The second important Vihara in West Bengal is Baudha Dharmankur Vihara, No. 1, Buddhist Temple Street, Calcutta-12. This Vihara was the first modern Buddha Vihara to be established in West Bengal. It was established by Ven. Kripasaran Maha Thera, the founder of the Bengal Buddhist Association. The present Bhikkhu-in-charge of the Vihara is Ven. Dharmapal Maha Thera.

The other Buddha Viharas in Calcutta are : Japanese Buddha Vihara, 60 Lake Road; Chinese Buddha Vihara, 426 Jasshre Road; Buddha Vihara, Talliganj; Himalayan Buddhist Gonpa; Venuban Vihara, Dum Dum Cantt; Buddha Vihara, Garia; Dharmachakra Vihara, Dum Dum; Burmese Buddhist Temple, Eden Hospital Road; Chinese Buddhist Temple, Tangra; Bodhichariya Vihara, near Dum Dum Air Port.

The Viharas and monasteries at Darjeeling are : Ghoom Monastery; Bhotia Basti Monastery; Thubten Sangag Choeling Monastery, West Point; Dromo Dongkar Monastery; Guru Lhakhang; Du Chu Monastery; Mem Monastery; Gandhamadan Vihara, Chota Kagjhora; Ananda Vihara, Sonada. Some other Viharas in Darjeeling district are : Triyâna Vardhana Vihara, Kalimpong; Dharmodaya Vihara Kalimpong; Tharpa Choling Monastery Kalimpong; Sangdo Peri, Kalimpong Dongser Gon Sum Monastery, Kalimpong; Buddha Vihara, Sevoke Road, Siliguri; Buddha Vihara, Kuresong; Buddha Vihara, Pradhan Nagar, Siliguri.

In the district of 24 Pargans the Buddha Viharas are : Buddha Vihara, Gautam Nagar, Maheshtala; Sakyamuni Vihara, Rampur; Bodhi Vihara, Shyam Nagar; Kunjaban Vihara, Mohan Pur; Tathagata Vihara, Ichapur; Ratnakur Vihara, Sodepur; Triratna Vihara, Vivek Nagar; Jetavan Vihara, Duttapukur.

Elsewhere in West Bengal, the Buddha Viharas are : Gautam Vihara, Durgapur; Buddha Vihara, Kalna; Buddha Vihara, Burnpur Asansole in Distt Burdwan; Dharmoday Vihara, Rishra; Jetavan Vihara, Rishra; Santivan Vihara, Deulpara in Distt. Hoogly; Buddha Vihara, Rajchandrapur in Distt. Howrah; Buddha Viharo, Mal, Jalpaiguri, Buddha Jayanti Vihara, Nagarkata, Santi Vihara, Niketan Damdin, Santi Vihara Maynagari, Maitri Vihara, Binnaguri, Buddha Vihara, Hasiwara in Distt. Jalpaiguri and Buddha Vihara, Deshbandhu Nagar in Distt. Midnapur.

CHAPTER V

Societies and Institutions

1. Societies

No movement worth its name can make headway until and unless it is pursued vigorously in an organised and systematic manner. Today, there are about one hundred Buddhist Societies engaged in the propagation of the Dhamma in various parts of India. This indicates the vitality of the contemporary Buddhist movement as well as the earnestness of the Indian Buddhists to guard their religious interests.

The Maha Bodhi Society was the first Buddhist Society to be established in modern India. It was established by Anagarika Dharmapala on 31 May 1891 primarily with a view to resuscitating the Maha Bodhi Temple at Bodh Gaya which had been converted into a Hindu Shiva temple. Dharmapala fought vigorously to rescue Buddha Gaya, recalimed the sacred places, established a chain of centres of the Maha Bodhi Society, and kept up a continuous stream of propaganda with the result that within the next forty years. Buddhism in India made significant progress in all respects. The construction of Sri Dharmarajika Vihara in Calcutta and the Mulagandhakuti Vihara at Sarnath in 1920 and 1931 respectively were the greatest achievements of the first missionary of modern times. On his death in 1933, Devapriya Valisinha became General Secretary of the Maha Bodhi Society, and held that position for more than 35 years, i.e. upto 1968. Valisinha not only kept the tempo of revival movement but also put it on a more sound footing. He built two more Buddha Viharas (New Delhi and Sanchi) and also took over three Buddha Viharas built by other pioneers. These were, Bahujana Vihara, Bombay, Ananda Vihara, Bombay, and the Buddha Vihara, Risaldar Park, Lucknow. Ven.

N. Jinaratana Nayaka Maha Thera was the third General Secretary of the Maha Bodhi Society of India from 1968 to 1983. . At present, Ven. M. Wipulsara Maha Thera is the General Secretary of the Maha Bodhi Society of India.

The first President of the Maha Bodhi Society was Pradhana Nayaka H. Sumangala Maha Thera of Ceylon. Colonel H.S. Olcott was its Director and Chief Adviser, and Anagarika Dharmapala was the founder General Secretary. In 1916, Sir Ashutosh Mookerjee was elected its President. After Sir Ashutosh's death in 1924, Sir M.N. Mukherjee became the Society's President and continued to hold this position till his death in 1942. He was succeeded by Shyama Prasad Mookerjee who died in 1953. H.H. the Chogyal of Sikkim was the President of the Maha Bodhi Society from 1953 to 1982. In 1983, P.K. Thungan. M.P. (former Chief Minister of Arunachal Pradesh) became President of the Maha Bodhi Society.

The Maha Bodhi Society has made tremendous contribution to the revival movement in India. The flourishing condition of a number of ancient Buddhist shrines which meets the eye today is, directly or indirectly, the result of the hard work of the devoted and selfless workers of this Society during the last 100 years. Besides Calcutta, its headquarters, the Maha Bodhi Society has now a chain of centres all over the country. These are at Buddha Gaya, Sarnath, Sanchi, Bombay, New Delhi, Lucknow, Nowgarh (Lumbini), Ajmer, Bangalore and Madras. The Maha Bodhi Society has also a few centres outside India.

The Bengal Buddhist Association (Dharmankur Sabha) founded by Ven. Kripasaran Mahasthavir in 1892 has been quite active amongst the Barua Buddhists of Bengal. The credit for popularising the Buddha—Dhamma in South India goes to the South India Buddhist Association which was established at Madras by Pandit Ayodhya Dasa in 1900 A.D. Its second President, who succeeded the founder, was Prof. P. Lakshmi Narasu, the well-known author of the 'Essence of Buddhism'.

The Ladakh Buddhist Association (1937) has done laudable work amongst the Buddhists of Ladakh. The All Assam Buddhist Association, founded by Ven. Nandabansha in 1939, is a powerful organisation of the Buddhists of Assam. Besides the Viharas, it has also established a number of schools known as Pali Tools/ Vidyalayas for inculcating the spirit of Dhamma amongst the Buddhist youth. The Tripura Rajya Buddhist Association established by Ven. Aryamitra in 1954 has forged unity amongst the Buddhists of Tripura.

The religious affairs of the neo-Buddhists are primarily looked after by the Buddhist Society of India (Bhartiya Baudh Maha Sabha) founded by Dr. Ambedkar in 1955. It was under the auspices of this Society that Dr. Ambedkar publicly embraced Buddhism at Nagpur on 14 October 1956, and exhorted his people to seek refuge in the Buddha-Dhamma. After the Parinirvana of Dr. Ambedkar on 6 December 1956, his son, Yashwant Ambedkar, was elected President of the Buddhist Society of India. Under his guidance, the Society organised in Bombay the first All India Buddhist Conference to coincide with the inauguration of the Memorial Stupa at the Chaitya Bhoomi in November 1968. Bhaiyasaheb Yashwant Ambedkar passed away in 1977. Thereafter, his wife, Mrs. Miratai Ambedkar was elected President of the Buddhist Society of India. The second All India Buddhist Conference was held by the Society at Nagpur in October 1980. The third All India Buddhist Delegates Conference of the Buddhist Society of India was held at Ambedkar Bhavan, New Delhi, on 18-19 March 1989.

The Buddhist Society of India has its head office at Ambedkar Bhavan, Gokuldas Pasta Road, Dadar, Bombay-14. It has branches almost in every city, town and village in Maharashtra. It has also a network of branches in other States of India.

The names and addresses of the important Buddhist Societies in various States of India are given in Appendix I.

2. W.F.B. Centres

For the first time in the history of Buddhism, the Buddhists of the World were united under the six-coloured flag, of the World Fellowship of Buddhists at Colombo, Sri Lanka in 1950. The credit for establishing this unique organisation goes to Dr. G.P. Malalasekera, its Founder President, who convened the first general

Conference in May 1950. Dr. B.R. Ambedkar, the greatest Pioneer of Buddhist revival in India, also participated in this conference as a special invitee.

The aims and objects of the World Fellowship of Buddhists are :

1. *To promote* among the members strict observance and practice of the teachings of the Buddha ;
2. *To secure* unity, solidarity and brotherhood among Buddhists ;
3. *To propagate* the sublime doctrine of the Buddha ;
4. *To organise and carry on* activities in the field of social, educational, cultural and other humanitarian services ; and
5. *To work for Securing* peace and harmony amongst men and happiness for all beings and to collaborate with other organisations working for the same ends.

The permanent headquarters of the World Fellowship of Buddhists are at 41, Phra Athit Road, Bangkok, Thailand. This International Buddhist Organisation has now more than 60 centres in various parts of the World. In India, the Regional Centres of the World Fellowship of Buddhists (W.F.B.) are :

1. All Assam Buddhist Association, Desangpani, Sibsagar ;
2. Asoka Mission, New Delhi ;
3. Bengal Buddhist Association, Calcutta ;
4. Buddhist Society of India, Bombay ;
5. Ladakh Buddhist Association, Leh ;
6. Maha Bodhi Society of India, Calcutta ;
7. Maha Bodhi Ashoka Mission, Ajmer ;
8. South India Buddhist Association. Madras ; and
9. Tripura Rajya Buddhist Association, Agartala.

3. Meditation Centres

There are two forms of meditation in Buddhism, viz. Samatha (calm or development of mental concentration) and Vipassana (insight, to see things as they really are). After the downfall of Buddhism, the Vipassana technique also vanished from India. Luckily, it was preserved in its pristine purity in Burma. From Burma, the Vipassana technique was brought back to India in 1969 by S.N. Goenka, an Indian born in Burma, who had learnt the technique from Sayagyi U Ba Khin, a great teacher of Vipassana meditation in modern Burma. In 1976, Acharya S.N. Goenka founded the Vipassana International Academy at Igatpuri in Maharashtra. By now four Vipassana Centres have been established by him in India where atleast one ten-day course is held every month. These centres are :

1. Dhammagiri Vipassana International Academy, Igatpuri—422403, Distt. Nasik, Maharashtra.
2. Dhammathali Vipassana Centre, Sisodiabaug-Galtaji Road, Jaipur—302001, Rajasthan.
3. Dhammakhet Vipassana International Meditation Centre, Kusumnagar, 12.6 km Nagarjunsagar Road, Hyderabad—500661, Andhra Pradesh.
4. Dhammaganga Vipassana Kendra, Baro Mandir, Sodepur, Panihati, Distt. 24 Praganas. (Calcutta)—743176, West Bengal.

Some other Buddhist Meditation Centres are :

1. International Meditation Centre,
   Bodh Gaya, Distt. Gaya, Bihar.
   General Secretary : Ven. Dr. Rashtrapal Bhikshu.
2. Maha Bodhi Meditation Centre,
   14, First Main Road, Gandhinagar, Banalore-9, Karnataka.
   Branch at : Leh-Ladakh—194101, Jammu & Kashmir.
   Founder : Acharya Buddharakkhita.
3. Anagarika Dharmapala
   Meditation Centre, Calcutta.
4. Vidarsan Dhyan Ashram
   Haiderpara, Siliguri, Distt. Darjeeling.
   West Bengal.
5. Tushita Mahayana Meditation Centre,
   C34A, Nizamudin East,
   New Delhi—110013.

4. Educational Institutions

In the field of education, the People's Education Society, Bombay is leading all other Buddhist societies. It was founded by Dr. B.R. Ambedkar in 1945. Its head office is housed in Anand Bhavan, near Fountain, Dr. Dadabhai Naoroji Road, Bombay-1. By 1956, Dr. Ambedkar had established three colleges at Bombay (Siddharth College of Arts and Science, Siddharth College of Commerce and Economics, and Siddharth College of Law) and one college at Aurangabad (Milind Maha Vidyalaya) He had also established two High Schools, namely, Siddharth Night High School, Bombay and Milind Multipurpose High School, Aurangabad. The People's Education Society is now running eleven degree colleges — five in Bombay, four in Aurangabad, one each at Mahad and Pune. The Society is also running six High Schools—two in Bombay, two in Aurangabad, and one each at Dapoli and Pandharpur. It is also running Primary schools. The P.E.S. has also established hostels at various places for the benefit of the students coming from far-off places.

The Maha Bodhi Society of India has established three schools and colleges at Sarnath, the Holy Isipatana : Dharmapala Degree College, Maha Bodhi Higher Secondary School, Maha Bodhi Teachers Training College.

Kushinagar, the site of Buddha's Mahaparinirvana, has now a High School and a College, known as, Mahavira Vidyalaya, and Buddha College respectively. These were founded by Ven. U Chandramani Maha Thera.

The primary research institute in Pali is the Nalanda Institute of Research and Post Graduate Studies in Buddhist Learning and Pali, Nalanda, Distt. Patna in Bihar. The Nava Nalanda Mahavihara, as this institute is also known, has done a commendable job of producing the entire Pali Tripitaka in Devanagari script under the able guidance of Ven. Jagdish Kashyap.

The Vipassana Research Institute (V.R.I.), Dhammagiri, established by the Vipassana International Academy, Igatpuri Maharashtra has recently begun the immense job of entering the Tipitika and the commentaries (i.e. the entire Pali Scriptures related to the teachings of the Buddha) in transliterated Roman script in computors for future research purposes.

Another Pali research institute is the Mahabodhi Institute of Pali Studies and Buddhology, Saraswathipuram, Mysore-570009, Karnataka. This has been established by Acharya Buddharakkhita, Maha Bodhi Society, Bangalore.

Two other institute are : Nalanda Vidyabhavan, Calcutta—an institute of Buddhology founded by the Bengal Buddhist Assoeiation in 1935, and International Centre for Buddhist Studies and Research, Siliguri, founded by Ven. Prajnananda in 1984.

The important institutions engaged in research in Tibetan Buddhism are :

1. School of Buddhist Philosophy, Leh—Ladakh, Jammu & Kashmir.
2. Sikkim Institute for Tibetology ana Buddhist studies, Gangtok, Sikkim.
3. Central Institute for Tibetan Higher Studies, Sarnath, Uttar Pradesh.

CHAPTER VI

Modern Buddhist Literature

IN ancient days, the literary treasures of Buddhism were mostly preserved in the monasteries. When the monasteries fell prey to vandalism and Buddhism declined, the Buddhist literature also disappeared. Thus whatever Pali and Sanskrit Buddhist literature we now have, it has come to us from Sri Lanka, Burma, Nepal and Tibet—where it was preserved with care and reverence.

The researches of the Western scholars, particularly the works of early Indologists like Sir William Jones (1746-94) and Sir A. Cunningham (1814-1893) who unearthed the priceless treasures of Buddhism, brought about an awakening among the Indian scholars as well. The pioneer Indian scholar was Rajendra Lal Mitra (1824-1891). His works, particularly, 'Buddha Gaya', The Hermitage of the Sakya Sage (1877), Sanskrit Buddhist Literature of Nepal (1882) and Lalitavistara (1887) aroused considerable interest in Buddhist studies. Two other pioneers in this field were : Hara Prasad Shastri and Sarat Chandra Das, both younger contemporaries of Rajendralal Mitra. While H.P. Shastri concentrated on Sanskrit Buddhist literature, Sarat Chandra Das specialised in Tibetan studies. His travelogue 'Indian Pandits in the Land of Snow' written after his visit to the interior Tibet opened a new vista for the scholars. In the year 1892, S.C. Das, H.P. Shastri and others founded the Buddhist Text Society at Calcutta. Under the aegis of this Society, a number of unknown Buddhist Texts were published. Some of the important being: Bodhicaryavatara and Visuddhimagga (in Sanskrit, first few chapters only) by Sarat Chandra Das ; Svayambhu-Purana and Asta—Sahasrika—prajna—Paramita by Hara Prasad Shastri ; and translation of Chandrakirti's Madhyamika—Vrtti (some portions only) by Harimohan Vidyabhusan.

The first Pali scholar of repute in India was Satish Chandra Vidyabhusan who was the first Indian to obtain an M.A. degree in Pali from the Calcutta University in 1901 where a new Department of Buddhist Studies had been established at the instance of the Buddhist Text Society, and the Maha Bodhi Society. Dr. Vidyabhusan concentrated his attention on the Buddhist logic and philosophy. His works included Kaccayana's Pali Grammer with an English translation (1907), the Buddha—Stotra – Sangraha (1908), Nyayabindu (1917), and the Monumental History of Indian Logic (1922). He also brought out editions of the Madhyamika and wrote about 150 essays on various aspects of Buddhist philosophy. Dr. Vidyabhusan's emphasis on logic and philosophy revolutionised research in Buddhism.

Dr. Beni Madhab Barua (1888-1948) was another eminent Indian scholar who contributed much to the Buddhist philosophical studies. His first work, The History of Pre-Buddhist Philosophy, placed early Buddhism in its proper perspective. His other works included Ajivikas and Prakrit Dhammapada. Dr. Barua also wrote many valuable works on Buddhist inscriptions and history. Dr. B.C. Law, a worthy colleague of Dr. Barua, has to his credit more than fifty volumes. His important works on Buddhism are : History of Pali Literature in two volumes, Buddha-ghosa. Study of Mahavastu, Women in Buddhist Literature, Concept of Buddhism, and translation of Buddhavamsa, Ccriyapitaka, Katha-vatthu etc.

Another eminent scholar who succeeded Prof. Barua as the head of the Pali Department at Calcutta University and enriched the Pali Studies was Dr. Nalinaksha Dutt. The credit of discovering a large collection of Gilgit manuscripts and publishing the same in eight volumes goes to him. His most valuable works are : 'Aspects of Mahayana Buddhism and its Relation to Hinayana' (1930) and 'Early Monastic Buddhism' in two volumes (1941-45). His last publication 'Buddhist Sects in India' is also worthy of note. Dr. Nalinaksha Dutt (1893-1973) was also the Chairman of the Editorial Board of the Maha Bodhi, monthly Journal of the Maha Bodhi Society of India.

The first Indian scholar to introduce Pali in Devanagari Script was the late Prof. Dharmananda Kosambi (1876-1947). In 1902, he went to Ceylon, took robes and learnt Pali at the Vidyodaya College under the Ven. Hikkaduwe Sri Sumangala Maha Nayaka Thera. From

1912-1918 he served as the Professor of Pali in the Fergusson College in Poona which laid firmly the foundation of Pali Studies in Western India, Ven. Dharmananda Kosambi also wrote a number of books on Buddhism in Marathi and Gujarati. His greatest work was the Devanagari edition of the Visuddhimagga which was published in 1940.

Professor N.K. Bhagwat (1887-1962), a worthy disciple of Dharmananda Kosambi, was another Pali scholar of distinction. He edited a number of Pali texts in Devanagari characters and published the same on behalf of the University of Bombay. The important works in this series were : the Nidanakatha (of the Jatakas), the Mahavamsa, the Digha Nikaya (Vols. I and II), the Majjhima Nikaya the Theragatha, the Theri-gatha and the Mahavagga in two volumes. Prof. Bhagwat also translated the Dhammapada, the Khuddakapatha and a few selections from the Jatakas.

Coming to modern Indian languages, we find that to begin with the Sacred Scriptures were translated by various Savants. The real help to the masses, however, came from the literature written in simple and intelligible modern languages. The pioneer in this field was Mahapandit Rahul Sankrityayan (1893-1963), the giant intellectual and creator of enormous Buddhist literature (about 175 books and pamphlets) in Hindi, the National Language of India.

Rahul Sankrityayan was a prolific writer, and besides Buddhist literature, canonical as well as non-canonical, he wrote histories, scientific and philosophical books, travel records and biographies etc. He was a great explorer also. Thrice he undertook the hazardous journeys to Tibet and brought back a large collection of valuable old manuscripts, some of which he himself edited and published. Verily, Rahul Sankrityayan was an institute in himself. Recognising his services in the literary field, he was awarded the title of Padma Bhushan by the Government of India.

Among the other Buddhist scholars, the most eminent ones are : Bhadant Anand Kausalyayan and Ven. Dr. Dharmarakshita. They have dozens of books, (including translations from Pali) to their credit, Recognising their valuable services to the Hindi and Pali literature, both of them were awarded the Degree of Vidyavaridhi (Doctor of Literature) by the Patna University, Nava Nalanda Mahavihara, Nalanda. Another eminent Buddhist scholar of repute is Ven. Nandabansa Mahasthavir. He has given us a number of books in the Assamese language.

The large mass of canonical and non-canonical literature produced by various savants and scholars in the wake of the Buddhist renaissance has had its effect on the other Indian writers as well. Among a host of literary figures whose writings echo the Buddhist themes, the prominent ones are : Gurudev Rabindranath Tagore, India's poet laureate and the Noble Prize winner; Acharya Chatursain Shastri and Yashpal, two top Hindi writers ; and Kumaran Assan, one of the greatest modern Malayalam poets.

Lord Buddha eschewed Sanskrit, the language of the educated few, and took up the spoken language of the people in order to convey His teachings directly to the masses. This language later became the common vehicle of communication in Buddhist India under the name of Pali. Pali, the language of the Tipitaka (Sanskrit : Tripitaka) is once again a living language in India. As a language, Pali is an archaic Prakrit and is now written in Devanagari script. The study of Pali in India is closely associated with the revival movement. The Calcutta University was the first University to establish a separate Pali Department. The first M.A. degree in Pali was awarded by this University in 1901. The Bombay University was the next to provide facilities for the study of Pali. The Fergusson College, Poona, where Dharmananda Kosambi was a Professor of Pali from 1912-18, was the principal College teaching Pali in Deccan. Now there are distinct Buddhist Departments in the Universities of Calcutta, Delhi and Sanskrit University, Varanasi. Further in the Universities of Andhra, Allahabad, Baroda, Banaras, Lucknow, Magadha, Marathwada, Patna etc., adequate arrangements exist for teaching Pali. As for the teaching of Pali in the schools, Pali has been recognised as one of the classical languages taught in the schools in Assam, Maharashtra, Uttar Pradesh and West Bengal.

As will be noticed from the bibliography, a number of Buddhist canonical works are now available in Hindi, Assamese, Bengali, Gujarati, Marathi, Telegu and Urdu. The Dhammapada is the most popular Text with the translators. This is, at it should be, because of its sublime message which has moulded the lives of the millions of people through the ages. The Buddhist literature is now available in all the major languages. It is worth noting that since the beginning of the 20th century nearly 500 books have been written by Indian authors. Of all these works, Dharmananda Kosambi's Marathi work 'Bhagwan Buddha' is the most translated work It has been translated into almost all the Indian languages by the Sahitya Akademi. Dr. B.R. Ambedkar's famous work 'The Buddha and His Dhamma' (commonly known as Buddhist Bible) is studied with reverence by the Indian Buddhists. It has been translated into Hindi and Punjabi by Ven. Bhadant Anand Kausalyayan.

Besides a select list of books in various languages, we have also included here particulars of the Journals which are primarily devoted to Buddhism. There are a few more periodicals also which are espousing the cause of Buddhism.

(i) PALI SCRIPTURES

Till recently, India did not possess the Sacred Scriptures of the Buddhists in any modern script. Thanks to the co-operation of the Government of India and the Government of Bihar, India has now the entire Pali Canon in Devanagari Script. It has been published by the Pali Publication Board, Government of Bihar, Nalanda under the General Editorship of Ven. Jagdish Kashyap. Each volume has been prefaced with a brief introduction in Hindi and English.

The Pali Tipitaka (Tripitaka) in Devanagari script has the following 41 volumes of about 400 pages each :

SUTTA PITAKA

1. Digha Nikaya in 3 volumes.
2. Majjhima Nikaya in 3 volumes.
3. Samyutta Nikaya in 4 volumes.
4. Anguttara Nikaya in 4 volumes.
5. Khuddaka Nikaya, which contains the following fifteen books :

(i) Khuddakapatha (ii) Dhammapada (iii) Udana (iv) Itivuttaka (v) Suttanipata	in one volume
(vi) Vimanvatthu (vii) Petavatthu (viii) Theragatha (ix) Therigatha	in one volume

(x)	Jataka	in 2 volumes
(xi)	Niddesa	in 2 volumes
(xii)	Patisambhidamagga	
(xiii)	Apadana	
(xiv)	Buddhavamsa	in 2 volumes
(xv)	Cariyapitaka	

II. VINAYA PITAKA

1. Mahavagga
2. Cullavagga
3. Parajika
4. Pacittiya
5. Parivara

III. ABHIDHAMMA PITAKA

1.	Dhammasangani	
2.	Vibhanga	
3.	Dhatukatha	in 1 volume (3–4)
4.	Puggalapanni	
5.	Kathavatthu	
6.	Yamaka	in 3 volumes
7.	Patthana	in 6 volumes

The following are the translations so far published in various Indian languages of some of the Sacred Books of the Tripitaka :

HINDI

1. **Anand Kausalyayan, Bhadant, Ven.**
   - (i) Anguttara Nikaya—Parts I—IV.
   - (ii) Jataka—Parts I—IV.
   - (iii) Abhidhammathsangho
   - (iv) Dhammapada

2. **Chandrika Prasad Jagiasu.**
   Dhammapada
   (Translation with Atthkatha)

3. **Dharmarakshita, Dr. Ven.**
   - (i) Samyutta Nikaya—Parts I—II.
   - (ii) Dhammapada (Translation only)
   - (iii) Dhammapada
     (Text and Translation)

(iv) Dhammapada
(Text and Translation with legends)
(v) Itivuttaka
(vi) Mahaparinirvana Sutta

4. **Dhammaratna, Dr. Ven.**
(i) Sutta Nipata
(Text and Translation)
(ii) Khuddak Paath
(Text and Translation)
(iii) Ther Gatha
(Translation)

5. **Inder, Prof.**
Dhammapada

6. **Jagdish Kashyap Ven.**
(i) Samyutta Nikaya—Parts–I–II.
(ii) Udana

7. **Kitima, Ven.**
(i) Sigala Sutta
(Text and Translation)
(ii) Mahaparinirvana Sutta
(Text and Translation)

8. **Pragyanand, G., Ven.**
Kalama Sutta

9. **Rahul Sankrityayan**
(i) Digha Nikaya
(ii) Majjhima Nikaya
(iii) Vinaya Pitaka
(iv) Ambattha–Sutta
(v) Dhammapada
(Pali Text, Sanskrit Text and Translation)
(vi) Khuddaka—Nikaya—(11 books with the exception of No. 10—13).

10. **Upadhaya, Bharat Singh**
Theri—gatha
(Translation)

11. **Vanshinarayan Lal**
Dhammapada
(in Poetry)

ASSAMESE

1. Nandabansha, Ven.
   Dhammapada
2. **Upendracandra Lekharu**
   Dhammapada

BENGALI

1. **Bhikkhu Silabhadra**
   (i) Dharmapada
   (ii) Digha Nikaya—Parts I—III.
   (iii) Theri Gatha
   (iv) Sutta Nipata
   (v) Dharma Chakkapavattana—Sutta
   (vi) Majjhima Nikaya
   (vii) Udana
2. **Bejoy Chandra Ghosh**
   (i) Ther Gatha
   (ii) Theri Gatha
3. **Charu Chandra Bose**
   Dhammapada
   (Text with Sanskrit and Translation)
4. **Ishan Chandra Ghosh**
   Jatakas
5. **Praganloka Sthavir and Bhikkhu Anomadarshi**
   Dhammapada
6. **Vidhushekhar Shastri**
   Patimokkha

GUJARATI

1. **Dharmananda Kosambi**
   (i) Sutta Nipata
   (ii) Abhidharma
2. **Mani Lal Nathubhai Dosi**
   Dharmanam Pado Dhammapad

MARATHI

1. **C.V. Rajvade**
   Digha Nikaya
2. **Dharmananda Kosambi**
   Sutta Nipata

3. **Dharmarakshita, Bhikshu**
   (i) Dhammapada
   (ii) Khuddak Paath

4. **Kunder Balwant Divan**
   Dharmapada

5. **Narayan Vasudev Tungar**
   Jatakas

PUNJABI

6. **Lal Mani Joshi**
   Dhammapada (Pali text in Gurmukhi script and translation)

TELEGU

7. **Sumedha Vimalksha**
   Dharmapada

URDU

8. **Bisheshwar Prasad Mannawar, Lacknavi**
   Dhammapada Ya Sachi Rah
   (Translation in verse)

ENGLISH

1. *Dhammapada*—Edited by C. Kunhan Raja.

(a) Pali text in Devanagari script with English translation.

(b) Palit text in Roman characters with an English translation.

(c) Englsh translation only.

2. *Dhammapada* – Pali text, in Devanagari script with introduction, English translation and notes – by P L. Vaidya.

3. *Dhammapada*—Pali text in Devanagari script with introduction, English translation and notes – by N.K. Bhagvat.

4. *The Dhammapada*—Pali text, in Roman characters, with introductory essays, English translation and notes.

– by S. Radhakrishnan

5. *Dhammapada* – translation by Acharya Buddharakkhita.

6. *Prakrit Dhammapada*—with translation and notes by B.M. Barua.

7. *Sermons and Sayings of the Buddha*—The Buddha's teachings drawn from Digha—Nikaya, Majjhima—Nikaya and other

original sources and presented in simple lucid language—by Sudhakar Dikshit.

8. *Cariya Pitaka*—Text in Devanagari script with English translation—by B.C. Law.

9. *Datthavamsa*—Text in Devanagari script with English translation—by B.C. Law.

10. *Buddhavamsa*—translation by B.C. Law.

11. *Sasanavamsa*—translation by B.C. Law.

12. *Katha*—vatthu (Debates Commentary—translation by B.C. Law.

13. *Sutta-nipata*—by Prof. P.V. Bapat.

14. *The Kalama Sutta*—translation by Ven. Soma Thera.

15. *Sakka's Quest*—translation of Sakka—Panha Sutta by Sister Vajira.

16. *Arthapada Sutra*—A translation of the Chinese version of the Pali Atthakavagga by P.V. Bapat.

(ii) SANSKRIT LITERATURE

1. *Abhidharma Samucchaya of Asanga*, Sanskrit text in Devanagari script, restored from the Tibetan and Chinese translations. Critically edited with introduction—by Prahlad Pradhan.

2. *Abhidharmakosa Samucchaya*, Sanskrit text in Devanagari script prepared from the Tibetan by Prof, Prahlad Pradhan.

3. *Abhidharmakosa—Karika*—Sanskrit text restored with the help of Yasomitra's commentary, Sphutartha—Abhidharma—kosa—Vyakhya, by Rahul Sankrityayan.

4. *Abhidharma—Kosa—Karika*, Full text based on an actual Sanskrit text—by Dr. V.V. Gokhale.

5. *Abhidharmamrta by Ghosaka*—Translated into Sanskrit from the Chinese by Shanti Bhikshu Shastri.

6. *Abhidharma—Kosha* (Acharya Vasubandhu) Ed. by Swami Dwarka Das Shastri.

7. *Abhisamayalankaravrittih Sphutartha of Acharya Haribhadra*—(Tibetan Text, Sanskrit Restoration) by Acharya Ram Shankar.

8. *Abhidharma—Pradipa*—Prepared from the Tibetan by Prof. Padmanabh Jaini.

9. *Abhisamacarika*—edited by Dr. B. Jinananda.

10. *Advayavajra—Sangraha*—edited by Mahamahopadhyaya Hara Prasad Shastri.

11. *Alambana—Pariksa and its Vrtti by Dinnaga*—retranslated from Tibetan into Sanskrit and edited by Prof. N. Aiyaswamy Shastri.

12. *Asta—Sahasrika—Prajna—Paramita*—translated by Hara Prasad Shastri.

13. *Avadanakalpalata Kshemendravirachita*—P-L. Vaidya.

14. *Bodhicaryavatara by Santideva*— restored into Sanskrit by Sarat Chandra Das. (Hindi translation by Shanti Bhikshu Shastri).

15. *Bodhicharyavtara by Santideva* (Sanskrit text with Hindi translation by Swami Dwarka Das Shastri.

16. *Buddhcharitram* (*kavya*) *Ashvaghosha* (with Hindi commentary) by Ram Chandra Das Shastri.

17. *Bodhicittotpada—Sutra—Sastra by Vasubandhu*—retranslated into Sanskrit from the Chinese by Shanti Bhikshu Shastri.

18. *Buddha Charit by Asvaghosha*—Sanskrit text and Hindi translation by Surya Narayan Chaudhary.

19. *Catuhastaka of Aryadeva*—retranslated from Tibetan into Sanskrit edited by Vidhushekhar Bhattacharya Shastri.

20. *Catuh-Sataka* (Along with the Chandrakirti Vritti and Hindi translation) by Bhag Chandra Jain.

21. *Citavisuddhi Prakarana of Aryadeva*—A critical edition of the Madhyamika philosophy of Aryadeva—by P.B , Patel.

22. *Dharmottara—Pradipa of Durveka.* edited by Prof. Mulavana.

23. *Dvadasamukha—Sastra by Nagarjuna*—retranslated into Sanskrit and edited by Aiyaswamy Shastri.

24. *Gilgit Manuscripts in eight volumes*, including Vinaya—vastu of the Mula—Sarvastivada School—by Dr. Nalinaksha Dutt.

25. *Jatakamala by Aryasura*—Sanskrit text and Hindi translation by Surya Narayan Chaudhary.

26. *Jatakamala of Aryasura*—Text with English and Hindi translation—by Dwivedi and Bhatt.

27. *Jatakamala by Aryasura* (Hindi translation) by Jagdish Chander Misra.

28. *Jnanaprasthana—Sastra of Katayaniputra*, Sanskrit rendering from the Chinese by Shanti Bhikshu Shastri.

29. *Karatalaratna by Bhavaviveka*– retranslated into Sanskrit from the Chinese by Aiyaswamy Shastri.

30. *Lalitavistara*– Sanskrit text critically edited in Devanagari with introductions in English and Hindi by P.L. Vaidya.

31. *Lalitavistara* –Text with English translation by Rajendra Lal Mitra.

32. *Madhyamaka Shastram of Nagarjuna*. Vol. I (With the Commentary Akutobhaya of Nagarjuna, Madhyamakavritti of Buddhapalit, Prajna Pradeep of Bhavaviveka and Prasannapada of Chandrakirti : Text in Sanskrit and Commentary restored from Tibetan Texts) by R.N. Pandeya.

33. *Madhyanta Vibhanga Sastra* (of Vasubandhu with the Karikas of Maitreya and Bhasya of Vasubandhu. Text in Devanagari) by R.N. Pandeya.

34 *Madhyamaka Shastra* (Archarya Nagarjuna) Ed. by Swami Dwarka Das Shastri.

35. *Madhyamikamate—Shikshasamuchchyah Shantidevavirachitah*—P.L. Vaidya.

36. *Mahayanasutrasangrah -Prathamah Khandah*: Suvikrantavikramiprajnaparmita, Vajrachhedika, Shalistambasutram, Sukhavativyuh, Karandavyuha, Praityasamutpadasutram, Bhaishajyaguruviduryaprabhasutram, Rashtrapalaparipraccha, Arthavinishchyasutram, Ratnagunasanchyah—P.L. Vaidya.
Dvitiyah Khandah : Aryamanjushrimulakalpah—P.L. Vaidya.

37. *Madhyamika-Vrtti of Chandrakirti*—by Harimohan Vidyabhusan.

38. *Mahayana--Vimsaka of Nagarjuna*—retranslated from Tibetan into Sanskrit and edited by Vidhushekhar Bhattacharya.

39. *Navadharma*
Lalitavistara—P.L. Vaidya
Samadhiriajasutram—P.L. Vaidya
Lankavatharasutram—P.L. Vaidya.
Ashtasahastrika Prajnaparamita Alokvyakhyaya Sahita—P.L. Vaidya
Gandavyuhasutram P.L. Vaidya
Sadharmapundarikasutram – P.L. Vaidya
Dashabhumikasutram—P.L. Vaidya
Suvarmaprabhasasutram—S. Bagchi
Guhyasamajatantra—S. Bagchi

40. *Nyaya Bindu* (Acharya Dharmakirti) Ed. by Swami Dwarka Das Shastri

41. *Nairatmyapariprooha of Asvaghosha,* (Sanskrit—Tibetan) edited by Sujitkumar Mukhopadhyaya.

42. *Nayayapravesa,* (treatise on Buddhist logic) edited by A.B. Dhruv.

43. *Pancavimsati Pranjnaparamita,* edited by Nalinaksha Dutt.

44. *Pramanavartika*—Sanskrit text restored and edited by Rahul Sankrityayan.

45. *Parmana-Vartika* (Acharya Dharmakirti) Ed. by Swami Dwarka Das Shastri.

46. *Parmartha-Chintana* (Dharma) Ed. by Swami Dwarka Das Shastri.

47. *Pratimoksha of the Mulasarvastivada School*—edited by Anukul Chandra Banerjee.

48. *Sadhana—mala*—edited by B. Bhattacharya.

49. *Saddharma—Pundarika*—edited by Nalinaksha Dutt.

50. *Saundarnanda by Asvaghosha*—Sanskrit text and translation by Surya Narayan Chaudhary.

51. *Sphutartha—Abhidharmakosa—Vyakhya* by Nalinaksha Dutt.

52. *Sardula—Karnavadana*—translated into Sanskrit from Tibetan and edited by Sujit Kumar Mukhopadhayaya.

53. *Sphutartha Srighanacarasangraha—tika,* edited by Dr. Sanghasena.

54. *Sri—Guhyasamaja—tantra,* edited by B. Bhattacharya.

55. *Tattvasangraha of Santaraksita* with the commentary of Kamalasila—Tattvasangraha (Compendium of True Doctrines)—edited by Embar Krishnamacharya. (Translated into English—by Ganganatha Jha. 2 Vols.)

56. *Tattva-Sangraha* (Shantarakshita) Ed. by Swami D.D. Shastri.

57. *Trisvabhavanirdesa of Vasubandhu*—Sanskrit text, Devanagari script, edited with introduction, English translation, by Sujit Kumar Mukhopadhyaya.

58. *Upasampadajnaplih*—edited by Dr. B. Jinananda.

59. *Vadanyaya*—Sanskrit text restored and edited by Rahul Sankrityayan.

60. *Vartika—alankara*—edited by Rahul Sankrityayan.

61. *Vadanyaya and Sambandha Pariksha* (Acharya Dharmakirti) Ed. by Swami Dwarka Das Shastri.

62. *Vagracchedika Prajnaparamtaisutra* (Sanskrit text, Hindi translation) by L.M. Joshi.

63. *Vimalakirtinirdesa Sutra* (Tibetan Text, Sanskrit Restoration and Hindi Translation) by Bhikshu Prasadika and L.M. Joshi.

64. *Vinayah* Mahavastu-Lokottaravadinam Vinayah—S. Bagchi. Mulasarvastivadinam Vinayah (Gilgit Mss.) 2 Vols—S. Bagchi.

65. *Yogacharamate* Sutralankarah Acharya Sangavirachitah—S. Bagchi.

66. *Yogacarabhumi—Sastra* edited by Vidhushekhar Shastri.

(iii) MODERN LITERATURE

HINDI

1. **Acharya Narendra Deo**
   Baudh Dharma Darshan

2. **Ambedkar, Dr. B.R.**
   (i) Bhagwan Buddha aur unka Dharma (Translation by Bhadant Anand Kausalyayan)
   (ii) Baudh Dharma hi Manav Dharma
   (Compilation and translation by Bhikshu Dharmarakhsita)

3. **Anand Kausalyayan, Bhadant**
   (i) Buddha Vachan
   (ii) Bhikshu Ke Pattar
   (iii) Samyojan
   (iv) Mahavansa (Translation)
   (v) Moggallana Pali Veyakarana
   (vi) Baudh Dharma (Ek Buddhivadi Addhyan)
   (vii) Kranti Ke Agardut—Bhagwan Buddha
   (viii) Anatamvada
   (ix) Sri Lanka
   (x) Tathagat Ka Shashwat Sandesh

(xi) Bhagwan Buddh Ka Dharam
(xii) Baudh Gyan
(xiii) Baudh Jeevan Padhiti
(xiv) Baudhdharam aur Marxwad
(xv) Bhagwadgita Tatha Dhammapada
(xvi) Darshan

4. **Anand Commarswamy and I.B Horner**
Bhagwan Buddha
(Translation by Dr. Devesh Chandra)

5. **Ariyawansa Bhikkhu and D.C. Ahir**
Baudh Jeevan Path

5.A **Ariyawansa, Bhikkhu**
(i) Tathagata Ka Updesh
(ii) Buddhwani aur Vandana Vidhi

6. **Bodhanand, Bhadant**
(i) Panch Sheel aur Buddh Vandana
(ii) Bhagwan Gautama Buddha
Co-author : Chandrika Prasad Jagiasu
(iii) Baudhchariya Padhiti

7. **Baldev Upadhaya**
Baudh Darshan Mimansa

8. **Bharat Singh, Upadhaya**
(i) Baudh Darshan Tatha
Ann Bhartiya Darshan—Vols. I & II.
(ii) Buddh Aur Baudh Sadhak
(iii) Pali Sahitya Ka Ithas

9. **Chandrika Prasad Jagiasu**
(i) Bhagwan Gautama Buddha
(ii) Baudhchariya Vidhi (Baudhon Ke Naiymik Karm)
(iii) Baudh Grihstyon Ke liye Nitya Upasana Path
(iv) Angulimal (Natak)

10. **Chatursain Shastri**
Buddha aur Baudh Dharma

11. Dharmananda Kosambi

(i) Visuddhimaggadeepika
(Commentary on Visuddhimagga)
(ii) Bhagwan Buddha.
Translation : Sahitya Akademi, New Delhi
(iii) Bhartiya Sanskriti aur Ahimsa

12. Dharmarakshita, Bhikkhu Dr.

(i) Visuddhimagga
(Translation) Parts I & II
(ii) Acharya Buddhaghosh
(iii) Sarnath Ka Ithas
(iv) Baudh Yogi Ke Pattar
(v) Baudhchariya Viddhi
(vi) Chariya Pittak
(vii) Baudh Bibhutiyan
(viii) Tathagat Hirdya
(ix) Baudh Dharma Ke Mul Siddhant
(x) Pali Veyakarna
(xi) Jati Bhed aur Buddha
(xii) Baudh Sanskar Padhiti
(xiii) Pali Path Mala
(xiv) Kushinagar Ka Ithas
(xv) Tathagat Ka Pratham Updesh
(xvi) Telkatah Gatha
(xvii) Mahavanso
(xviii) Buddha Kaiin Bharat Ka Bhaugolak Parichay
(xix) Sarnath Digdarshan
(xx) Pali Sahitya Ka Ithas
(xxi) Baudh Dharma Darshan tatha Sahitya
(xxii) Sarnath –Varanasi
(xxiii) Bhikshu Pratimoksha
(xxiv) Sramner Vinaya
(xxv) Baudh Dharma Ke Updesh
(xxvi) Kalama Gantantra Ka Kesaputra

13. Dhamma Darshi Baudh (Devi Dayal)

Baudh Upasakon Ke Dhamma

14. Dhammaratana, U. Ven.

Visuddhimagga Ki Ruparekha

15. Havaldar Tripathi 'Sahadya'

Baudh Dharma Aur Bihar

16. Jagdish Kashyap, Ven.

(i) Milinda—Panha
(ii) Moggallana—Veyakarana

17. Kumari Vidyavati Malika

(i) Baudh Kala Kritiyan
(ii) Purnima (Poems)
(iii) Hindi Sant Sahitya par Baudh Dharma ka Prabhav
(iv) Archana (Dramas)
(v) Adarsh Baudh Mehlain
(vi) Bhagwan Gautama Buddha

18. Lama, Rigjin Lunduv

(i) Bodhipath Pradeep
(ii) Arya Angulimal Sutra

19. Mangal Hridya, Bhadant

Tathagat Garbhsutra
(Translation from Tibetan)

20. Nagendra Nath Upadhaya

Tantrik Baudh Sadhna aur Sahitya

21. Nagendra Nath Vasu

Bhaktimarg Baudh Dharma
Tr. by Namradeshwar Chaturvedi

22. Nalinaksha Dutt and K.D. Bajpai

Uttar Pradesh Mein Baudh Dharma Ka Vikas

23. Prem Singh Chauhan

(i) Buddharchan
(ii) Buddh Kirtan

24. Parkhurst, C.A.

Gautam Ki Rah Par
Tr. by Shrimati Prem Srivastava

25. Pragyanand, G. Ven

Vajrasuchi-upanishad
(Translation)

26. **P.V. Bapat**

Baudh Dharma Ke 2500 Varsha

27. **Rabindranath Tagore**

Buddhadeva
(Tr. from Bengali by Kamla Roy)

28. **Rahul Sankrityayan**

(i) Sutraduyam
(Translation from Chinese)

(ii) Buddhchariya

(iii) Mahamanav Buddha

(iv) Baudh Sanskriti

(v) Darshan Dig Darshan

(vi) Pali Sahitya Ka Ithas

29. **Ramchandralal**

Buddh Charitaravali

30. **Ram Bahadur Sharma**

Nand Katha
(Asvaghosha's Saundarnanda)

31. **Ramakant Tripathi 'Prakash'**

Bhagwan Buddha

32. **Satyanarain Goenka**

(i) Dharam Jeevan Jeene Ki Kala

(ii) Atama Darshan

(iii) Dharam Jyoti

33. **Shanti Bhikshu Shastri**

(i) Bodhichariyavatara

(ii) Mahayana

34. **Shasansri, Bhadant**

(i) Buddha Ki Den

(ii) Buddha Vachanamrit

35. **Sitaram Chaturvedi**

Baudh Dharma Ka Kendra : Sarnath

36. **Siva Narayan Gupta**
Buddha Vachan

37. **Upali, Bhikshu**
Buddha Sandesh

38. **Vedraj Prasad**
Buddha Jivani

39. **Vijay Srivastava**
Kapilavastu—Lumbini Dig Darshan

40. **Vyogi Hari**
Buddha Bani

ASSAMESE

1. **Bandaloi Gopinath**
Buddhadeva.

2. **Bhikshu Nandabansha**
(i) Buddha—Charit
(ii) Buddha Vandana
(iii) Baudha Sishu Bodh
(iv) Baudha Mahila
(v) Angulimala (Drama)
(vi) Siddharth Charit
(vii) Vishva Baudha Pataka
(viii) Buddhar Samo Jivani

Brinchi Kumar Barua
Sariputta and Moggallana

4. **Dharmananda Kosambi**
Bhagwan Buddha
Translation : Sahitya Akademi

5. **Sasanbansha, Bhikshu**
(i) Sadharma Siksha
(ii) Lok Niti
(iii) Nabin Pali Vyakarana and other Pali Text Books for High Schools

BENGALI

1. **Anagarika Dharmapala**
Bhagwan Buddher Updesh

2. **Bikkhu L. Ariyawansa**
   (i) Subodha Lankar
   (ii) Baudh Niti Siksha

3. **Bhikkhu Dharam Pal**
   Saddharmaratna Mala

4. **Bhikkhu Silabhadra**
   (i) Buddha Bani
   (ii) Buddha Niti Siksha
   (iii) Banchiter Sandhani

5. **Bhikkhu Silacara**
   (i) Isipatana
   (ii) Sarnath Tirath
   (iii) Buddha Vandana
   (iv) Sivali Brat Katha
   (v) Buddha Gaya

6. **Bimlcaran**
   Buddha Ramani

7. **Brahmachari Silananda**
   Sambodhir Pathey

8. **Hara Prasad Shastri**
   Bauddha gana O Doha

9. **Jainik Udasin**
   Rajgriher Indragupta

10. **Jyotish Chandra Ghosh**
   (i) Char punyasthan
   (ii) Teen Buddhasthan

11. **K.C. Gupta**
   Sariputta and Moggallana

12. **Manindra Nath Chakraborti**
   Buddha Charit

13. **Nalinikanta Dasgupta**
   Buddha Dharma

14. **P.C. Barua**
   Vidarshan Bhavana

15. **Prabodhchandra Bagui**
    Buddhadharma O Sahitya
16. **Praganaloka Sthavir**
    Paticca Samutpada
17. **Satyandranath Thakur**
    Buddha Dharma
18. **Sridhar Chandra**
    Abhisambuddha
19. **Subhuti Ranjan Barua**
    (i) Saddharma Niti Ratnamala
    (ii) Buddha Path
20. **Sudhansha Bimal Barua**
    Rabindrannath O Buddha Sanskrit
21. **Sujit Kumar Mukhopadhaya**
    Santideva's Bodhicaryavatara
22. **Tribhang Roy**
    Gautama Buddha
23. **Visuddhachar Sthavir**
    (i) Sivali Brat Katha
    (ii) Mara Vijaya
    (iii) Ashoka Charit
24. **Vidhushekhar Shastri**
    (i) Pali Prakasa (a Pali grammer)
    (ii) Milinda – Panha

GUJARATI

1. **Dharmananda Kosambi**
    (i) Buddha Dharma ani Sangha
    Translation from Marathi by
    Hargovind Singh Pathak
    (ii) Buddha Lila Sar Sangh
    (iii) Buddhasangha na paricay
    (iv) Samadhimarga
    (v) Bhagwan Buddha na dharmasamvad
    (vi) **Bhagwan Buddha**
    Translation : Sahitya Akademi

KANNADA

Dharmananda, Kosambi

Bhagwan Buddha

Translation : Sahitya Akademi

MALYALAM

Dharmananda Kosambi

Bhagwan Buddha

Translation : Sahitya Akademi

MARATHI

1. **Ambedkar, Dr. B.R.**
   (i) Baudh Dharma hach Manav Dharma
   (ii) Baudh Upasana Paath
   (iii) Bhagwan Buddha ani Tvancha Dhamma

   Translation : Ghanshyam Talwatkar, M.B. Chitnis, S.S Rege

2. **Dharmarakshita, Bhikkhu**
   (i) Baudh Dharmachi Multattven
   (ii) Jati Bhed ani Buddh
   (iii) Baudh Sanskar Padhiti

3. **Dharmananda Kosambi**
   (i) Bhagwan Buddha
   (ii) Buddha-lila-sara sangraha
   (iii) Buddha Dharma ani Sangha
   (iv) Samadhimarga
   (v) Buddha-Sanghaca Paricaya
   (vi) Hindi Sanskriti ani Ahimsa.

4. **Kolangande, Ramchandra Govind**

   Tyagraj Bhagwan Gautam Buddha

5. **Ponchurang Sadashiv Sane**

   Mahatma Gautama Buddha

Shankar Dattararaye Dev

Bhagwan Buddha

6. **P.L. Vaidya**

   Baudha Dharmaca

   Abhiudaya ani Prasara

ORIYA

Dharmananda Kosambi

Bhagwan Buddha
Translation : Sahitya Akademi

PUNJABI

1. **Mohan Singh**

Asia da Chanan
Translation of the Light of Asia
by Sir Edwin Arnold.

(ii) **Ambedkar, Dr. B.R.**

Bhagwan Buddha ate Unah da Dharam
Translation : Bhadant Anand Kausalyayan

SINDHI

Dharmananda Kosambi

Bhagwan Buddha
Translation : Sahitya Akademi

TAMIL

1. **Ayodhya Dasa, Pandit**

Buddhadharma Adivedam

2. **Appadhurai, Pandit**

Buddharadu Arulasam

3. **Dharmananda Kosambi**

Bhagwan Buddha
Translation : Sahitya Akademi

4. **Harman Hesse**

Siddhartha

TELEGU

1- **Adavi Bapiraja**

Himabindu

2. **Daggisala Gopala Krishnaih**

Baudha Vangmayam

3. **Karunagree**

(i) Saundaranandamu
Translation of Asvaghosha's
Saundarnanda

(ii) Buddha Charitha
Translation of Asvaghosha's
Buddha—Carita

4. **Veerabhadra Rao, B.**

(i) Russailo Bauddham

(ii) Bauddha Dharma Parichayam
Translation from English : H H. Dalai Lama

URDU

1. **Dharmananda Kesambi**

Bhagwan Buddha
Translation : Sahitya Akademi, New Delhi

2 **K.L. Chibber and B. Dhamma Siri**

The Buddhist Catachism
(Translation in Urdu of Henry S. Olcot's English Treatise)

ENGLISH

A

Abhidhamma Philosophy Volume I—Bhikshu Jagdish Kashyap
Abhidharmakosa of Vasubandhu : Some Psychological Aspects of Early Buddhist Philosophy—Aruna Halder
Adi Buddha—Kanai Lal Hazra
Ajanta Ellora and Aurangabad Caves—R.S. Gupte and B.D. Mahajan
Amala Prajna—Aspects of Buddhist Studies—Prof. P.V. Bapat Felicitation Vol. Ed. N.H. Samtani
Amaravati—H. Sarkar and B.B. Misra
Amaravati Sculptures in the Madras Government Museum—C. Sivaramamurti
Dr. Ambedkar on Buddhism—Ed. D.C. Ahir
Amitabha and His Family—Santipriya Mukhopadhayay
Amitabha Buddha—S.N. Dixit
Analytical Study of Abhidharmakosa—Sukomal Chaudhuri
The Arya Dharma of Sakya Muni, Gautama Buddha—Anagarika Dharmapala
Asoka—Radha Kumud Mookerjee
Asoka's Edicts—Amulya Chandra Sen

Asoka and his Inscriptions—B.M. Barua
Asokan Inscriptions—R.G. Basak
Asoka and the Decline of the Mauryas—Romila Thapar
Aspects of Buddhism in Indian History - L.M. Joshi
Aspects of Buddhist Culture—V. Subramaniam
Aspects of Mahayana Buddhism and its relation to Hinayana—Nalinaksha Dutt
Asvaghosha : A Monograph—B.C. Law
Asvaghosa and his Times—Sarla Khosla
Atisa and Tibet—Alaka Chattopadhyaya

B

Basic Conceptions of Buddhism—Vidhushekhar Bhattacharya
Bharhut, The Great Buddhist Stupa—B.M. Barua
Bharbut Inscriptions—B.M. Barua
Bodh Gaya The Land of Enlightenment - Dipak Kumar Barua
Bodh Gaya-Shiva-Buddha—Sachindra Narayan
Bodhisattva Doctrine in Buddhist Sanskrit Literature—Hardayal
Buddha, His Life, His Teachings, His Order—Manmatha Nath Shastri
Bhagwan Buddha - R.K. Diwakar
The Buddha—Papul Jayakar
The Buddha, The Life and Teachings—Devamitta Dharmapala
The Buddha—written as autobiography—J. Vijayatunga
The Buddha and Buddhism B.R. Barua
The Buddha and His Dhamma—B.R. Ambedkar
The Buddha and His Message—N. Gangulee
The Buddha and His Message - Ven. Dhammaratana
The Buddha and Five After Centuries—Sukumar Dutt
Buddha and Bodhisattva—A.K. Biswas
Buddha, The Trimurti and Modern Hinduism—A.R. Kulkarni
Buddha and Caste System—Ven. Dr. U. Dhammaratana
Buddha Dharma (A Higher Affirmation) G.C. Lal
Buddha Jayanti Souvenir - Buddha Jayanti Celebrations—Committee, Jaggayyapeta - Ed. P. Srinivasachary
Buddha Relics from Kapilavastu—K.M. Srivastava
Buddha's system of Meditation (4 vols) A.P. Pradhan
Buddha Gaya—Rajendralal Mitra
Buddhaghosha B.C. Law
Buddhism—Pandit Sheo Narain
Buddhism : Dance and Drama—V. Subramaniam
Buddhism : My conception—Dr. R.L. Soni

Buddhism—The Path of Enlightenment—Acharya Buddharakkhita
Buddhism : A Select Bibliography—Satyaprakash
Buddhism in the Capital of India – D.C. Ahir
Buddhism in Central Asia—B.N. Puri
Buddhism in the Classical Age—Sudha Sengupta
Buddhism in East Asia —D.P. Singhal
Buddhism in India and Abroad—A.C. Bannerjee.
Buddhism in India as Described by the Chinese Pilgrims – K.L. Hazra
Buddhism in Kashmir—Nalinaksha Dutt
Buddhism in Kashmir and Ladakh—J.N. Ganhar and P.N. Ganhar
Buddhism in Kerala—P.C. Alaxendar
Buddhism in Ladakh—Nawrang Tsering
Buddhism in Malwa—S.M. Pahadia
Buddhism in Maharashtra : A History—B.G. Gokhale
Buddhism in Modern India—D.C. Ahir
Buddhism in North India—D.C. Ahir
Buddhism in the Punjab, Haryana and Himachal Pradesh—D.C. Ahir
Buddhism and Ambedkar—D.C. Ahir
Buddhism and Asoka – B G. Gokhale
Buddhism and Buddhist Civilization in India – R.C. Dutt
Buddhism's Contribution to World Culture and Civilization—Ed Ananda W.P. Gurge, D.C. Ahir
Buddhism and its Development —Bhikshu Buddharakkhita
Buddhism and the Indian Outlook R.L. Soni
Buddhism and Jainism – Ed. Harish Chandra Das
Buddhism and Marxism : A Study in Humanism—V. Banerjee
Buddhism and Other Religious Cults – S.S. Tripathy
Buddhism for Every Body—Bhikshu Jagdish Kashyap
2500 Years of Buddhism—Ed. P.V. Bapat
Buddhist Art of Mathura—R.C. Sharma
Buddhist Avadanas—S. Sharma
The Buddhist Conception of Spirits—B.C. Law
Buddhist Conception of Mara—B.C. Law
Buddhist Contribution to Sanskrit Poetics—Moolchand Shastri
Buddhist Culture in Tibetan Sources—A.C. Bannerjee
Buddhist Iconography, 2 Vols. Ed. Lokesh Chandra
Buddhist Kashmir—F.M. Hussnain

Buddhist Logic : A Fresh Study of Dharmakirti's Philosophy—L. Bapat
Buddhist Manual for Every Day Practice—Acharya Buddharakkhita
Buddhist Monasteries in Himachal Pradesh—O.C. Handa
Buddhist Monasteries in Western Himalaya—Romi Khosla
Buddhist Monks and Monasteries of India—Sukumar Dutt
Buddhist Monuments—Mrs. Debala Mitra
The Buddhist Philosophy : As Presented in Mimansaloka Vartika—Vijaya Rani
The Buddhist Philosophy of Universe—Radhakamal Mookerjee
The Buddhist Philosophy of Universal Flux—Satkari Mookerjee
The Buddhist Philosophy of Theravada School—N.K. Bhagwat
Buddhist Remains in India—A.C. Sen
Buddhist Remains in Andhra—K.R. Subramaniam
Buddhist Remains in South India and Early Andhra History—K.S. Subraminian
Buddhist Savants of Kashmir—Their Contribution Abroad—A Kaul
Buddhist Sects in India—Nalinaksha Dutt
Buddhist Shrines - D.C. Bhattacharya
Buddhist Shrines in India—D.C. Ahir
Buddhist Studies - B.C. Law
Buddhist Studies in India—R.C. Pandeya
Buddhist Stupa of Amaravati and Jaggayyapeta—C. Sivaramamurti

C

The Capital of Buddhism : Sarnath—Acharya Sitaram Chaturvedi
The Central Philosophy of Buddhism—T.R.V. Murti
Chakradhvaja : The Wheel-Flag of India (Being a History Exposition of the Meaning of Dharmachakra and Sarnath Capital—V.S. Agarwala
Chinese Monks in India—Latika Lahiri
A Comparative Study of Jainism and Buddhism - Sital Prasad
Concept of Buddhism—B C. Law
Constitution of the Buddhist Sangha—K.L. Hazra
A Critical Study of Milindapanha—R. Basu
Cross Currents in Early Buddhism—S.N Dube
Cultural Heritage of India—Aspects of Buddhist Culture—V. Subramaniam.

D

Dalai Lamas of Tibet : Succession of Births—Inder L. Malik

Dialectics Method of Nagarjuna, Vigrahavyavartani, text, Eng. translation—K. Bhattacharya
The Dialectics of Nagarjuna—Ramendra Nath Ghosh
The Decline of Buddhism in India—R.C. Mitra
Democracy in Early Buddhist Sangha—Gokuldas De
Development of Buddhism in U.P.—Nalinaksha Dutt and K.D. Bajpai
Developments of Buddhist Ethics—Girja Prasad Misra
Development of Buddhist Iconography in Eastern India—A Study of Tara, Prajnas of Five Thatagatas and Bhirukti—Mallar Ghosh
Dhamma As Told By Dr. Ambedkar - Ed. D.C. Ahir
Discerning the Buddha. A Study of Buddhism and of the Brahamanical Hindu Attitude to it—Lal Mani Joshi
The Discovery of Kapilavastu --K.M. Srivastva

E

Early Buddhism and the Bhagwad Gita—K.N. Upadhayaya
Early Buddhism and its Origins—Vishwanath Nath Varma
Early Buddhist Monachism - Sukumar Dutt
Early Buddhist Mythology—J.P. Halder
Early History of the Spread of Buddhism and the Buddhist Schools—Nalinaksha Dutt
Early Monastic Buddhism—Nalinaksha Dutt
Edicts of Asoka—G. Srinivasamurti and A.N.K. Aiyangar
The Elements of Early Buddhist Psychology—S.K. Ramachandra Rao
The Essence of Buddhism—P. Lakshmi Narasu

F

In the Footsteps of the Buddha—T.L. Wasvani
Foundations of Tibetan Monasticsm—Anagarika Govinda Lama
Framework of Nagarjuna's Philosophy—A.M. Padhya
Future Buddha (Bodhisattva)—Shamu T. Merani

G

The Gandhara Sculptures—K. Krishna Murthy
Gautama Buddha and the Parbrajakas—B.C. Law
Gautama the Buddha—S. Radhakrishnan

Gautama the Buddha : The Incomparable Physician—S.L. Bhatia
Gautama the Buddha—Akshaya Kumar Debi
Gautama : The Story of Lord Buddha—Shakuntala Masani
Gaya and Bodh Gaya—B.M. Barua
Geography of Early Buddhism—B.C. Law
Gilgit Manuscripts—Nalinaksha Dutt
A Glimpse of Buddhism—R.L. Soni
Glimpses of Buddhism—N. Ramesan
Glimpses of Buddhist Culture in India including Four Dances—V. Subramaniam
A Guide to Bodh Gaya—Devapriya Valisinha
Guide to Buddhist Ruins of Sarnath—Daya Ram Sahni
A Guide to Kushinagar—Bhikshu Dharmarakshita
Guide to Nalanda—A Ghosh

H

Heaven and Hell in Buddhist Perspective—B.C. Law
The Heart of Buddhist Philosophy : Dinnaga and Dharmakirti—Amar Singh
Heritage of Buddhism—D.C, Ahir
The History of Buddha's Religion (Sasanavamsa)—B.C. Law
History of Buddhism in Assam (C. 300 B.C. to 1200. A.D.)—S. Sasanananda
History of Buddhism in Kashmir—S. Khosla
History of Central Asia—Rahul Sankrityayan
History of Indian Buddhism—S.R. Goyal
The History of Orissa—Harekrushna Mahtab
History of Pali Literature (2 Volumes) B.C. Law
History of Researches on Indian Buddhism—N.N. Bhattacharya
The Historical Evolution of the Buddha Legend—Sarla Khosla
Historical Study of the terms of Hinayana and Mahayana and the origins of Mahayana Buddism—R. Kimura
History of Theravada Buddhism in South-East Asia, with special reference to India and Ceylon—Kanai Lal Hazra
How and Why Buddhism Declined in India—D.C. Ahir
Human Life and the Teachings of Buddha—M.N. Pathak

I

India's Debt to Buddhism—D.C. Ahir
India and China—P.C. Bagchi

Indian Buddhist Iconography—B. Bhattacharya
Indian Pandits in the land of Snow—Sarat Chandra Das
Insights into Buddhism—Ed. S.K. Gupta
An Intelligent Man's Guide to Buddhism—Bhadant Anand Kausalyayan
An Introduction to Buddhist Esoterism—B. Bhattacharya
An Introduction to Buddhism—H.H. Dalai Lama
An Introduction to Lamaism—R.R. Anurudha
Introduction to Madhyamika Philosophy—Jaideva Singh
An Introduction to Pali Literature—S.C. Banerjee
An Introduction to Tantrik Buddhism—Shashi Bhushan Dasgupta
An Introducation to Visuddhi Magga—Ven. U. Dhammaratana
Inscriptions of Asoka—D.C. Sircar
Institute of Asoka—S.K. Sen Gupta

K

Kusinagara—D.R. Patil

L

The Legend of the Topes (Thupavamsa) Translated into English—B.C. Law
Life of Buddha in Indian Sculpture—Ratan Parimoo
Life's Highest Blessings—Dr. R.L. Soni
Life in Sanchi Sculptures—A.L. Srivastava
Literary History of Sanskrit Buddhism—C.K. Nariman
Living Legacy of the Buddha—Acharya Buddharakkhita

M

Maharashtra The Land of Buddhism—D.C. Ahir
Mahayana Buddhism—Nalinaksha Dutt
The Mahayana Buddhist Ideals of Ksemendra—N.S. Shukla
Madhyantra Vibhanga Sastra—R.C. Pandeya
Madhyamaka Shastram of Nagarjuna Vol. I—R.C. Pandeya
Manual of Buddhist Historical Traditions—B.C. Law
A Manual of Pali (Grammer Book)—C.V. Joshi
The Message of Buddha—A.P. Wadia
Mind : Overcoming its Cankers—Acharya Buddharakkhita
Milindapanha—R. Basu
Modern Buddhism and its followers in Orissa—Nagendra Nath Vasu

N

Nagarjuna's Philosophy as Presented in the Maha-Prajnaparamita Sastra – K. Venkata Ramanan
Nagarjunakonda—T.N. Ramachandran
Nagarjunakonda --H. Sarkar and B.N. Misra
Nature of Bondage and Liberation in Buddhist System—K. Shukla
Nibbana in Early Buddhism (Based on Pali Sources)—H.S. Sobti
Notion of Truth in Buddhism and Pragmatism—Kamla Kumari

O

Origins of the Buddha Image—Adris Bannerjee
Origin and the Development of Pali language—R. Siddhartha
Outline of Early Buddhism—Ajay Mitra Shastri

P

A Pali Grammer—N. Chakravarti Vidyabhushan and M.K. Ghose
Pali Language and Literature-Wilhelm Geiger, Translated by Balkrishna Ghosh
Pali Sangraha (Selections from early Buddhist Texts)—Ed. P.V. Bapat
The Pioneers of Buddhist Revival in India—D.C. Ahir
The Pramamanavarttikam of Acharya Dharmakirti—Ed. R.C. Pandey
Pre-Buddhist India—Ratilal Mehta
Prolegomena to History of Buddhist Philosophy—B.M. Barua
The Psychological Attitude of Early Buddhist Philosophy—Anagarika Govinda Lama

R

Rajgir—K.M.H. Kuraishi and A. Ghosh
Rajgriha and Nalanda—Amulya Chandra Sen
Royal Patronage of Buddhism in Ancient India—K.L. Hazra

S

Sanchi—Mrs. Debala Mitra
Sanskrit Buddhism—Nihar Ranjan Ray
Sanskrit Buddhist Literature of Nepal—R.L. Mitra
Sariputta and Moggallana—Ven. N. Jinaratana
Sarnath—V.S. Agarwala

Sarnath—Pandit Sheo Narain
Sarvastivada Literature—A.C. Bannerjee
Sarva –Tathagata –Tattva—Sangraha—Ed. Lokesh Chandra
Sculptures of Vajrayana Buddhism—K. Krishna Murthy
Significance and Importance of Jatakas—Gokuldas Dey
The Social Dimensions of Early Buddhism—Uma Chakravarti
Some Fundamental Values of Buddhism—R.L. Soni
The Spirit of Buddhism – Hari Singh Gaur
Spokes of the Wheel (Studies in Buddha's Dhamma)—Arvind Sharma
Sravasti – M. Venkataramayya
Story of Buddhism with special reference to South India—A.A. Aiyyapaan and P.P. Srinivasan
Study of the Mahavastu—B.C. Law
A Study of Patisambhidamagga—Ven. U. Dhammaratana
Studies in Buddhism and Sikhism—H.S. Sobti
Studies in Buddhist Art of South Asia—A.K. Narain
Studies in Buddhist Culture of India – L.M. Joshi
Studies in Buddhist Iconography – D.C. Bhattacharya
Studies in the Buddhist Jatakas - R.C. Sen
Studies in Chinese Buddhism—A.C. Bannerjee
Studies in Early Buddhist Architecture of India—H. Sarkar.
Studies in Early Buddhist Monuments and Brahmi Inscriptions of Andhradesa – I K. Sarma
Studies in the Origin of Buddhism – G.C. Pande
Studies in Pali and Buddhism : A Memorial Volume In Honor of Bhikkhu Jagdish Kashyap – A.K. Narain
A Survey of Buddhism—Bhikshu Sangharakshita

T

Tarkabhasa : A Manual of Buddhist Logic—B.N. Singh
Taranatha's History of Buddhism in India. Trs. from the Tibetan by Lama Chimpa and Alka Chattopadhyaya – Ed. Debiprasad Chattopadhayaya
Tathagata Buddha : The Untold Story of the Enlightened One—P.Y. Deshpande
Theatres of the Buddhists—H.V. Sharma
Theravada Buddhism—Nihar Ranjan Ray
Theory of Buddhist Relations in Buddhist Philosophy – Bimkendra Kumar
Tibetan Studies—S.C. Das

U

An Unforgettatble Inheritence (Stories of Dhammapada)—Parts I, II, III, IV—Acharya Buddharakkhita

V

The Vajrayana Works—Ed. B. Bhattacharya

Viharas in Ancient India—Dipak Kumar Barua

Vimuttimagga and Visuddhimagga—A Comparative Study—P.V. Bapat

The Voice of Buddha : The Eternal Truth—Pranab Bandhopodhay

W

The Way of the Buddha—Publications Division, Ministery of Information and Broadcasting

What is Buddhism—P. Lakshmi Narasu

Women in Buddhist Literature—B.C. Law

Y

Yogacara Idealism—A.K. Chatterjee

Z

Zen Buddhism : Analysis of the Main Themes—L.P. Singh and B.M. Sirisena

(iv) Buddhist Journals

The foremost Buddhist journal is *The Maha Bodhi*, a monthly in English published by the Maha Bodhi Society of India, 4-A, Bankim Chatterjee Street, Calcutta. It was founded by Anagarika Dharmapala in May 1892, and is the only Buddhist journal to have survived for nearly a century whereas many other journals founded after it have ceased publication.

The second oldest Buddhist journal in India is *Jagajjyoti* which was founded in 1908 by Venerable Kripasaran Maha Thera, the founder of the Bengal Buddhist Association. When founded, the Jagajjyoti was a monthly in Bengali but now it is published quarterly in English and Bengali, under the Editorship of Hemendu B. Chowdhury, by the Bengal Buddhist Association, I. Buddhist Temple Street, Calcutta.

The third important Buddhist journal is the monthly *Dhamma* in English published by the Maha Bodhi Society, 14, Kalidasa Road, Gandhinagar, Bangalore, Karnataka. It was founded by Ven. Acharya Buddharakkhita in 1976. The venerable is also its founder Editor.

Some of the other Buddhist journals currently in circulation in India are: I, *Samyak Drishti* (Right View), Monthly, Hindi-English Maha Bodhi Ashoka Mission, Ajmer, Rajasthan. 2. *Bodhipath*, Annual, Hindi-English, Vaishali International Buddhist Society, Muzaffarpur, Bihar. 3. *Nalanda*, Quarterly, Bengali, Nalanda Vidya Bhavan, Calcntta, West Bengal. 4. *Vipassana.* Monthly Hindi, Vipassana International Academy, Dhammagiri, Igatpuri Maharashtra. 5. *Pragaya Vijaya,* Monthly, Hindi, Bhoor, Bulandshahahr, Uttar Pradesh. 6. *Dhammakirti*, Quarterly, Hindi, Jalandhar, Punjab. 7. *Baudh Dhuram Prachark*, Monthly, Hindi, Anandgarh, Distt. Hoshiarpur, Punjab. 8. Dhammalipi, Monthly, Marathi, Bombay, Maharashtra.

CHAPTER VII

Buddhist Customs and Manners

1. The Buddha

THE Buddha means the Enlightened One, the Awakened One. Generally, it refers to Gautama the Buddha who was a historical Personage and sanctified the soil of India more than 2,500 years ago. The Buddha is also known as the Tathagata – the Perfect One ; Bhagava—the Blessed One ; Sambuddha—the Perfectly Enlightened One ; Sammasambuddha—Perfectly All Enlightened One ; Sakyamuni—the Sage of the Sakyas ; and Sugata – the Hapyy One or the Accomplished One. In the Buddhist tradition, mention is also made of some previous Buddhas as well as of the Buddha Maitreya who is said to be the next Buddha to appear in this world at some future time.

2. Triple—Gem

Buddhism stands on three Pillars : the Buddha, the Dhamma, and the Sangha. Gautama the Buddha, the Fully Enlightened One is the founder of Buddhism. His ethical and philosophical Teachings are the Dhamma, and the Order of Buddhist monks and nuns is the Sangha. Together, the Buddha, the Dhamma and the Sangha are known as the Triple – Gem (Ti-Ratana).

3. The Buddhists

A Buddhist is a person who revers the Buddha, the Enlightened One, as the highest spiritual guide, and strives to live according to His Teachings.

The Buddhists are divided into two classes i.e. the upasakas and the monks. The term upasaka (fem. upasika) literally means 'sitting close by' a lay adherent, a lay devotee, or a lay follower who has deep faith in Buddhism and has taken refuge in the Buddha, the Dhamma, and the Sangha. Those who renounce the life of a householder and take to the life of a recluse by joining the Sangha are known as monks (Bhikkhus). In Buddhism, women have equal rights. They can take part in any religious, social or political activity. If desired, they can even join the Sangha and attain the highest spiritual bliss.

4. Bhikkhus

A Bhikkhu or Bhikshu is a member of the Buddhist Order of monks, the Sangha. The word 'Bhikkhu' means mendicant, a monk living on alms. A Bhikkhu is not a priest in the sense of theistic religions. He being the torch-bearer of the Dhamma acts as a friend, philosopher and guide of the laity in all religious and social matters. Every Buddhist monk has to be a Samanera (Sramanera) before being ordained as a full fledged member of the Sangha. The higher ordination of a Bhikkhu is called Upasampada. The ordination can only be taken at the hands of the Bhikkhus.

5. The Three Refuges

A Buddhist takes refuge in the Buddha, the Dhamma and the Sangha. A person taking refuge in the Triple-Gem (Ti-Ratana) not only revers the Buddha but also undertakes to follow the Dhamma in his daily life, and to support the Bhikkhu Sangha. The Three Refuges in Pali are :

Buddham saranam gacchami
Dhamman saranam gacchami
Sangham saranam gacchami

(Translation)

To the Buddha I go for refuge.
To the Dhamma I go for refuge.
To the Sangha I go for refuge.

6. The Five Precepts

The Three Refuges are usually followed by the Five Moral Precepts (Panca Sila) which form the bed-rock of the Buddhist way of life. The Five Precepts are; to abstain from killing, stealing, adultery, lying and intoxicants.

The Refuge-cum-Precepts formula is recited in Pali by the devout Buddhists daily in the morning as well as in the evening. It is also recited at all the religious and social functions. The complete formula is as follows :

Vandana

Namo tassa bhagavato arahato samma sambuddhassa
Namo tassa bhagavato arahato samma sambuddhassa
Namo tassa bhagavato arahato samma sambuddhassa

Tisarana

Buddham saranam gacchami
Dhammam saranam gacchami
Sangham saranam gacchami

Dutiyam pi Buddham saranam gacchami
Dutiyam pi Dhummam saranam gacchami
Dutiyam pi Sangham saranam gacchami
Tatiyam pi Buddham saranam gacchami
Tatiyam pi Dhammam saranam gacchami
Tatiyam pi Sangham saranam gacchami

Panca Sila

1. Panatipata veramani sikkhapadam. samadiyami
2. Adinnadana veramani sikkhapadam samadiyami
3. Kamesu micchacara veramani sikkhapadam samadiyami
4. Musavada veramani sikkhapadam samadiyami
5. Sura-meraya-majja-pamadatthana veramani sikkhapadam samadiyami.

(Translation)

Homage to Him, the Blessed One, the Exalted One, the Fully—Enlightened One.

The Three Refuges

To the Buddha I go for refuge.
To the Dhamma I go for refuge.
To the Sangha I go for refuge.
For the second time to the Buddha I go for refuge.
For the second time to the Dhamma I go for refuge.
For the second time to the Sangha I go for refuge.
For the third time to the Buddha I go for refuge.
For the third time to the Dhamma I go for refuge.
For the third time to the Sangha I go for refuge.

The Five Precepts

1. I take the precept to abstain from killing.
2. I take the precept to abstain from stealing.
3. I take the precept to abstain from adultery.
4. I take the precept to abstain from lying.
5. I take the precept to abstain from liquor that causes intoxication and heedlessness.

7, Symbolic Veneration

Buddhism attaches no importance to the rites and rituals as these are not necessary for the attainment of Nirvana, the eternal bliss. However, to give expression to their veneration and gratitude to the Great Buddha who showed the way of emancipation, they do offer flowers, incense etc., and light lamps and candles before the the images of the Lord in the Viharas as well as in the homes on auspicious days. The beautiful flowers which will fade soonafter symbolize and remind them that every thing is impermanent; destined to fade into oblivion. The lighting of lamps, candles are meant to dispel the darkness (of ignorance).

8· Sacred Days

The Buddhists have four sacred days in a month which are observed as days of fasting. These days are the new moon, full moon and the two quarter-moon days. They are called Uposatha or fast days. The Dhammika Sutta enjoins the observance of the 14th day from the new moon in the short month and 15th day in the long month as fast days. On the Uposatha days, the devout

Buddhists follow the Eight Precepts and abstain from worldly pleasures. They visit Viharas and offer Dana to the Bhikkhus. Confession of sins, absolution by the Bhikkhus present, and recital of the Patimokkha are an important feature of Uposatha or Poya days.

9. Sacred Shrines

India, the birth place of the Buddha and Buddhism has many sacred shrines. The four places Lumbini, Bodh Gaya, Sarnath and Kushinagor, where the Four Principal events of Buddha's life, *viz.* Birth, Enlightenment, First Sermon and Maha-Parinirvana took place are looked upon with greatest reverence by the Buddhists. The Buddha Himself says in the Maha Parinibbana Sutta : "There are four places that a pious man should visit and look upon with feelings of reverence. What are the four ? Where the Tattagata was born ; became fully enlightened, in unsurpassed, supreme Enlightenment ; set rolling the unexcelled Wheel of the Law, and passed away into Nibbana". To these be added, four other places which were also intimately associated with the Buddha. These places are Sravasti, Sankasya, Rajgir and Vaisali. These eight places have all along been considered as the eight holy places, celebrated alike in Buddhist lore as well as art.

10. Sacred Bo-Tree

The Pipal is the most sacred tree for the Buddhists as it was under this tree that Siddhartha attained the 'Supreme Enlightenment at Bodh Gaya and became a Buddha. This tree is thus called the Bodhi Tree or Tree of Enlightenment. It is venerated and watered ceremoniously on the occasion of the Buddha Jayanti. Because of its sanctity and hitorical importance, saplings of the Bodhi Tree are planted almost in all the Viharas. Its leaves are also used in many social and religious ceremonies.

11. Dhamma-Dana

Dana means charity, generosity or liberality, especially the philanthropic and liberal support of the Bhikkhus. Every Buddhist is expected to contribute some thing out of his honest income for the propagation and preservation of the Buddha-Dhamma, as Dhamma-dana, the gift of the truth, surpasses all other dana. The dana is of three kinds ; Dhamma-Dana, Abhaya-dana and Vastu-dana. To propagate and preach the Dhamma is called 'Dhamma-dana'. To give protection to the unprotected and to help those in distress is known as Abhaya-dana. The dana of the articles of daily necessity such as food, clothes, medicines and books etc., is called Abhikha or Vastu-dana. The dana to an individual is called Pudgal dana. Giving of alms and material gifts to atleast five monks at a time is called 'Sanghadana'. (According to tradition, at least 10 monks constitute Sangha in a city and 5 monks constitute Śangha in a village.). Amongst the specific articles to be given to the Bhikkhus, mention may be made of eight items of chivara, alms-bowl, blade, needle, belt, bedding, food and medicines.

12. Buddhist Era

The Buddhist Era commemorates the Maha Parinirvana of the Buddha. The Buddhist New Year day is the first day of Vaisakha. On the basis of the Buddha Sasana Era, the calendar was framed by the early Buddhists, and time used to be reckoned, as the date, month or year such and such of the Parinirvana of the Blessed One. This Era was in use in India and Burma for several centuries. According to tradition, the Buddha attained Maha-parinirvana in B.C. 544. Hence, the Buddhist Era completed 2,500 years in 1956. In that year, Buddha Jayanti was celebrated throughout the Buddhist world with great zeal, enthusiasm and happiness.

13. Buddhist Flag

The Buddhist Flag has five colours of the Buddha's aura, namely, royal blue, golden yellow, dark red, white and magenta orange. It has six vertical strips representing the five colours in the above order in the first five strips and a composition of all the five colours in the last strip. The blue strip is near the flag staff and the composite one constitutes the free margin.

When Lord Buddha attained Enlightenment under the sacred Bodhi Tree at Bodh Gaya, five colours emanated from His body-royal blue from his hair, golden yellow from the skin, red from the flesh and blood, white from the teeth and bones, and orange from the palms, heels and lips. As they became blended together, a sixth composite colour was formed. An aura of these six colours surrounded Buddha's person. The five colours : blue, yellow, red, white and orange also represent the noble qualities of the Buddha-blue for Confidence, yellow for Holiness, red for Wisdom, white for Purity, and orange for Desirelessness Hence, the Buddhist flag is a reminiscent of the spiritual aura of the Blessed Buddha.

Not only that, it is also a vital symbol of the Buddhist renaissance in modern times. This Flag was first of all hoisted on 28 April 1885, the Buddha Purnima day, at Kotahena in Sri Lanka by the famous Buddhist monk, Venerable M. Gunananda. Though born in Sri Lanka, this flag has been in regular use by the Maha Bodhi Society of India since its very inception. At the First Conference of the World Fellowship of Buddhists held at Kandy, Sri Lanka in 1950, it was accepted as the World Buddhist Flag. Thus the six-stripped Buddhist flag is a universal symbol of faith.

14. Salutation

The Buddhists, while meeting each other, salute with folded hands or shake hands and say 'Namo Buddhaya' or the usual secular form of salutation prevalant in their country of residence. The upasakas salute the venerable monks in two ways i.e. Anjali and Panchang ways. To salute the monks with folded hands raised to the fore-head and bending slightly is called Anjali salutation. To salute with the knees and the hands on the ground and keeping fore-head on the hands is the way of Panchang.

The lay Buddhists address the Bhikkhus respectfully as 'Bhante'. In the Himalayan region, where Mahayana Buddhism is prevalent, Buddhist monks are known as Lamas, and are addressed as such.

15. Festivals

Every Full-Moon day is an auspicious day for the Buddhists. They observe this day with due solemnity, visiting Viharas, hearing the discourses on the Dhamma and giving dana to the Bhikkhus. On festivals days, the lay men and women throng the Viharas and take the Precepts from the Venerable monks. They also worship the Buddha with perfumes and flowers etc. Almost all the Buddhist festivals are the festivals of light as countless lights are enkindled by the devout Buddhists on the occasion.

The following are the principal festivals associated with the Buddha :

(1) *Buddha Jayanti* : The most sacred and the most important festival for all the Buddhists is Vaisakha Purnima, known in India as Buddha Purnima or Buddha Jayanti. It is fixed by the full-moon day of Vaisakha which falls in May. This day is the Thrice Blessed day as Lord Buddha was born (at Lumbini), attained Enlightenment (at Bodh Gaya) and entered into Maha·parinirvana (at Kusinara) on this day. Of all the three events, the Enlightenment is of utmost significance as 'birth' and 'passing away' are common to all human beings but the attainment of Enlightenment, Supreme Badhi, is the rarest and it happens only once in millions of years. No wonder, thousands of pilgrims from India and abroad throng Bodh-Gaya on the Vaisakha Purnima day or the Buddha Day to worship the Vajrasana, Seat of Enlightenment, in person. On this auspicious occasion the Buddhists take pleasure in feeding the poor; in providing succour to the sick; and in freeing the birds and fishes as the cultivation of compassion and love is considered the highest virtue. The Buddhists also exchange mutual Greetings on the Vaisakha Purnima.

(2) *Ashadi Purnima* : The fullmoon day of Ashada, which falls in July, is known as the Dharma-Chakra Pravartana day as on this auspicious day the Buddha had preached His First Sermon at the Deer Park at Isipatana, modern Sarnath. This sermon, entitled the Dhamma-Cakkappavattana Sutta or Turning of the Wheel of the Law, marked the beginning of the Buddha Sasana as well as the establishment of the Buddhist Sangha. The missionary activities of the Blessed One also commenced on this day. The celebrations at Sarnath on this occasion are naturally the most important.

(3) *Sravana Purnima* : The full-moon day of Sravana which falls in August, is associated with the memory of the First Buddhist Council which was held immediately after the Mahaparinirvana of the Buddha. This Council was held in Sapatparni Cave at Rajagriha (Rajgir) under the Presidentship of Maha-Kashypa and it codified Buddha-Dhamma which was mainly recited by Venerables Upali, and Ananda.

(4) *Madhu Purnima* ; The full-moon day in the month of Bhadra, which usually falls in September, is known as Madhu Purnima. The scriptures tell that once the monks became very quarrelsome and split up into factions. Lord Buddha and His

senior disciples tried in vain to pacify them. The Buddha decided to teach them a lesson. Leaving the monastery He went away alone into the forest. There He literally lived with the animals. The wild animals of the forest. elephants, monkeys and parrots, brought Him food and enabled Him to live in peace which human beings had denied to Him. Madhu, honey, was the chief food the animals provided for the Buddha. Madhu Purnima commemorates this event and even today it is customary to offer honey on this day to the Buddhist monks.

(5) *Pavarana Purnima* : The full-moon day in the month of Aswina, corresponding to October, is regarded as the Pavarana Purnima by the Buddhists. It marks the end of Vassavaso, the Buddhist 'Lent'. The word 'Pavarana' means the 'satisfaction of desire', 'fulfilment of wish', or 'the day of completion of study and meditation'. During the rainy season (Vassa period) which begins on the full moon day of Asadha, the monks live in retirement, seldom moving from their monasteries. They spend the whole period in retreat giving themselves upto meditation, study, spiritual training and intellectual development. On the full-moon day at the end of the Vassa, the Buddhist laity hold a festival in honour of the monks who have been residing in their monastery. They offer them food and gifts of robes. This ceremony is known as Kathina. For the Bhikkhus the Pavarana has a solemn close as it is the day of confession of sins followed by atonement.

The Kathina or 'Kathina Chivara Dana' ceremony can be observed at any time between Aswina Purnima and Kartika Purnima. Since in ancient days the robes were made of cotton, it was called Kathina. The robes are traditionally supposed to be made from the raw materials, dyed and stitched all on the same day, and in many places this custom is still observed. The Pavarana-Kathina festival has many picturesque traditional features. The Viharas are decorated in splendid manner with many coloured lamps, flowers, balloons and garlands. Sometimes it is accompanied with 'Kalpa tree' festival as well. The legendary 'Kalparukka' is celestial tree which gives anything one desires. The Kalpa tree or lucky tree is decorated with all kinds of pleasant things.

(6) *Maghi Purnima* : The full-moon day in the month of Magha (January-February) marks the day when Lord Buddha

announced in the Chapala Chaitya at Vaisali that at the end of three months He would attain Parinirvana. This announcement of the Buddha reminded His followers that all life is impermanent, that all things must pass away and that all conditioned beings are Anicca, Dukkha, Anatta-Impermanent, subject to suffering and devoid of reality. The Buddha told them that at the end of three months He would pass out of conditioned existence into the final Nirvana after fulfilling His mission and that He was leaving them His Teaching (Dhamma) which they should in turn pass on to others. Thus Maghi Purnima is celebrated with this spirit of preserving and propagating the Dhamma.

(7) *Other Full-Moon Days* : The significance of the six Full-moon days of Vaisakha, Asadha, Sravana, Bhadra, Aswina and Magha has already been explained. Of the remaining, Jaistha Purnima is associated with Mahinda, son of Asoka, as on this day he reached Sri Lanka and met Devanampiya-Tissa, king of that Island, at Mihintale, about eight miles to the east of Anuradhapura. The Kartika Purnima is associated with one of the chief disciples of Lord Buddha, Mahamoggallana. He attained Parinirvana on the Kartika full-moon day. The Falguna Purnima is associated with Lord Buddha's first visit to Kapilavastu after His Enlightenment. On this occasion, Rahula approached the Buddha and claimed his patrimony as directed by his mother Yashodhara. Lord Buddha made him a novice monk.

Other Festivals

1. *Ambedkar Jayanti* : On 14 April in 1891 was born Dr. B.R. Ambedkar, who has been hailed as a modern Bodhisattva. He was the greatest Pioneer of Buddhist revival in India. Hence, Indian Buddhists celebrate his birthday to pay homage to the great leader, their liberator and emancipator.

2. *Dhamma-Vijaya* : On Vijaya Dashami day in the third century B.C. Asoka the Great embraced Buddhism and declared that thenceforth he would conquer the people by love and persuation, instead of by force ; thus giving it the title of 'Dhamma-Vijaya'. This auspicious day was also chosen in 1956 (October 14) by Dr. Babasaheb Ambedkar for embracing Buddhism and leading his people to the refuge of the Buddha-Dhamma. The Vijaya Dashami is, therefore, now celebrated as the twin Dhamma Vijaya festival. The Deeksha Bhoomi, the site where Dr. Ambedkar

had given a clarion call to his countrymen to adopt the Buddhist way of life, has since become a sacred shrine for the Indian Buddhists. Every year, in October, on Vijaya Dashami day, all roads lead to Nagpur. And lakhs of people from all over India throng the Daeksha Bhoomi in prayerful mood to celebrate the Dhamma-Vijaya festival.

16. Social ceremonies

Man is a social being. To give vent to his feelings of joy or sorrow, he has instituted certain ceremonies, rites and rituals connected with the various events in a person's life. In the religion of the Buddha, there is no place for superstition or blind faith as it is the religion of wisdom, rationalism and common sense. Simplicity is also the keynote of the Buddha's Teachings. The Buddhists are, therefore, enjoined to celebrate their social functions in a simple and dignified manner on any suitable day convenient to the parties concerned.

The two important social ceremonies are those connected with the birth and marriage :

1. Name-giving Ceremony.

After the birth of a child, this is the first ceremony to be performed. It can be performed on the fifth day after birth or any other day thereafter, in the presence of Bhikkhu or any respectable Upasaka (lay-man). The purpose of this ceremony is to ensure that the new-born is given a name which is buddhistic in sense and import. Another purpose is to bless the infant child and to pray that he may live long and serve the Buddha-Dhamma.

2. *Marriage*

Marriage is the basis of family life, and without the family there could be no preservation of the species and culture. Hence, the marriage ceremony is an important ceremony in every society. Some aspects of marriage in Buddhism are explained below :

(1) *Form of Marriage* :

Generally, the marriages amongst the Buddhists are arranged by the parents in consultation with the parties concerned. The Brahma form of marriage, in accordance with which the bride is given away as a gift (Kanyadana) by her parents to the selected bride-groom, is the most popular form of marriage.

(2) *Qualifications of parties*

Buddhists have no caste restrictions. Hence, the only qualifications and dis-qualifications to be noted generally in the bride and the bridegroom before the marriage is contracted are the following :

(a) Character.
(b) Education.
(c) Absence of disease.
(d) Age and bodily stature.
(e) Earning capacity of the bridegroom.
(f) Family antecedents, and
(g) No family blood relation.

(3) *Marriage vows* :

In Buddhism, there is no disparity between man and woman. Husband and wife are Co-equal. No one is superior to the other. Each one is to perform his or her own duty. A woman being Grih-Lakshmi—'wealth and honour or the house' has special responsibility in managing the household, and a husband being Grihpati, 'head of the family' is supposed to provide sufficient funds for the purpose. Therefore, the essential ingredient of Buddhist marriage ceremony is taking of vows or precepts by the couple which were prescribed by the Buddha Himself. These precepts lay down the duties of the husband and wife to each other.

The husband's duties to his wife are :

(i) To treat his wife with respect.
(ii) To treat her with kindness.
(iii) To be faithful to her.
(iv) To keep her content by having adequate source of income.
(v) To provide her with ornaments and clothes.

The duties of the wife to her husband are :

(i) To keep the management of her household in perfect order.

(ii) To keep all family members happy by good behaviour.
(iii) To be a faithful wife.
(iv) To be a thrifty housekeeper.
(v) To show skill and diligence in discharging her duties.

(4) *Marriage Ceremony*

The priests do not play any prominent role in the marriage ceremony of the Buddhists. A Bhikkhu cannot solemnise the marriage. However. in practice the Buddhist monks are invariably invited at the time of marriage and they bless the couple, and recite certain appropriate Suttas. The actual marriage ceremony is performed by a competent layman selected from the gathering.

Epilogue

PROGRESS is the Key-note of modern Buddhism. By now Buddhism in India has regained much of its lost prestige. The Buddhist Sacred Shrines have since been repaired and renovated to a great extent, and are once again humming with the sweet sound of 'Buddham Saranam Gacchami'. Also, the Blessed One is now the guiding star of a vast multitude in India. Not only that, the Buddha and the Buddhist heritage now command respect and reverence which was their due, among all Indians. In fact, with the Lion Capital of Asoka's Pillar at Sarnath as the National Emblem and the Buddhist Wheel of Law (Dharma-Chakra) in the National Flag, Lord Buddha can be regarded as the ruling deity of modern India. Verily, Buddhism is once again a living spiritual force in India.

As is well-known, soon after the Mahaparinirvana of the Buddha, differences arose among His followers as to the interpretation of the Master's teachings. At the Second Council held, after 100 years of the Mahaparinirvana of the Buddha, at Vaisali, two schools of thought—the Theravada and the Mahasanghika—came into being. By the time of Asoka, there were as many as eighteen schools, each with its own interpretation of canonical teachings. In the ultimate, in the first century AD, Mahayana emerged as the main school of thought as a powerful rival to the Theravada, the original school which adhered to the Pali scriptures. Primarily, the Mahayanists differed from the Theravadins in three respects : (i) the conception of Bodhisattva, (ii) the goal of Buddhahood, and (iii) the conception of Trikaya. The Mahayanists gave prominence to the Bodhisattva ideal, and laid emphasis at liberating all the sentient beings rather than salvation of an individual, the ideal of arhatship in Theravada. The Mahayanists further gave prominence to the

Eternal Buddhas, who look like the God of theistic religions. In due course, this trend gave birth to a vast pantheon of Buddhas and Bodhisattvas. Among the most popular Bodhisattvas who were widely worshipped were Avalokiteshvara (personification of Compassion), Manjusri (personification of eternal Wisdom), and Vajrapani (personification of Power). As a result of further intermingling of Buddhistic and Brahamanical speculations, the Mahayana paved way for Vajrayana or Tantric Buddhism. The Vajrayana (the Vehicle of Spells) flourished in eastern India in the eighth century A.D., and it was this form of Buddhism which was introduced into Tibet by Padmasambhava and other Indian savants.

In modern India, both the Theravada and the Mahayana traditions of Buddhism are prevalent. 92% of the Indian Buddhists follow the Theravada tradition, and the remaining 8% who live in the high Himalayas, are Mahayanists. The Indian Buddhists can be further divided into four distinct groups. Firstly, there are survivals from the Buddhist period. Mainly this type is represented by the Barua Buddhists of Bengal, the Chakma tribe of Tripura and Mizoram, and the Buddhists of Ladakh, Himachal Pradesh (Lahul, Spiti, Kinnaur and Pangi valleys) and Arunachal Pradesh (NEFA). Secondly, there are the ethnic over-laps from Nepal, Thailand and Burma such as the Tamangs and Sherpas who are mainly settled in the Darjeeling and Jalpaiguri Districts of West Bengal; and the Tais of Assam. The third category of Buddhists is represented by those who were attracted towards Buddhism as a result of the missionary movement spearheaded by the Maha Bodhi Society. The followers of Dr. Ambedkar, who adopted the Buddhist way of life in October 1956 and after, form the fourth group. The Tibetans, who followed in the footsteps of His Holiness the Dalai Lama in 1959 and after, form yet another group. Of all the groups, the followers of Dr. Ambedkar or the neo-Buddhists as they are some times called, form the most dominant group. They are over 90% of the total population of Buddhists in India. Majority of the neo-Buddhists are in Maharashtra (40 lakhs). The rest are scattered throughout India. As the mass movement launched by Dr. Ambedkar is still making steady progress, the position of this group is likely to improve further.

In 1891, India had 50,000 Buddhists and, after sixty years, in 1951, the Buddhist population in India had risen only to 1,80,823.

Thus till then, impact of the revival movement was not much. Then came Dr. B.R. Ambedkar, the modern Bodhisattva, who performed a miracle at Nagpur on 14 October 1956 by bringing about five lakh people to the fold of Buddhism. In fact, it was a great miracle. Never before in the history of any religion in the world, so many people, at one time and at the instance of one man had changed their religion. Unfortunately, Dr. Ambedkar suddenly passed away on 6 December 1956. Inspite of this tragedy, the conversions continued unabated. No wonder, the 1961 Census revealed a still greater miracle. The Buddhist population in 1961 showed an unprecedented increase of over 1661%, that is, from 1,80,823 it rose to 32,50,227 just in five years (1956-61). In the case of Maharashtra, the home state of Babasaheb Ambedkar, the increase was the maximum ; from a meagre figure of 2,487 in 1951, the Buddhist population there rose to 27,89,501 in 1961. In 1981, the population of Buddhists in India was 47,19,796 constituting 0.71% of the total population of the country (665 millions). Maharashtra has the largest Buddhist population; 39,46,149 or 83.60% of the total Buddhist population in India. Eight other States having Buddhist population of more than 50,000 are : West Bengal (1,56,296), Sikkim (90,848), Arunachal Pradesh (86,483), Madhya Pradesh (75,312), Jammu and Kashmir (69,706), Tripura (54,806), Uttar Pradesh (54,542) and Himachal Pradesh (52,629). Six other States have more than 5.000 Buddhists. These are : Karnataka (42,147), Mizoram (40,429), Andhra Pradesh (12,830), Orissa (8,028), Gujarat (7,550) and Delhi (7,117).

Notwithstanding the unique restoration, regeneration and rejuvenation, Buddhism in India is yet shorn of its ancient grandeur and glory ; its spiritual force and practical vitality ; and is still to be animated with the ever fresh vitality of a living religion. However, as more and more Indians are seeking refuge in Buddhism in order to enjoy the bliss of Nibbana ; to do away with social distinctions ; and to cast aside irrational beliefs and customs, the future of Buddhism in India seems bright ; and the hopes are that the Buddha-Dhamma will hence-forth shine for ever like a beacon-Light in this sacred land of the Buddha.

Our belief in the bright future of Buddhism in India is strengthened by the growing interest in the life and teachings of the Buddha among all sections of society. To make our point clear, here is an anthology of the tributes paid to the Buddha and Buddhism by some eminent personalities of modern India.

Rabindra-nath Tagore

In these days of the world-wide indignity of man, it is meet that we should say: Buddham Saranam Gacchami. He will be our refuge who manifested the ideal of Man in himself, who spoke of the liberation which is not a negation but a positive reality-the liberation that comes not by abjuring work, but by the practice of self-giving through right action, and which consists not merely in the rejection of anger and malice but in the cultivation of immeasurable love and good-will towards all creatures.

Jawaharlal Nehru

Buddha had the courage to attack popular religion, superstition, ceremonial and priestcraft, and all the vested interests that clung to them. He condemned also the mataphysical and theological outlook, miracles, revelations, and dealings with the supernatural. His appeal was to logic, reason, and experience ; his emphasis was on ethics, and his method was one of psychological analysis, a psychology without a soul. His whole approach comes like the breath of the fresh wind from the mountains after the stale air of metaphysical speculation.

In this world of storm and strife, hatred and violence, the message of the Buddha shines like the radiant sun. Two thousand five hundred years have only added to the vitality and truth of the message. So, on this memorable occasion while we pay homage to the Buddha, let us remember that immortal message and try to fashion our thought and actions in the light of that teaching.

Dr. B.R. Ambedkar

We must embrace such a religion in which there is no distinction between man and man; which is based no equality and universal brotherhood. These high ideals are to be found only in Buddhism. As the various streams and rivers become one after they have fallen into the great ocean, so after embracing Buddhism all become equal; there is no unequality, no distinctions in Buddhism.

Dr. S. Radhakrishnan

The Buddha has given us a message, which is of permanent value, which is an eternal message, which is of a timeless character, but we are unworthy descendents of that Great Master. He was a man who was superior, ahead of his time, a man who came out and told us what we should do if we want to recover our balance, our harmony, our love, our friendship. If we wish to live in brotherly love, we must develop the 'Bodhi Hridya' the heart of Enlightenment, the heart of love, the heart of understanding.

Dr. Rajendra Prasad

While the Buddha's teachings were considered revolutionary in his own time, it is absolutely essential to apply them now to bring an end to communal and caste feelings in the country.

Dr. Kailash Nath Katju

I verily believe (that) the loss of freedom and independence by the Indian people was hastened by their lessening attachment to and reverence for the person of Lord Buddha and His excellent doctrine.

Dr. H.C. Mookerjee

It is India's glory that it gave birth to the Blessed One and this was the land where Buddha gave the message which has proved a healing balm down the centuries to men and women in distress and pain. With the emergence of a free India, the figure of Gautama Buddha has also emerged in greater effulgence to point out for all time the noble eight-fold path which leads to the safety and security of mankind.

Dr. H.K. Mahtab

The world today is in the most urgent need of the message of Buddha so that the mind of the man may be freed from fear and suspicion and then plunge in love and compassion. How one wishes tha India could set right the irony of history and carry to the whole world the message of compassion which Buddha preached on her soil. It is said that history repeats itself in course of time. I believe India will again take up the mission of Buddha for the sake of the world.

Sri Prakasa

Free India must remember with reverence and gratitude, all the great heroes that have brought lustre to the land; and among them the noblest of her sons and her teachers, the Buddha must stand foremost. We must bring Him back to the land of His birth and His illumination, His preaching and His passing.

May we make ourselves truly fit-physically, mentally, morally and spiritually to sing in all humility and in all sincerity :

Buddham Saranam Gacchami

Dhammam Saranam Gacchami

Sangham Saranam Gacchami

APPENDIX I

Given below are the addresses of the important Buddhist Societies in India :

Andaman And Nicobar Islands

Andaman Buddhist Mission,
Vishva Shanti Vihar,
Port Blair.

Andhra Pradesh

Buddhist Cultural Organisation
26-14-14, Alankar Theatre Side Lane,
Nagarampalem, Guntur-522 004.

Andhra Buddhist Society,
Siddhartha Vihara.
Kancheralem. Visakhapatnam.

Buddhist Society of India
Andhra Pradesh Branch,
Siddharth Niwas,
Hyderabad-4.

Arunachal Pradesh

Lohit Bodhi Society,
Chowkham Raj Vihar,
P.O. Chowkham.

Assam

All Assam Buddhist Assciation,
Desangpani Buddhist Temple,
P.O. Desangpani,
Distt. Sibśagar.

All Assam Bhikshu Sangha Samiti
Chalapather Buddhist Temple,
P.O. Chalapather, Sibsagar.

All Assam Buddhist Students Union,
Chalapather,
P.O. Chalapather, Sibsagar.

Note : There are a number of Societies (Baudh Samitis) in various towns of Assam.

Bihar

Maha Bodhi Society of India,
Buddha Gaya,
District Gaya.

Burmese Buddhist Society,
Burmese Buddhist Temple,
P.O. Rajgir,
District Patna.

Vaishali International Buddhist Society,
Buddha Ashram, Bhagwan Buddha Chowk,
Muzaffarpur.

Japan Buddha Sangha
Japanese Buddhist Temple,
P.O. Rajgir,
District Patna.

Chandigarh

Buddhist Association
H.N. 1880 F, Sector-C,
Chandigarh.

Delhi

Maha Bodhi Society of India,
Buddha Vihara,
Mandir Marg,
New Delhi-110 001.

Asoka Mission
P.O. Mehrauli,
New Delhi-110030.

Bhartiya Baudh Maha Sabha
Ambedkar Bhavan,
Rani Jhansi Road,
New Delhi-110055.

Gujarat

Buddhist Society of Gujarat
Bakul Bhavan,
Behind Gujarat Vaishya Sabha
Jamalpur Road,
Ahmedabad.

Bhartiya Baudh Maha Sabha
Babar Bhai Ka Pitha,
Madan Jhampa Road,
Baroda.

Himachal Pradesh

Himalayan Buddhist Society.

Head Office :	In Summer :	Manali
	In Winter :	Kulu
	Distt. :	Kangra

Council of Religious Affairs of His
Holiness The Dalai Lama,
Dharamsala Cantt.
Distt. Kangra.

Shri Siddhartha Saddharm Sangam
12, Brockhurst,
Simla-171002

Jammu and Kashmir

Ladakh Buddhist Association,
Leh-Ladakh

Branches : Padam, Zanskar, Wakha Kargil, Skurbuchan, Khaltse, Nimoo, Chemrey, Hyimia, Tanntse, Doskit, Nobra, Panamik Nobra and Nyuma.

Wings :
1. Ladakh Buddhist Association Youth Wing, Leh-Ladakh.
2. Ladakh Buddhist Association Women Wing, Leh-Ladakh.

Karnataka

Maha Bodhi Society of India
14, Kalidasa Road, Gandhinagar,
Bangalore-560 009

The South India Buddaist Association,
Champion Reef, Kolar Gold Fields.

The South India Buddhist Association,
Ganeshpet, Hubli.

Madhya Pradesh

Maha Bodhi Society of India
Cetiyagiri Vihara,
Sanchi (Bhopal)

Maharashtra

Buddhist Society of India,
Dr. Ambedkar Bhavan,
Gokuldas Pasta Road,
Dadar,
Bombay-400014.

Maha Bodhi Society of India,
Bahujana Vihara,
Parel,
Bombay-12.

Maha Bodhi Society of India,
Ananda Vihara,
Nair Hospital Compound,
Dr. Anand Rao Nair Road,
Bombay-8.

Japan Buddha Sangh
Japanese Buddhist Temple
Worli Naka,
Bombay-18.

World Buddhist Cultural Foundation
3-A, Cama Industrial Estate,
Sun Mill Compound,
Lower Parel (West),
Bombay-400 013.

Dr. Ambedkar Smarak Samiti
Deeksha Bhoomi,
Nagpur-10.

Buddhist Training Institute,
Buddha Bhoomi,
Kamptee Road, Khairi, Nagpur

Meghalaya

Meghalaya Buddhist Association
Buddhist Temple, Shillong.

Mizoram

All Mizoram Buddhist Assciation,
Kamlanagar, P.O. Chuntu,

Orissa

Maha Bodhi Society of India
Plot 4-Unit 9,
New Capital, Bhuvaneshwar.

Punjab

Punjab Buddh Mahasabha
Nawan Shehr Doaba,
District Jalandhar.

Buddhist Society of India (Punjab Branch)
Buddha Vihara
5, Siddharth Nagar,
Jalandhar-144 003.

Rajasthan

Maha Bodhi Ashoka Mission
Buddha Vihara,
Maha Bodhi Marg,
Gautamnagar, Ajmer.

Sikkim

Sikkim Buddhist' Association
Gangtok.

Tamil Nadu

The South India Buddhist Association
Mrs Foster's Buddhis Hall,
41, Paddy Field Road,
Perambur, Madras-11.

Maha Bodhi Society of India
17, Kennet Lane,
Egmore, Madras-8.

Tripura

Buddha Bharati Mission,
Venuvan Vihara,
Agartala.

All Tripura Rajya Buddhist Association,
Venuvan Vihara,
Agartala.

Uttar Pradesh

Maha Bodhi Society of India,
Mulagandhakuti Vihara,
Sarnath (Varanasi).

Maha Bodhi Society of India,
Buddha Vihara,
Risaldar Park, Lucknow.

Maha Bodhi Society of India,
Lumbini Road,
Srinivasa Ashram, Nowgarh.

Bhartiya Pragaya Mission,
Maha Pragaya Buddha Vihara,
Bhoor, Bulandshahr-203001.

West Bengal

Maha Bodhi Society of India,
4-A, Bankim Chatterjee Street,
Calcutta-700073.

Bengal Buddhist Association,
1, Buddhist Temple Street,
Calcutta-7000012.

APPENDIX-II

Population of Buddhists in India-1951-1981

S. No.	State/Union Territory	Population 1951	1961	1971	1981
	INDIA	180,823	3,256,036	3,852,377	4,719,796*
	States				
1.	Andhra Pradesh	230	6,753	10,035	12,930
2.	Assam	22,628	36,513	45,212	**
3.	Bihar	1,092	2,885	4,806	3,003
4.	Gujarat	198	3,285	5,469	7,550
5.	Haryana	***	***	845	761
6.	Himachal Pradesh	N.A.	6.308	35,937	52,629
7.	Jammu & Kashmir	N.A.	48,360	57,956	69,706
8.	Karnataka	1,707	9,770	14,139	42,147
9.	Kerala	90	228	605	223
10.	Madhya Pradesh	2,251	1,13,365	81,823	75,312
11.	Maharashtra	2,487	2,789,501	3,264,223	3,946,149
12.	Manipur	33	325	495	473
13.	Maghalaya	****	****	1,878	2,739
14.	Nagaland	47	42	179	517
15.	Orissa	969	454	8,462	8,028
16.	Punjab	1,660	14,857	1,374	799
17.	Rajasthan	4,361	759	3,642	4,427
18.	Sikkim	39,397	49,894	62,617	90,848
19.	Tamil Nadu	1,179	777	1,148	735
20.	Tripura	15,403	33,716	42,285	54,806
21.	Uttar Pradesh	3,221	12,893	39,639	54,542
22.	West Bengal	81,665	112,253	121,504	156,296
23.	Andaman & Nicobar Islands	1,604	1,707	103	127

24.	Arunachel Pradesh	N.A.	5,809	61,400	86,483
25.	Chandigarh	**	**	92	454
26.	Dadra & Nagar Haveli	—	2	73	189
27.	Delhi	503	5,466	8,720	7,117
28.	Goa, Daman & Diu	56	189	260	302
29.	Lakshadweep	—	—	—	—
30.	Mizoram	***	***	22,647	40,429
31.	Pondicherry	N.A.	25	21	75

* Exludes Assam

** In 1971, Assam had 45,212 Buddhists. By adding average increase of 22.52% in Buddhist population during 1971-1981, it comes to 55,393

*** Included in Punjab

+*** Included in Assam

SOURCE : Census of India, Paper I of 1963, 1961 Census—Religion.
Census of India—1981, Series 1, India, Paper 3 of 1984.
Census Commissioner for India, New Delhi.